Routledge Revivals

Coins of Japan

Coins of Japan

Neil Gordon Munro

First published in 1904 Isha Books

This edition first published in 2019 by Routledge
2 Park Square, Milton Park, Abingdon, Oxon, OX14 4RN
and by Routledge
52 Vanderbilt Avenue, New York, NY 10017, USA

Routledge is an imprint of the Taylor & Francis Group, an informa business

© 1904 by Taylor and Francis

All rights reserved. No part of this book may be reprinted or reproduced or utilised in any form or by any electronic, mechanical, or other means, now known or hereafter invented, including photocopying and recording, or in any information storage or retrieval system, without permission in writing from the publishers.

Publisher's Note
The publisher has gone to great lengths to ensure the quality of this reprint but points out that some imperfections in the original copies may be apparent.

Disclaimer
The publisher has made every effort to trace copyright holders and welcomes correspondence from those they have been unable to contact.
A Library of Congress record exists under ISBN:

ISBN 13: 978-0-367-24871-0 (hbk)
ISBN 13: 978-0-367-24875-8 (pbk)
ISBN 13: 978-0-429-28483-0 (ebk)

Treasure of Books
Under One Roof

Demand Any Rare Book at
www.facsimilepublisher.com

Demand Any Rare Book at:
www.facsimilepublisher.com
if not available, give information,
our team will search and update you.

Promote Knowledge:
If you have any rare book
which is not available at
www.facsimilepublisher.com,
offer it to other readers so that others can also be
benefitted with your cooperation.
The book will be printed with your courtesy.

Print & Publish:
If you wish to get your book printed or published,
we have the service for you.

Customization on Demand:
We offer customization of books
as per the demand of the customer.

COINS OF JAPAN

COINS OF JAPAN

Neil Gordon Munro

COINS OF JAPAN

Neil Gordon Munro

ISBN : 4444006382092PB

First Published 1904, reprint 2013 in India by

Isha Books
B-69, New Gupta Colony,
New DDA Market, New Delhi - 110009

Printed at : Sagar Color Scan, New Delhi.

COINS OF JAPAN.

AN OMEN.
INCIDENT IN THE LIFE OF INOUYE GENI
Introduction, page xx.

PREFACE.

With the object of shewing the characters on the various coins of Japan in as clear a manner as possible, tracings were made which were afterwards photographed and reproduced by half tone process. By this means the shadows of the characters in relief on the coins have been eliminated. If the resulting illustrations are more of the nature of sketches than full pictures, they may at least claim to shew the coins in their true proportions, both with regard to size and the delineation of the characters. In a few instances, where the half tone figures have been imperfect, wood cuts have been used to replace them. If some of the characters are not clear in every detail, I would plead that it is not always possible to obtain perfect specimens. The best available ones have been drawn upon for this purpose, from my own collection and those of my friends Mr. Morita Jihei and Dr. Majima, to whom I extend my hearty thanks.

I wish also to express my appreciation of the work done by Messrs. Yuzawa and Takechi in preparing translations and to thank Miss Sato for the preparation of the index. To Mr. Yuzawa especially, am I much indebted for careful and conscientious labour and particularly for his assistance in elucidating the archaic characters to be found in an appendix to this volume. To Professor Chamberlain, for kind advice and the loan of historical works, and also to Mr. Mason for much generous help in the correction of proofs, my indebtedness is great.

For the knowledge of the coins themselves, I am mainly under obligation to Mr. Muramatsu, the well known antiquary, who imparted to me, in the most frank and generous manner, the results of a ripe experience, extending for thirty years and ranging over all the coins of China, Annam, Corea and Japan. He

PREFACE.

has been no less kind in the help which he has given in the preparation of this work.

As I have stated elsewhere, the translation of the year names is a matter of peculiar difficulty, because it is often impossible to bring their self contained announcements into line with each other. My attempt to do so may be held by those of high scholarship to be improper. On these and other matters I shall esteem it a favour to receive criticism and suggestions.

The pronounciation of the Japanese words will be facilitated if the reader remembers that the vowels have the Italian sound, that the letter *G* may soften to the sound of *Ng* in *going*, but never takes the place of *J*. Full details will be found in any good Japanese grammar, such as those of Chamberlain or Aston. I have not attempted to distinguish between the long and short pronounciation of the letter O. There are many shades of emphasis given to this, and it would have been difficult to ensure perfect accuracy when so many other points need attention.

I may add that the many details incidental to a work of this nature have been gathered and arranged in the leisure moments of professional life. If the healthful counterpoise which this has afforded to the more serious work of a physican can contribute its quota, through this volume, to the relaxation of other brain workers, I shall feel that the drudgery of seeing it through the press has not been useless. In this respect my labours have been lightened by the attention and consideration of Messrs. Thorn and Son, who have undertaken the printing, not only of the text, but of nearly all the illustrations, and whose lithographic reproductions of the gold and silver coins have contributed much to the value of this work.

N. GORDON MUNRO.

Yokohama.

CONTENTS.

		PAGE
	Introduction	vii
I.	Prehistoric and Protohistoric	1
II.	The Antique Coins	22
III.	Mediæval Coins	79
IV.	From Tensho to Meiji	100
V.	Provincial Coins	155
VI.	Gold and Silver Currency	186
	Meiji Currency	210
VII.	Experimental and Ornamental Coins	215

INTRODUCTION.

There is something very fascinating in the study of Far Eastern coins. They do not appeal to us through any pictorial effect, but a subtle and impersonal charm pervades their inscriptions and the sentiments which they set forth.

They are written in characters which are a manifest survival of the picture writing of early man. He wrote, that is to say, scored or scratched,* various outline sketches of his doings and the more intimate facts of his surroundings, on bone, clay or other material. Previous to this, he had learned to utter speech sounds, (names *nouns*, by which things are *known*), in association with the various objects of his environment. Originally, these names were short and simple sounds, given probably, in imitation of some notable feature in the thing which they served to distinguish. Longer words were formed by joining the simpler ones, and thus it is that language is capable of being resolved into simple sounds or syllables, which latter are again into elementary sounds, namely vowels and consonants.

The primitive pictures of objects have also undergone further development, but this did not keep pace with the evolution of language. As speech is more important than writing, which, in early times was a crude and inefficient adjunct to it, it has resulted that many nations have reached quite an advanced stage in the arts of life without developing the art of writing to a useful degree. This art has always been of very slow growth, its progress being impeded in its early stages by reason of its

---

1. In Japanese also, the word "Kaku" means both to write and to scratch. The characters for Kaku, to write and Kaku, to scratch, are different because they were adopted in Japan long after the ideas were differentiated. Still, the character Sho or Kaku, to write, also means to sketch or draw.

clumsiness and incompetency to fully express the spoken idea. It is obvious that the change from the representation of the thing in itself to that of some special quality which it possessed, must have taken a long time to effect. To illustrate this by a familiar example, the sun in archaic Chinese is represented by ☉ and the moon by ☽, which are pictorial outlines, (See appendix A) though they are now written 日 and 月. It is easy to understand why the symbol ☉ or 日 came to be used for day, which is equivalent to one sun, but it probably was long before it occurred to any one to place the characters for sun and moon together to signify light, or brightness.

From the idea of brightness to that of enlightment in the intellectual sense, is a still wider step, but the same character is used to convey this idea and may be seen on any of the Japanese coins of the present era of Meiji (明治), which means "Enlightened Government". Thus it is that the pictorial writing of early man has gradually come to adapt itself to the expression of ideas other than those of the object which they originally delineated. It will interest the reader no doubt and assist his memory, to trace back the origin of the characters on the Japanese coins, to their archaic forms. With this object I have placed in an appendix a list of the characters on the antique coins with their primitive pictorial forms, as far as I can trace them, and the meanings which they probably conveyed.

It is generally supposed that the written language of the Chinese presents such a forbidding aspect and bristles with technical difficulties of almost insurmountable extent, so that none but those who devote their whole lifetime to the task, can hope to have more than a nodding acquaintance with it. To learn to write the characters is no easy matter, but it is not essential to

INTRODUCTION.

master the *writing* of Chinese, while simply to *read* them is a good exercise for the attention, involving little or no fatigue. To be able to read the inscriptions on the coins of Japan involves a very limited area of ideographic acquirement, yet it is an end in itself and no one need feel incapable of quickly mastering it. This result achieved, the reader will have the satisfaction of having got to the root of his subject, and the pleasure of viewing or collecting these coins will be greatly enhanced.

The mottoes are often of great interest. They belong to the order of sentiment which is based partly on theological, and partly on purely human interest. "The First Treasure of Divine Merit", "The Eternal Treasure of Prosperous Peace", are examples of the earlier mottoes, whose grandiose sentiments were often sadly at variance with the actual state of the coinage, or the conditions that attended its debut. Many of these coins bear the name of the "Nengo" or year period in which they were issued, and serve in this way to punctuate Japanese history. It has been the custom, from very early times in Japan, to mark the occurrence of special events, such as an accession to the throne or some other fact of real or fancied significance, by changing the name of the period in which it occurred. The new period thus inaugurated, was named so as to conform in some way with the new event; thus the period Taiho, or Great Treasure (A. D. 701) marks the discovery of gold, or (more correctly perhaps) silver; Wado, or Japan Copper, the finding of this useful metal in notable amount; while Genwa (1615) or Commencement of Concord, celebrates the peace which though temporary, practically established the Tokugawa Dynasty on the throne of the Shogunate.

The coins themselves are especially interesting on account of their variety of design and motto, while those

INTRODUCTION.

of the antique group carry us back over a thousand years to the dawn of Japanese history. Those little relics, precipitated as it were, from the obscurity of the past, beg to assure us that the civilisation of that time was no myth, but a real if elementary fact, and that they came into being in order to further the needs of a progressive people. To the Japanese collector, those coins of earlier origin are particularly fascinating on account of the "Sabi" which has formed upon them and which bears testimony to their antiquity. The word "verdigris" may be used to convey an idea of this "Sabi" which is found on these bronze coins, but it does not quite cover all that is implied in this expression. The "basic acetate of copper" is doubtless apropos when the door plate is neglected and the copper stew pan wears bare, but I am convinced that this chemical substance is not the whole of "Sabi".

Even in its literal sense, the expression "verdegris" is not always appropriate, for there is a blood-red Sabi which is supposed to take about a thousand years to form and which is found especially on those coins which have been buried with the dead. I do not know whether that time is absolutely necessary for the production of this red colour, but I have only seen it on coins of venerable age. As many of the antique coins in existence have been recovered from old graves, it is evident that some special condition must encourage this red Sabi, which is but seldom found. Of the green Sabi there are many kinds and varied hues. Sometimes it is of a dark olive tint, sometimes it is almost black, or it may be grass green or even blue. The best of all, no matter the colour, is when it lies on the coin with a thick glaze upon it, like the varnish of a Cremona violin. Rarely it is almost transparent and I have seen it fill up the body of the coin, so that the characters were covered, though plainly to be seen underneath the translucent coating. Here probably, some silicate (perhaps of lead) had formed a glassy covering. Indeed it may be questioned whether the word Sabi does not include many chemical compounds of the various metals which are to be found on the bronze of these coins. When one has been long buried in lime soil, it acquires a Sabi of green mixed with creamy filling, often crystalline. In water containing iron, it becomes coated with a thin yellowish film and it is astonishing how very fresh and new may be the appearance of coins which have been immersed for centuries in water.

The antique coins are frequently very brittle and require careful handling, while one wonders often at their exceedingly light weight. Five specimens of nearly or quite the same size, of a coin called the Jinko Kaiho, in my collection, weighed respectively in centigrammes, 500.5, 465.5, 456, and 355, whereas the book called the Dai Nihon Kwaheishi gives the heaviest weight of this coin as 1.05 fun, which is about 394 centigrammes. This difference of 21 per cent in the weight of coins which present not more than five per cent variation in size, is remarkable and at first sight might be attributed to some dissimilarity in the quality of the metal of which they were made. The reason however is to be found in the action of the earthy salts with moisture, and perhaps the action of free ammonia in the soil, which combine to dissolve the metals (especially the baser ones) of which the coin is made. Thus it acquires a spongy consistence and becomes both light and brittle. Another factor in lessening the weight of these coins accounts also for the frequency with which one comes across coins which have no Sabi at all. Japan is a country of earthquakes and consequently wooden houses, and it is not surprising that conflagations are very common. Many genuine old coins have been burnt in this manner and the softer metals have been melted or vaporised, leaving the copper and some other residum behind. The Sabi has of course shared the fate of the above and disappeared. It is an unwritten law that this garb of antiquity cannot be bestowed more than once upon the same coin, but it may happen that an attenuated and inferior Sabi forms on a coin which has been burnt, so that the above statement must not be taken as absolute. For a reason which will presently be mentioned, the collector of Japanese coins looks with suspicion upon such burnt coins, though many of them are quite genuine.

The earliest record of coin collecting in Japan, appears to have been written before the period of Keicho, 1596, 1615, but it was not until the Genroku period 1681-1704- that it became a regular cult. At this time the family of the Tokugawa was established in the office of Shogun and invested with the control of affairs, and the Daimyos were beginning to settle down to something like a peaceful life. The collecting of coins soon became a fashionable craze, and the active Japanese mind found some vent for its surplus energy in the classification of these tokens of civilisation. The coins of China were especially sought after: even those of Annam and Corea seem to have been held in greater esteem than those of Japan itself. Like the "Tulip craze" in Europe, this enthusiasm affected all classes of society from the Daimyo to the artisan. Rare coins were enthroned in ivory boxes, decorated with lacquer of gold, the pride and joy of their owners and winners of the respectful admiration of the select few who were permitted to view their charms. Much literature was devoted to the subject and though mistakes were not few, still there was much accurate work done in the classification, not only of Japanese but of other ideographic coins. Indeed, with the exception of the Chinese work entitled the "Ko Sen Wai", it may be said that the accuracy of the classification by Japanese collectors and scholars has not been approached by those of the greater empire. From the period of Bunsei, 1818-30, many works have appeared which would do credit to any learned society of Europe. It is from these that I have gleaned in the following pages most of the information which is contained therein.

It will be understood that such enthusiasm and zeal in the acquistion of coins, of which many were rare and some were scarcely to be duplicated, led to their imitation on a very wide scale. As the Chinese coins were held in greater estimation than those of Japan, it follows that these have been mostly the subject of imitation, but the rare coins of this counry have also been forged for the delectation of the unwary collector. It is well to be specially careful therefore, when offered these rare specimens, most of which are no longer obtainable in the market. The beginner would do well to confine his attention to those that are easily procurable. Specimens even of the antique coins can be had for a few shillings each, though the better and rarer kinds are very expensive. From a respectable dealer one can purchase "models," imitations, of the rare varieties, some of which are "really old" (but made within the last two hundred years) and he can trust to time and extended experience to acquire some of the genuine ones.

Until the present era of Meiji, the government coins of Japan, with the exception of some gold and silver ones, have been cast, not struck. The currency was copper diluted with other metals that is to say, bronze, and the quality was rather inferior in many of the coins, so that the metal was not suited to the process of stamping. When a coin was to be made, a sample was engraved and submitted to the officials in charge of the currency. From the impression of this on clay, a certain number of "Tane" or "Seed" coins were made of the best finish, and these were used for the purpose of "sowing" or impressing the surfaces of the coin on clay moulds. They are therefore much rarer than the ordinary coins and are surrounded by the halo of original sanctity. These moulds were then cut out so as to form connecting channels between each coin impression. After the mould was heated, the molten metal was poured in. It will be understood that one side of the mould contained the obverse and the other the reverse, which were apposed, so that the resulting cast was a complete coin, or rather a series of coins arranged in rows and connected by the metal which had been poured through the connecting channels. These were broken off and filed so as to have uniform edges.

It should be well kept in mind that the coins of Japan have a flat edge like this ⊓; not rounded like this, ⌒. This point is of great importance, for coins which are forged or imitated have been cast on a smaller scale and in doing so it is very difficult to get this flat edge. The filing of the edges quite flat, was done with many coins in rouleaux, so that many edges were finished at one time. This art is said to have been specialised in certain families. This may be so; at any rate it is certain that this edge is something quite special, and not to be easily imitated. When the edge of an imitation coin has been flattened it may usually be noticed that it is not perfectly even, the result of filing it as an individual coin. The body of the coin is less likely to be of uniform thickness, especially at the edges, owing to imperfection of the mould and the smaller quantity of metal used. The bronze coins have almost always a square central hole. In the case of the antique coins this was not filed, so that early coins with marks of the file on the edges of this hole are to be regarded with suspicion.

The quality of the metal used is also of much importance in deciding the reliability of the older coins, it being less brassy in colour in the genuine than in the imitated ones. The mould which was used in the making of government coins was usually of the finest clay, so that but few marks were left on the surface of the resulting coin. This is not the case with imitation coins. In the vast majority of these a distinct sandy appearance is to be noticed in the field of the coin, as if cast from a course grained mould. Then there is something quite characteristic about the appearance of the writing in the genuine government coins, which I can scarcely describe, but which like the expression of a face, gives at the first glance, an indication as to their real nature. The characters are cleaner cut, and less rounded on the surface than those of imitated coins, but wear and tear effect a certain degree of obliteration which is apt to be mistaken for this. In such cases however, attention to the above points will enable the connoisseur to distinguish almost infallibly between true and false coins. Some of the imitations which have been made during the last two centuries are so exactly like the genuine coins that a careful scrutiny is essential and here the condition of the Sabi is of importance, for it is most difficult to imitate. Like the famous Cremona varnish, it imparts to an antique coin the semblance of authentic age and like it, has had many imitators. Chemical treatment has not reached such a degree of perfection that an expert can be deceived. The best substitute hitherto found, and a good one, is the coating of the coin with coloured lacquer. To detect this it is usually necessary to scratch the coin, and owners are naturaly unwilling to permit their treasures to be injured.

There are three methods by which the best imitations are made. The first consists in making an impression of the real coin in clay, which is then used as a mould. The resulting coin is an exact model of the true one, but is slightly smaller, because the clay mould, which has to be heated for the reception of the molten metal, contracts somewhat in the process. This is sometimes counteracted by increasing the width of the rim; hence suspicion is apt to attach to unusally wide margins in certain coins, though there are some varieties which are specially characterised by this feature. There is something about the appearance of such coins, as above stated, which leads one to suspect them, the characters having a lack of definition and the body a want of uniform surface. The second method consists of taking a real coin and either renovating an indistinct character, or cutting out one or two characters and replacing them by others, so as to change the coin to the likeness of a rarer one. Sometimes a portion of a coin is broken off, and one character altered so as to make it appear as an imperfect specimen of a rare variety. The character can be replaced by excavating the site of the new character, which is then filled in with molten metal and carved out, after hardening. The third plan is to paint with lacquer one or more characters on a coin, or to alter the style of writing in this way. Some of these imitations are perfect works of art, and not at all easy to detect. Poorer imitations are made by pasting a tracing of a genuine coin on wood, which is then engraved and used to make the impression on the clay mould. They have even been made by being copied from the illustrations in works on numismatics, but are then easily detected. It is not uncommon to see specimens which some painstaking person has evolved from his inner consciousness, no such coin having been

INTRODUCTION. xvii

in existence. Probably these had their moment of triumph, followed by exposure and disgrace. Some of them are nicely made and may belong to the order of fancy coins or medals, of which there is a superabundance. Many of the latter were made of silver, in imitation of noted coins. Together with the picture coins of Japan, they have a place in a work of this kind, though not current coin, nor properly speaking, coin at all. Illustrations of these will be found in the last chapter.

Tracings on paper are of great value to the collector of ideographic coins, who cannot always possess genuine specimens. At first these were made by painting ink on the coins, which were then covered with tissue paper, which shewed the impression in an incomplete way, on the other side. The present method was first used by the Daimyo Masatsuna Kuchiki, ruler of Fukuchiyama, who adapted it from the old method of taking impressions of ancient tiles. The coin is placed on a piece of wooden board, covered with three or four layers of Japanese paper. This is slightly moistened at the spot where the coin is to be placed, so that the latter may not slip during the process. A piece of thin tissue paper, preferably of the finely ribbed variety known as "Hakushi," is moistened with water and after being half dried, is placed over the coin and pressed closely to it with a small pad of cotton wool. Any excess of moisture is removed by pressing another piece of tissue paper upon it. The clearness of the impression is thus secured, as the paper will not take the ink properly if too damp. The ink used is of that pasty kind, called "Niku," having an oily menstruum which is made to saturate the fibres of a plant called the Mogusa (Artemesia moxa). This is covered with silk, to prevent the fibres from getting on to the pad which transfers the ink to the coin.

xviii   INTRODUCTION.

This pad is made with cotton wool, about three quarters of an inch in diameter and is covered with fine silk. By pressing it on to the ink, removing excess by rubbing it against another pad, and then lightly touching with it the paper covering the coin an excellent impression is obtained, which, after, drying, is indelible. Before drying, the slip of paper is pressed between blotting paper, so as to take out any creases that remain. In this manner I have prepared most of the illustrations for this work.

I would advise collectors of coins to adopt the method above outlined, so that they may have correct delineations for reference. To take the impression of a coin in this manner, occupies not more than three minutes for both obverse and reverse. Societies exist throughout Japan for the study of numismatics. These publish at varying intervals, journals which are illustrated simply by pasting these slips of tissue paper or "Uchigata" as they are called, on to the leaves. These might be exchanged for similar impressions of the coins of other lands and thus the science of numismatics could not fail to benefit.

The first book writtten on the coinage of Japan was called the "Kwacho Ruien",* or "Classified Collection of Coins", but it only appeared in manuscript. It was written about the period of Tenwa, 1681-83. The story goes that the Daimyo Toyama of the Province of Etchu was asked to write it, but being unable, or unwilling he asked one Tennojiya Chozaemon of Osaka,. to do so. The dislike of high, or military personages to have their names even academically associated with filthy lucre,

*. The origin of the word Kwacho, as a synonym for coin, dates back to the time of the To Dynasty of China. The Emperor Bokuso, so says the legend, gave a great reception at court, during which many butterflies entered the palace and clung to the flowers which decorated the reception hall. The courtiers and ladies had some difficulty in capturing these, and the Emperor ordered the butterflies to be caught in nets and sent to the houses of his guests. Imagine the surprise of the latter, when they found that they had turned to gold coins! Hence the word "Kwacho," which means "Disguised Butterfly."

INTRODUCTION.

was most marked. The next work of any note was entitled the "Hanji Roku," or "Catalogue of Coins". It was also written by hand and appeared in 14 volumes, during the period of Kyoho, 1716-35. The author was Senoo Ryusai. The "Wakan Kohodzukan," or "Illustrations of Japanese and Chinese Coins," is another work of the same period, written by Nakatani Kozan. On account of the lack of reference, there are mistakes in these early works, but they are evidence of the keen spirit of enquiry and scientific investigation which was abroad in the land a century and a half before the "civilisation" of the Meiji period.

About the period of Meiwa, A. D. 1764-71, Fujiwara Teikan, a learned man and ardent antiquarian, wrote several books on coins, his work on the Kwanei coins being still regarded as the classical treatise on the subject. About this time or a little earlier, Unno Somin of Osaka, who had acquired a very complete collection of Chinese and Japanese coins, wrote a "Continuation of the Kacho Ruien", but it was not printed. Towards the end of the eighteenth century the daimyo Kuchiki Masatsuna, better known by his nom de plume Riukyo, ordered one of his retainers to publish the "Kokon Senkwa Kan" in his own name, as it was then considered beneath the dignity of one of his rank to write on matters, connected with money. This work is in twenty volumes and is of great assistance to collectors. In the latter part of that century too, the celebrated book called the "Wakan Sen Ji" or "Collection of Japanese and Chinese Coins" was written by Yoshikawa Iken. The first volume, dealing with the Coins of Japan was alone issued; it is a comprehensive treatise on the Japanese sen, but does not go into the varieties of the Kwanei coins.

Other notable numismatists were Kawamura Hadzumi, who wrote the "Kisei Hyaku En," a well known work; Omura Naritomi, author of the accurate and useful book, the "Chin Sen Kihin Dzuroku"; Kariya Kwaishi, who produced the "Shin Kosei Koho Dzukan"; Narushima Ryuhoku, who wrote the very accurate work "Meiji Shin Sen Sempu", the last volume of which was compiled by Morita Jihei. Nor must one forget to mention that luminous and voluminous book (in thirty six volumes), the "Ko Sen Tai Sen" the work of Imai Teikichi. A list of these and other works on numismatics will be found in the appendix.

Amongst professional experts too, are some who have illuminated the subject of far Eastern coins. Quite a romantic story attaches to the entry of Inouye Geni into the profession of coin expert. Having lost his fortune and being reduced to poverty, he sought inspiration at the shrine of Kwannon in Asakusa. For seven days he went without food and for seven days he prayed fervently for a sign. On the seventh day while absorbed in his devout supplication, something struck him on the neck and fell down his back within the loose garment worn by Japanese. This something was a coin which some one, whom we will suppose to have been an elderly female, had tried to throw into the Sai Sen Bako, or offering box of the Temple. (See Frontispiece). Now this very coin is illustrated in Plate 1, No. 5, chapter 4, and is excessively rare; indeed there are not supposed to be more than two in existence. It is mentioned at page 13. Inouye who had considerable knowledge of coins, was, we may be sure, struck with wonder when he inspected this rare specimen and immediately regarded it as an omen from the deity. With confidence and determination he established his office near the entrance to the Temple and for three generations this family carried on the business of Kosensho or coin merchant.

Mr. MURAMATSU,
Japanese Antiquary and Coin Expert.

I.

PREHISTORIC AND PROTOHISTORIC.

IT may be taken as an axiom, that in no time or place, have the capabilities of man, and the opportunities of his environment, been so evenly distributed that all products of human industry were fashioned exactly alike, in quality or number, by each individual member of the race. There must always have been a time when some one was able to make a certain article of better quality, or more abundantly than his neighbours. Even in the most rudimentary stage of culture, to-wit, the early paleolithic age, when rough splinters of stone did duty for weapons and implements wherewith to cut sticks and to carve bone and horn, some one must have been able to make or to use these splinters with greater facility than those around him. Thus the original craftsman came to have a surplus which he could exchange for other commodities of which he stood in need, but could not so easily produce. In this way, the earliest act of commerce was initiated, to which we now give the name of barter. The boy at school, who exchanges a top and four marbles for a two-bladed knife, illustrates the principle of barter as carried on by the primeval savage. Without committing ourselves to a statement of relative values, we may suppose that those remote ancestors of ours might have exchanged ten stone arrow-heads, (counted on the fingers,) for a shoulder of venison, a couple of skins to cover the body and, at a later period, some vessels of wood, or rude pottery.

A decided advance on this trading by barter was accomplished when arrow-heads, which were necessarily in the possession of all, came to be recognised as a convenient medium which could be stored until required, and exchanged at will for other commodities. In this way arrow-heads might acquire a value quite apart from their utility as weapons. They would in fact constitute money, of a very primitive kind, but serving all the purposes of a medium of exchange: that is to say, having a fairly constant value in themselves, they would gradually come to bear a recognised ratio to other commodities, whose value could thus be adjusted on the principle that things which were equal to a given number of arrow-heads were equal in value to each other. Tylor, in his "Anthropology" gives an excellent illustration of such primitive standards of value at a period, which, though much later and higher than the above, still lacked what we are accustomed to regard as essential to trade, namely, a metallic currency. "In the old world" he says, "many traces have come down of the times when value was regularly reckoned in cattle; as where in the Illiad, in the description of the funeral games, we read of the great prize tripod that was valued at twelve oxen, while the female slave who was the second prize was worth only four oxen. Here the principle of unit of value is already recognised, for not only could the owner of oxen buy tripods and slaves with them, but also he who had a twelve ox tripod to sell could take in exchange three slaves reckoned at four oxen each." In the later neolithic, and certainly in the bronze and early iron stages of European civilisation, cattle were a favourite medium of exchange. The English word "fee" which was also an equivalent for money, was derived from the Anglo-Saxon "feoh," meaning cattle, while every one knows that the expression "pecuniary" comes from the Latin "pecunia," money, itself being derived from "pecus", cattle. In 430 B.C., the Lex Julia Papiria ordered that fines should be paid in money instead of cattle. It is possible that the word "oof", vulgarly applied to money, might be traced to "hoof," which is used to designate the foot of certain animals, but was formerly applied to the animals themselves, especially when counting them for sale or exchange. The common Japanese word for money is "O Ashi," honourable foot.

Various are the commodities which, in different times and places, have done duty as currency. Fur, amongst the people of Northern Europe and America, olive oil in the Mediterranean, salt in Abyssinia, in Iceland dried fish, in Africa the iron blades of hoes, brass wire, beads,* cloth and shells have been, and in some places still are used as money. In Asia and the East of Africa, the cowrie shell was employed for a similar purpose, while in North America the haiqua shell and wampum served the same object. It is interesting to note that those words in Chinese relating to money

---

* In plate 1, fig. G, are seen four beads of blue glass, from the dolmens of Japan, with a bead of carnelian. These, with fig. F, were possibly in use as money, 2000 years ago or more.
Fig. H. of the same plate, illustrates the cut shell money of Micronesia.

usually have the character "kai" (貝) meaning a shell, as a component, surely a suggestive survival! The Indians of America used discs and other shapes of "lignite, coal, bone, shell, terra-cotta, mica, pearl, cornelian, chalcedony, agate, jasper, native gold, silver, copper, lead and iron, which were fashioned into forms evincing a skill in art to which the descendants of the aborigines now surviving are strangers."* These specimens of "money" are often inscribed with archaic drawings and hieroglyphs, and some with characters which were identified by Schoolcraft as those of the "ancient rock alphabet" used by the Pelasgi and other Mediterranean nations.

The rings of silver and gold, used by the Celts, and other early nations of Europe, as well as amongst the people of Asia and America, seem to have been used as money in the days of primitive civilisation. Dr. Moritz Hoernes says "Ornament was equal to riches, since it frequently constituted a man's sole possessions. Much decoration signified a well filled purse, for the ornaments mostly in use were the representatives of money, for which more useful articles were exchanged. Nor could a more secure place for them be found than on the person of the owner. For this reason the most ancient money recognised as European has the form of rings."†
He goes on to say, "They are recognised as money by the fact that they are all of different weight, whilst an additional proof is furnished by the circumstance that

---

* "The American Numismatic Manual" by M.W. Dickeson, M.D.
† "Primitive Man" P. 13

PREHISTORIC AND PROTOHISTORIC.

they are held together by another ring which takes the place of the purse." What he probably intended to say was that though of different weight, these rings are proportioned to a definite standard of weight, true at least with regard to the Celtic rings, whereas the fact of their all being of different weight would by no means prove their claim to be regarded as money. Rings resembling these have been in use in Eastern Asia, including Japan, for at least 2500 years, but in the latter country at least, gold seems to have been very scarce and copper to have been rather a precious metal, for they are usually made of the latter covered by beaten gold, or silver. Sometimes, probably for the sake of lightness, they were made hollow and covered in the same manner with beaten gold. They are found in the ancient stone sepulchres of Japan which are akin to the dolmens of Europe. They are called "Kin Kwan" and "Gin Kwan" according to whether they are made of gold or silver. (Figs. B & C, Plate 1.)

From the great numbers which have been found, it might also be argued that the cut crystal beads, called "Kiri Kodama," (Fig. D) the claw or comma shaped "Magatama"† (Fig. A) of agate, jade, &c., and the

---

† There has been much discussion as to the nature and significance of these Magatama. It has been suggested that they are embryonic forms, but it is more likely that they were shaped after the claw of some animal, possibly a tiger. This is supported by the existence of claw-shaped stones closely resembling the talon of the tiger, one in my collection being almost an exact model. The tiger's claw is the strongest of amulets even to this day in Corea. Lastly, the word "Magatama", which is supposed to come from "Maga," curved, and "Tama", a gem, may, with equal propriety, as it seems to me, derive its latter portion from the archaic form of "Tsume", namely "Tume", a talon or nail. The character in which it is written was given to it long after its coming into favour and about two centuries before the end of the dolmen period. The word "Kudatama" refers to its tube-like [kuda] form. "Kiri Kodama" means cut crystal jewels or gems.

cylindrical "Kudatama" (Fig. E) were used as a means as well as a token of wealth.

I am strongly inclined to believe also that the small arrow-heads of agate and other superior stone which existed in Japan previous to the dolmen age, may have been a form of primitive money (Fig. I). According to many archeologists, these have been used for the hunting of small birds, but it is scarcely credible that such superior stone, so difficult to obtain and to fashion into arrow-heads, could have been employed in shooting among shrubs and trees where, from their small size they were very likely to get lost. Besides, many of these "arrow-heads" are only shaped to suggest the title and not adapted to the purpose of shooting. Those illustrated in Fig. I appear somewhat larger than in reality.

Such considerations as the foregoing relate entirely to prehistoric civilisation and are applicable, in a work of this kind, only as a foundation on which to rest the more definite superstructure of knowledge gained by historical research. They belong to the domain of archeology, rather than to history which, rigidly defined, is the narrative of past events compiled from contemporary record. The written document is thus held to be the best witness of its truth. Judged by this standard, the dawn of Japanese history must be placed in the beginning of the eighth century of our era, for the first known record called the "Kojiki" was not completed till the year 712 A.D. The twilight which precedes the dawn had begun however, some three

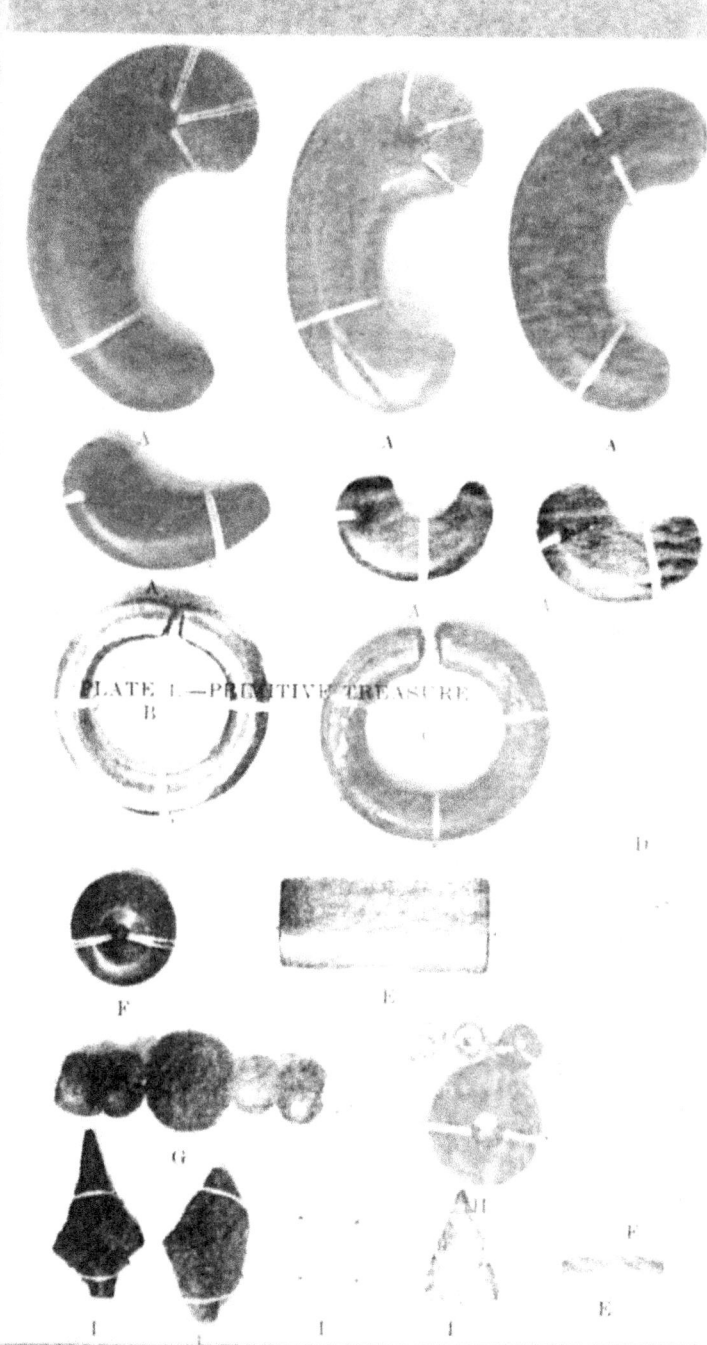

PLATE I.—PRIMITIVE TREASURE

hundred years previously, when the art of reading and writing arrived with the Chinese ideograph,* and it is safe to assume that the accounts given of this interval are not entirely legendary. It may be called the Protohistoric Period of Japanese civilisation. Its interest to the numismatist lies in this, that it has been credited with the production of a coinage which has fallen into oblivion, and left only the vestiges of its former existence. How far this surmise may be correct it is our present object to enquire. As the condition of the Japanese people however, prior to, and during these three centuries, is not without bearing on the question of the existence of protohistoric coins, I propose to give it some brief consideration.

The Japanese people are a mixture of various offshoots of the Mongolian race, but they possess distinct traces of Aryan blood. My present belief is that three and possibly more stocks are represented in the modern Japanese. There were first the autochthones or indigenes, who have disappeared or merged into the common blend, before rising out of the stone age, but whose knowledge of various arts of civilisation, such as the making and decoration of pottery was equal if not superior to that of the aborigines of America. They were probably a people of no great stature. Their remains have been found as far north as the Kurile Islands and might possibly be traced to the continent

*Wani, the first teacher of the Chinese character, mentioned in the Kojiki, is stated to have arrived at a date corresponding to 284 A.D., but Aston has shown that it should properly be placed about the beginning of the 5th. century.

of America while they extended to the southern islands (the Luchus), and similar remains have been found in Formosa. Next came the Ainu, a hunting race, probably from northern Siberia, who resemble the European rather than the Mongol, being very hirsute with wavy hair and horizontal eyes. This race still exists in Yezo, and the northern islands, to the number of sixteen thousand. They have no knowledge of pottery making, though they have, during the present era of Meiji taken on some of the arts of civilisation in a very limited way. Though this small remnant of original stock seems quite insignificant, still these people are largely mixed with the modern Japanese and it is probably from them that the Japanese derive their leaven of Aryan blood. Probably about, or a little previous to 1000 B.C. there came an invasion of virile stock, from the mainland of Asia, through, if not entirely from, what is now Corea. It is a moot question whether there were not two invasions, and I am even inclined to suppose that there was an anterior invasion, perhaps about 2000 B. C. or earlier, of a people in the bronze age, but this cannot be discussed here. The latter invaders used weapons of iron only, excepting bronze arrow-heads in limited numbers, and they (at least their chief warriors) were protected by iron armour and helmets, while they rode horses caparisoned with cloth and bells, with beautifully wrought ornaments of studded iron work, covered with silver and gold. Though probably much inferior in numbers, the great superiority of their weapons and military qualities gave them much the

PREHISTORIC AND PROTOHISTORIC.

same advantage over their foes as if half a dozen modern battleships were to engage the whole Armada. In time they blended with the indigenes and the conquered Ainu, and having killed most of their male opponents in battle, or massacre, it may be taken for granted that this mixture was accomplished with greater celerity than had the immigration been of a peaceful character. Whether these invaders were pure Mongols is doubtful.

A mythological account of the beginning of things and of the lineal descent of emperors from godlike ancestors (invaders), is contained in the "Ko-Jiki" or Records of Ancient Matters. It belongs to the same intellectual order as the Mosaic account of creation, but is less simple and refined. It was compiled by order of the Emperor Temmu, and written down, after his death, to the dictation of one Hiyeda no Are, who had memorised these ancient legends. It was completed as previously stated, in the year 712 A. D., and the later portions, say from the end of the 4th century, contain some true history. This has however been reduced to somewhat thin proportions by the criticism of such scholars as Chamberlain and Aston, who have shewn that many of its dates are not reliable and that its facts are as islands in a lake of traditional fiction. This work, unlike its younger and more fashionable sister, the "Nihongi" or Chronicles of Japan, completed in 720 A.D., is written mainly in archaic Japanese, and its originality may pass without question. By the use of the etymological spade, Professor Chamberlain has found, amongst the often incoherent language of the Kojiki, the material from which he has been able to sketch the surroundings of the prehistoric and protohistoric Japanese and to give us some idea of their mode of living, during at least the latter period. This is contained in the introduction to his translation of the Kojiki, and in the following account, his remarks are freely quoted.

"The Japanese of the mythical period, as pictured in the legends preserved by the compiler of the "Records of Ancient Matters," were a race who had long emerged from the savage state, and had attained to a high level of barbaric skill. The stone age was forgotten by them, or nearly so, and the evidence points to their never having passed through a genuine bronze age * * * They used iron for manufacturing spears, swords, and knives of various shapes, and likewise for the more peaceful purpose of making hooks wherewith to angle, or to fasten the doors of their huts. Their other warlike and hunting implements (besides traps and gins), which appear to have been used equally for beasts and birds, and for destroying human enemies), were bow and arrows, spears and elbow pads, the latter seemingly of skin, while special allusion is made to the fact that the arrows were feathered." Mention is made of the "pestle and morter, of the fire drill, of the wedge, of the sickle, and of the shuttle used in weaving." Boats were not unknown, but there is little reference, and that doubtful, to the art of sailing. This may possibly help to strengthen the supposition that their sea passage to Japan was a short one, that they were not a maritime people previous to the invasion, and that they came from the mainland and not from the Malay archipelago, as has been surmised. Their palaces were wooden huts, with a hole in the roof for the escape of smoke from the fire which was used in cooking. The doors opened and shut like those of Europe, rather than like the sliding doors of modern Japan. Rugs of skin, rush, matting and even of silk are mentioned. Personal cleanliness received some attention and latrines were in use. Fish, the flesh of wild animals, and rice were used, as well as the alcoholic beverage called sake. "Cooking pots and dishes, the latter both of earthenware and of the leaves of trees, are mentioned, but of the use of fire for warming purposes, we hear nothing. Tables are mentioned several times, but never in connection with food. * * * In the use of clothing and the specialisation of garments, the early Japanese had reached a high level. We read in the most ancient legends of upper garments, skirts, trowsers, girdles, veils and hats, while both sexes adorned themselves with necklaces, bracelets, and other ornaments of stones considered precious." Ear-rings of copper covered with gold (Kin Kwan) were in vogue and a clay image of the dolmen period in my possession illustrates their use in this respect. These, together with the "Magatama" and other ornaments of superior stone, probably took the place of money, the latter idea, it may be, having arisen from the similar use of arrow-heads of superior stone, in a previous age.

The protohistoric interval, of little over three centuries before the period of Wado, witnessed a gradual rise of culture to a higher level than that outlined in the above sketch. The arrival of Buddhism, about the middle of this interval, must have carried in its slow but steady progress, the elements of such enlightenment as the use of the ideograph and the inculcation of the higher moral precepts could bestow on those who came within its reach. In many other ways, the increasing intercourse between China and Corea, brought, not only such literature as the times afforded, but the knowledge of various arts, for instance, silk rearing and weaving and the working of metals. The constant warfare of these early times had, doubtless long ere this, developed the art of weapon making to a degree even superior to that of the great invasion. We are told also, that this interval produced a large image of Buddha, cast in bronze, and garnished with gold, so that the arts of metallurgy were not unknown. Most, however, of the copper and bronze ornaments, mirrors, etc., which have been found in the stone tombs, or dolmens, are of Chinese or Corean origin. The scarcity of iron and copper was such that weapons and mirrors were sometimes copied in soft stone and placed in tombs for the service of the dead, though it was considered of the highest importance to provide the departed with the proper equipment for their long voyage. The scarcity of gold and copper is a theme upon which the old historians have much to say. It would seem as if the efforts of the protohistoric Japanese were mainly directed to squeezing tributes of these metals from the minor kingdoms which now constitute Corea. Aston

PREHISTORIC AND PROTOHISTORIC.   13

and Chamberlain have shewn that these expeditions were neither so numerous nor so uniformly successful as the early accounts would lead us to suppose, but their object is none the less clear.

It may be that the influx of gold or copper was not entirely in the form of loot or compulsory tribute and that it was limited by reason of the fact that Japan was not always able to provide an acceptable *quid pro quo*. To this dearth of these metals we may trace the comparative rarity of bronze or copper ornaments of the protohistoric age, though we should not lose sight of the later conversion of such metallic objects into images of Buddha. What do remain are mostly of Chinese origin and bear out the supposition that until the period of Wado, copper was a rare and practically precious metal. The principal occupation of the Japanese at this time seems to have been fighting, with a background of agriculture to retire upon; and they probably had little opportunity, or taste for acquiring the higher arts of civilisation. The account given of the Anglo-Saxons by David Hume, in his History of England, is fairly applicable to the Japanese of the pre-Wado period. "The military profession alone was honourable among all these conquerors; the warriors subsisted by their possessions in land; they were in general a rude, uncultivated people, ignorant of letters, unskilled in the mechanical arts, untamed to submission under law and government, addicted to intemperance,* riot and disorder. Their best quality was their military courage, which

---
* This is supported by the account of a contemporary traveller from China.

yet was not supported by discipline or conduct." The government of the pre-Wado era, however, seems to have taken a fatherly, if selfish, interest in the welfare of its subjects, a virtue to which the Heptarchy in England has but little claim.

The dolmens, or stone sepulchral chambers of the early Japanese, ceased to be built about a century before the Wado period, and it is practically certain that no coins were then in existence. Mr. William Gowland, who had exceptional opportunities of studying this subject, and who examined no fewer than four hundred dolmens, states with regard to the burial of the dead, "When a warrior was laid in these rude stone chambers of the dead, his wants in a future world where he was supposed to continue his existence, were supplied in no unstinted measure. He was clothed in his robes, adorned with his personal ornaments, his implements of war and of the chase, and the bits and trappings of his horse were all placed near him. Around and at the entrance of the dolmen chamber were arranged offerings of food, water, wine and flowers, in vessels of pottery, some of which are of elaborate forms." But "coins are absent," he tells us. I have visited many of these dolmens and have made diligent enquiry in the neighbourhood of those that had been opened, as to whether any coins have been found, but have been unable to get one instance of their being exhumed from these stone tombs. We know that coins were made during the period of Wado. We know that they were then placed in the graves of the dead as a necessary part of their outfit.

PREHISTORIC AND PROTOHISTORIC.

Had they been in existence during the dolmen age, they would almost certainly have been found in these tombs.

During the century that elapsed between the end of the dolmen age and the beginning of Wado, there is no valid evidence that there had been a metallic currency in Japan. China had possessed such for *twelve centuries* before the Wado period, and I confess that I was greatly astonished to find that coins were lacking in this country so late as the beginning of the 8th century. It is stated in the historical works, "Nihon Shoki" and "Dai Nihonshi," that a silver coin was made as early as the reign of the Emperor Kenso, 485-487. The statement in the Dai Nihonshi however, has evidently been taken from the Nihon Shoki, and the latter has inferred it from an obscure passage in the Nihongi, the historical accuracy of which is very much open to question, even, as Mr. Aston has pointed out, as late as the 6th century. Several pieces of silver have been found, bearing the same badge or stamp, which have been claimed by many writers on numismatics as the coin in question. The first of these was found in the province of O-Sumi, during the period of Kyo-Ho, (1716-1735); then in the Settsu province, in the 11th year of Ho-Reki (1761) a number were found, while pieces of similar size, but with varying badge or marks, have since been exhumed in other places. Such a piece of silver (fig 1.) bears, as Dr. Enomoto Bunshiro has pointed

FIG. 1.

out, no written character whereby its age or identity might be ascertained, but only a crest or badge which has nothing to distinguish it from the stamps placed on precious metals as a guarantee of weight. Mr. Yokoyama, who has specially investigated this matter, found that nearly a hundred pieces were exhumed from a field at Shimpo-In, province of Settsu, in the above-mentioned period of Horeki, but that only two escaped destruction, one of which was owned by himself. He could not find any evidence that these coins were in circulation in the 5th century. One which is in my collection, is said to have been found in the soil at the village of Kawanishi, in the province of Yamato, in the 3rd year of Kei-O (1867); but as the Japanese are known to have been ardent collectors of coins, fifty years before the period of Kyoho, when the first silver coin was found, and as imitations of old and rare coins have been frequent since the end of the 17th century, it is more than likely that some at least have been made for the delectation of collectors. This one, illustrated

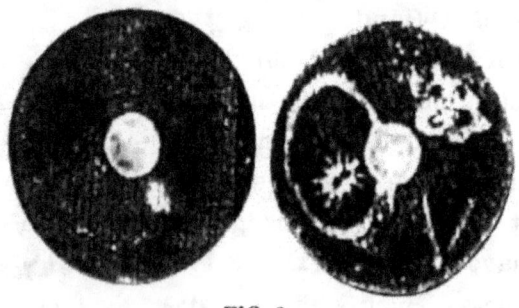

FIG. 2.

in fig. 2. is open to suspicion. The silver piece above-mentioned is known as the "Mu-mon Gin Sen," or non-inscribed silver sen, in recognition of the fact that it has no proper character or ideograph on its face, but inasmuch as the word "Mon" implies also a crest or badge, the definition "Mu-Mon," meaning without writing or badge, is regarded by Mr. Nakagawa as inappropriate; and he proposes the term "Kwammon Gin Sen" i.e. Flower Badge Silver Sen, which seems equally unsuitable. This piece has apparently been roughly cast, and then struck with a design that has been variously described as that of the sun, moon and three stars, a flower, a bunch of rice heads, etc., which similies are somewhat conflicting.* If it be symbolical of anything, the rice supposition may be near the truth, for it is probable that rice was used for money long after the Wado period. On the other hand, it may have been the trade mark of some merchant of advanced ideas, or of a local governor, or perhaps it corresponds to something like our hall-mark, and may have been intended as a guarantee of quality or weight.

Another so called coin (fig 3.) is said to have been of copper and is supposed by some authorities, without any serious reason that I can discover, to have been in circulation even before the silver one. It is illustrated in the older books, but no specimen of it is known to exist. It appears to have been round, with an oval hole in the centre, and the marks of four crosses, or what have been

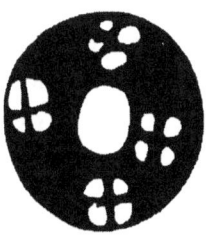

FIG. 3.

---

* On the reverse there is the mark of some stamp, but it is quite illegible.

called the "symbols of rice-plants," arranged around the circle. To my poor judgment, they might be taken for rice-fields as easily as rice-plants, or even the four leaved-shamrock. Possibly they were intended to depict the end of a rice bag with the straw rope tied crosswise over it, as is now usually the case, and thus we might suppose that these four marks represented four bags of rice, each bag having a definite weight. Mr. Hamada Kenjiro in an interesting little brochure entitled "Nihon Kodai Tsuka Ko," or Reflections on Ancient Japanese Coins, suggests that these are rice plant symbols, intended to shew that this token could be exchanged for a given amount of rice, which latter he shews to have been used as a medium of exchange. It is then possible that this, and also the silver coin, had some such function with regard to rice as a bank note has with regard to gold, namely, that they indicated a definite amount, for which they could be exchanged. This surmise seems more likely than the suggestion that one of them was a ticket for admission to the "No" dance, though such tickets were ih use. As it appears to me, the most that can be said about these medals is that they are probably pictorial, but as they do not correspond to any known ideograph and are not sufficiently distinctive, they cannot speak for themselves, and we cannot speak for them.

The written character was known at Court at least as early as A.D. 400 and the silver coin mentioned in the Nihon Shoki was produced, according to its account, more than 80 years later. Chinese coins, which, with the exception of their most primitive forms, are always inscribed, must have been known to the authorities, and it would be very remarkable if the government of Japan should have produced a coin at this date without the slightest sign of a written character thereon.* As I have pointed out, the historical reference to this supposed coin rests on a very slender foundation, and we shall see that even a thousand years later, history has mentioned a coin, the "Ken-Kon Tsu-Ho" which never went into circulation.

More interesting and more convincing to me, is the contention of Mr. Hamada that rice was the current medium of exchange during the later prehistoric and protohistoric age. He states that the word "ine," rice in the stalk, may be recognised in "nedan" value, price, and that the word "atai," also meaning value, price, worth, is derived from "ateshi", rice equivalent. He refers to the existence of markets during the protohistoric period, and argues that a medium of exchange was essential to commerce. Cloth, he says, has been credited with this function, but he believes that rice was a much more likely medium, owing to its general use and the facility with which it could be divided. He remarks that *after* the period of Wado, during which coins were plentiful, great difficulty was experienced in educating the people to their use, and many edicts were published with that object. "In the 'Ima Mukashi Mono Gatari,' or " Talks of Things Present and Past "

---

* According to the "Wakan Kisei Sempu" a copper coin called the "Kai Ka Jimpo" was minted in the second year of the reign of the Emperor Tenchi A.D. 669, but the statement is apocryphal.

he says "a certain person is stated to have said with one ryo of gold I bought three koku of rice and with the rice I bought a house," which would indicate that rice was more acceptable than gold as a purchasing factor. It cannot be said, however, to prove that it was the general medium of financial transactions. There is ample evidence that rice was used in payment of taxes after the Wado period.

The value of rice must have been subject to severe fluctuations from climatic and other causes, such as the devastation accompanying rude warfare; and this must have occasioned much inconvenience. During the latter part of the 7th century several appointments were made relating to the establishment of a mint, and the regulation of matters concerning taxation, weights and measures, precious metals, etc. There is no evidence, however, that coins were actually produced, for the reason probably that copper was not found in sufficient quantity to justify its employment as a circulating medium.

Perhaps the most notable event in the history of Japan, the physical basis indeed of her later civilisation, the auspicious omen which ushered in the accession of the Empress Gemmyo, was the discovery of copper in abundance in the province of Musashi. This occurred in A.D. 707-708, and on this account, following also the established custom of changing the year name on the accession of a new sovereign, the last year of the period Kei-Un was changed to Wa-Do (和同), meaning Japan Copper. At last the long deferred hope was realised.

The land had opened out its hoard of precious metal, the solid basis of wealth and prosperity. A metallic currency would remove the stigma of barbarism and advance the country in the esteem of China, the source of all its civilisation, than which no higher culture could be imagined at that time. Thus, under the feminine sovereignty of the Empress Gemmyo, Japan made her first firm stride in the march of civilisation.

II.

THE ANTIQUE COINS.

From the first year of Wado to the second of Tentoku, that is to say, from the year A.D. 708 to 958, a period of two hundred and fifty years, twelve coins of different denomination were issued by the government of Japan. These coins, together with those that follow, are called sen (Page 263), a word of Chinese derivation, meaning a fountain, hence something which flows. Our own word "currency" originates from the same basic idea. Sen, or "O Ashi", as they are called in common parlance, come under the heading of "copper coinage," but every one knows that the copper is diluted with tin, zinc, and sometimes lead in varying proportions, and should properly be called bronze. The quality of the bronze is liable to considerable variation, and in the case of the twelve antique coins, there is to be noticed a gradual deterioration from first to last, not only in size, but in quality of material. The cause of this deterioration is to be found in the fact that the copper of the Wado period became exhausted and great difficulty was experienced in getting fresh supplies for the mint. The great wave of Buddhism, which swept over the country, was responsible to a considerable extent for this scarcity, for vast amounts of coin, copper ornaments and utensils, as well as fresh supplies, went into the melting pot,

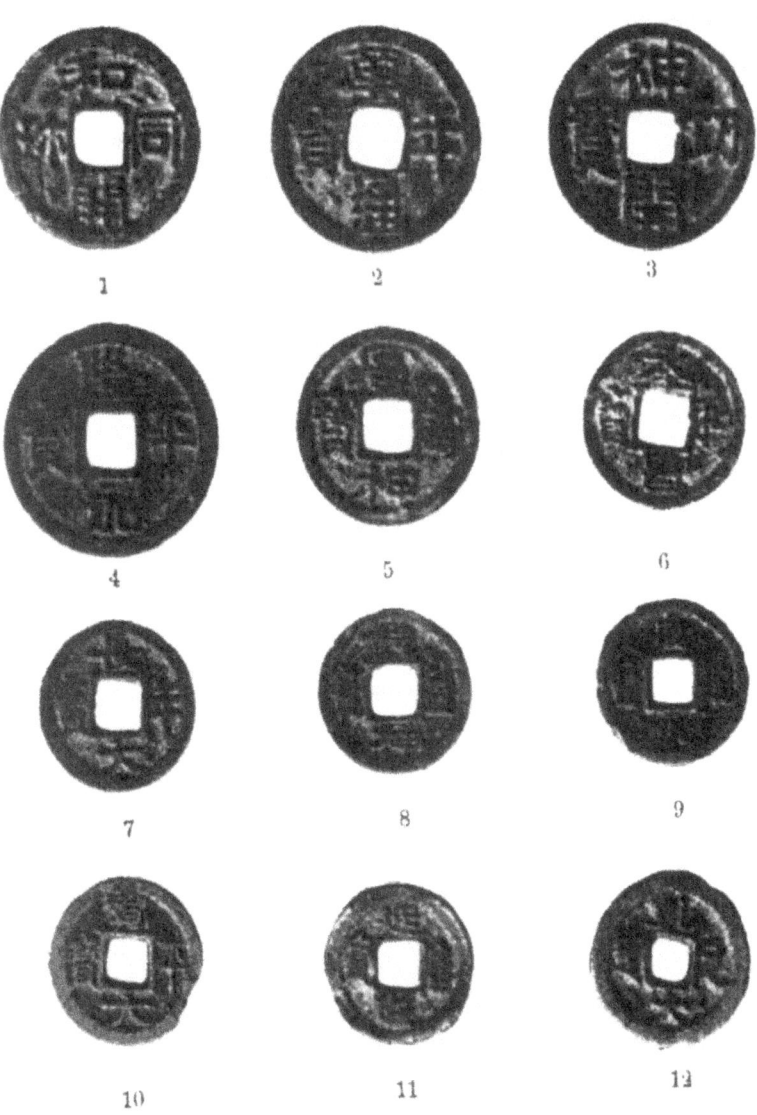

PLATE 1.—THE TWELVE ANTIQUE SEN.

THE ANTIQUE COINS. 23

in order to make images of Buddha. Some of these were of great size and many thousands were erected in various parts of the country. The copper sen which formed the currency of Japan from the period of Wado till the present era of Meiji, which began in 1868, are called by Japanese collectors, "Do Sen," copper sen. With the above qualification, we may state that the coinage of this country was essentially a copper one for eleven hundred and sixty years. Some gold and silver coins exist and they have even been made of iron, but they have been for the most part subsidiary to those of bronze.

The list of antique coins given below, is known to collectors as the "Jiu-ni Zene," or twelve sen, and though this number might be increased to fourteen by the addition of a gold and a silver sen, it is not likely that these were in general circulation, so it is advisable to adhere to the usual classification.

Name	Japanese Period	Year	Name of Sovereign
1. Wado Kaiho	Wado, 1st.	708	Gemmyo
2. Mannen Tsuho	Tempei Hoji 4th,	760	Junnin (Koken, in seclusion)
(Taihei Gempo) (Silver)	"	"	"
(Kaiki Shoho) (Gold)	"	"	"
3. Jingo Kaiho	Tempei Jingo 1st,	765	Shotoku (formerly Koken)
4. Ryuhei Eiho	Enryaku 15th.	796	Kwammu
5. Fuju Jimpo	Konin 9th.	818	Saga
6. Showa Shoho	Showa 2nd.	835	Nimmei
7. Chonen Taiho	Kasho 1st.	848	Nimmei
8. Nyueki Jimpo	Jogwan 1st.	859	Seiwa
9. Jogwan Eiho	Jogwan 12th.	870	Seiwa
10. Kampei Taiho	Kampei 2nd.	890	Uda
11. Engi Tsuho	Engi 7th.	907	Daigo
12. Kengen Taiho	Tentoku 2nd.	958	Murakami

24   *THE ANTIQUE COINS.*

WA-DOKAI-HO   This coin, the first of the Japanese sen,
和 同 開 珎 is usually called "Wado Kai-Chin" and is
A. D. 708   so named in the Japanese works on the
subject. The characters read round the coin, from the
top to the reader's right, then down and to the
left, like the figures on a clock (figs. 1 and 2.) The

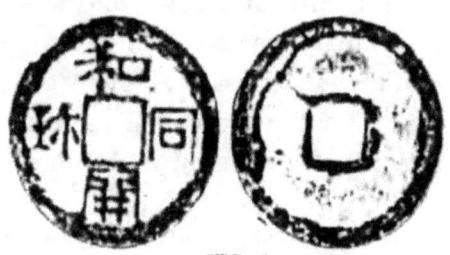

FIG. 1

twelve antique coins are alike in this respect, but from
the 15th year of Tensho (1587) onwards, the reading* is
crosswise, from the top downwards and from right to
left. The late Mr. Narushima Ryuhoku, an eminent
scholar and high official of the present era of Meiji, and
author of the authoritative work called the "Meiji Shin
Sen Sempu," noticed that the character "Chin" (珎) on
the Wado Kaichin coin is an abbreviated form of "Ho"
(寶), meaning treasure. The character "Ho" (寶), is
found on many of the Chinese, Annamese, Corean and
Japanese sen, and frequently occurs as a classical inscription "Tsu Ho" (通寶), which reads "current treasure."
Now, the character "Chin" (珎), which may be described
as the middle third of the character "Ho" (寶), means
precious or curious, and is not used on any of the Japa-

---

* See illustrations in Chapter 4. Note also that the Chinese coin shown in Fig. 3 is read crosswise.

nese or Chinese coins. This character was probably therefore intended as an abbreviated form of "Ho."

FIG. 2

This is the more likely, as the second character "Do" (同) on this coin, is certainly written in the abridged style, instead of in its usual manner (銅). In a variety of the last of the pre-Meiji sen, called the Bunkyu Eiho (Chapter 4), the "Ho" is also abbreviated, but in this case the roof, or top, and the left half of the middle third are retained. Compare (珎) and (寶).

It is reasonable to suppose that, at this period, artificers in metal were not expert in the engraving or casting of small objects in bronze; indeed the few specimens left of their handicraft in metal-work, are by

FIG. 3

no means souvenirs of skill. It is probable therefore, that the easier form was adopted at the expense of strict accuracy. This impression is borne out by a glance at the earlier Wado coins, (figs. 4, 5, 6, and 7). Compare them with figs. 1 and 2, which represent a later mintage. There is every reason to suppose that these later sen were cast by Chinese workmen, imported for the purpose. Their likeness to the Chinese coin "Kai-Gen Tsu-Ho", of the To dynasty, with regard to size, design of the face and reverse, and the exact likeness which the characters "Kai" (開) bear to each other is so striking that it is difficult to escape the deduction that they were minted by artificers from the mainland. I have introduced a specimen of the "Kai-Gen Tsu-Ho" (fig. 3.) for purpose of comparison. At that time, China was the fountain-head

FIG. 4

of Japanese civilisation. Previous to the Wado period, and long subsequent to it, skilled workers, male and female, came over from China to teach various arts to the eager Japanese.

There are other considerations which make it probable that the abbreviated characters "Do" (同) and "Chin" (珎), originated in the need for simplicity in the casting of the earlier coins. The very first Wado Kaiho coin, or Japanese Copper New (Initial or Commencing) Treasure, was not made from copper, but was cast in silver. Figs. 4 and 5 are taken from this silver coin which

THE ANTIQUE COINS.

was cast in the fifth month of the 1st year of Wado, while the copper one did not materialise till the eighth month of the same year. A glance at these, and a

FIG. 5

comparison with figs. 6 and 7 which shew the first copper, "Ko", or old Wado sen, proves their striking similarity in the writing and general clumsiness. The silver sen was really the advance agent of the copper coin. Like our modern bank-notes, it carried the name of the real metallic currency of the country but unlike them the material of the certificate was of greater value than the currency which it repre-

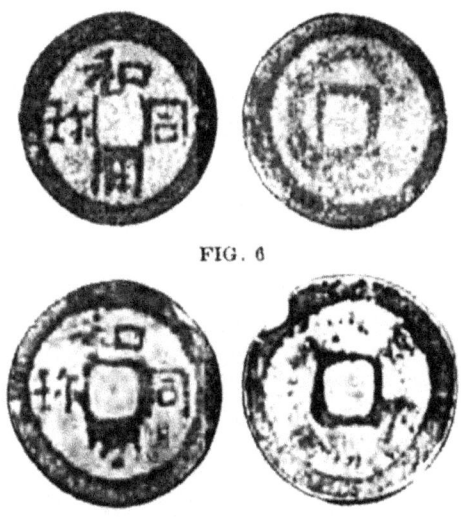

FIG. 6

FIG. 7

sented. At first this caused no inconvenience, for the simple reason that the currency in question was not yet in existence. If it be asked why the first Wado sen was not made of the metal whose name it bore, I can only surmise that Japanese officials of the mint may have found that the copper coin, which had been advertised, so to speak, to appear at a certain date, by government edict, was more difficult to make than had been anticipated. The characters "Wa-Do Kai-Ho" (和同開珎) stand for something like "Japanese Copper Commencing Treasure," a distinct announcement that the coin is of copper and that it is the first to be made of that metal. It is on record that the amount of copper which was discovered in the district of Chichibu, in the province of Musashi, was sufficient to justify the change of the year name from Keiun to Wado, Japan Copper. There is clear proof of the intention to make the coin of copper, and also of the supply for that purpose. Why was this intention not immediately carried out? We can imagine, that with feminine impetuosity and patriotic wish to uplift the name of her country and to celebrate her accession to the throne, the Empress Gemmyo ordered the coin to be cast at once. We may also believe, which is even more likely, that her advisers of the Fujiwara family, who practically controlled the affairs of state, were responsible for the decision to open the Wado period with a copper currency. Experience, however, in the extraction of copper from its ore presupposes the existence of that metal. As copper did not exist in any notable amount prior to Wado, it is probable that the first attempts to extract copper from its ore, or to refine and alloy it for the purpose of minting, were only partially successful. Not only the workmanship but the material of the copper "Ko" Wado sen is inferior to the later issues, and suggest that haste and self-confidence, rather than foresight and experience, were the guiding actors in its inception. On the whole, it may be supposed that the task of producing the first Wado coin proved more difficult than was anticipated and that, to simplify it as much as possible, the characters "Do" and "Ho" were cut down to their abbreviated proportions.

The old but favourite work on the Japanese sen called the "Wakan sen Ii," states, on what authority I do not know, that the characters of the earlier Wado sen were written by Fujiwara Gyoyo and Awata Mabito, while those of the later issues came from the pen of Ono Dofu. In figs. 4 and 5 representing the first or silver Wado coin, and in figs. 6 and 7, which shew the earliest copper issue, the two key-shaped parts of the character "Kai" (開), are closed above by each inner vertical stroke, while in the later issues (figs. 1 and 2) this stroke begins lower down, so that the upper end of each key-shaped part is open. Other differences exist, but this is distinctive. It is in this latter respect that the character "Kai" of the later issues resembles that of the Chinese "Kaigen Tsuho," (fig. 3.) Some experts maintain that both the silver and the copper "Ko" or old Wado sen are found with the open "Kai" but how this is determined I do not know. The Silver Wado is becoming rare, and the Copper one of the same style is much more so. It has usually a doubtful appearance, as if cast from the silver coin, but competent authorities maintain that a few are genuine relics of the first issue of the copper coin. It may be that their very paucity in number and quality attest their premature debut. They are inferior to those that follow, and to the contemporary coins of China, so that some disappointment must have been felt, and if the Empress Gemmyo was at all interested in the matter, no doubt her mint-master Tajihi Mabito Myaki Maro heard her opinion about these first attempts at coin making. It is perhaps not too much to suppose that a messenger was sent post haste to China to solicit from the Emperor Chu-So, the skilled artisans who cast the later Wado coins after the fashion of the beautiful "Kaigen Tsuho."

The later Wado sen are not all of the same standard either in size or quality. The existing specimens of the Wado Kaiho exhibit so much variety in size, width of outer or inner rims, position, size, and even minor differences in the style of the character, that it is sometimes a puzzle, even to an expert, to decide between the genuine and counterfeit coins of this period.

With regard to size, it may be stated generally, as applicable to all of the antique sen, that the first issue of each denomination is larger than those that follow. To some extent this is due to the shrinkage of the clay mould in heating it for the reception of the molten metal. If the sen which have been cast in one mould are used for making the impression on another, the coins from this second mould will be smaller than those

THE ANTIQUE COINS. 31

from the first. In the "Dai Nihon Kwaheishi," Mr. Yoshida Kensuke takes it upon himself to give the size and weight of the earlier as well as the modern coins. With respect to the former, such statements do not rest upon historical information, but on measurements and weights of such specimens as he or his authorities have had in their possession. As the earlier issues of cast coins are larger than those that follow, a fairly reliable indication of their relative age is thus available. In my own collection there are specimens of greater diameter, and probably therefore of earlier origin than some of those described in his work, which, I may state in passing, is by far the most complete and reliable on the subject, from the purely historical point of view. If we suppose that no larger ones have been lost, careful measurements of all the best specimens might give us reliable information with regard to size. The difficulty of ascertaining the exact weight must still remain. The peculiar verdigris or "Sabi," as it is called in Japanese, which forms on these bronze coins, must necessarily alter their weight, and the prolonged exposure to moisture and earthy salts when buried in the soil, dissolves some of the metals which are alloyed together. Owing to frequent conflagrations, too, which are numerous in this earthquake country as a result of the houses being built mainly of wood, many of the antique coins have been burnt. This results in loss of weight from the melting of the baser metals.

Variations in size may also be partly explained by the fact that this coin was not always minted at the same place. At first it was cast in the province of Omi, near the seat of government, but latterly it was found more convenient to make it nearer the sources of copper and therefore Dazaifu, Harima, and Nagato were chosen for the purpose. The intentional debasing of the coinage in order to reap a profit must however be regarded as the main reason for the progressive deterioration in size, from the first issue to later ones. The officials to whom the privilege of minting was entrusted were sometimes the highest in the land, and in these rude times their conduct was above effective criticism. This remark applies not only to the Wado sen, but to all the coins of the antique group.

The change of the mint from one place to another may also account for slight differences in the writing which are to be noticed in these coins. Sometimes the handwriting is quite distinctive and thus several varieties are recognised. Some of these are open to grave suspicion, for there is ample historical proof that as in England about the same time, the ignoble art of counterfeiting was carried on to a degree embarrassing to the government. During the two centuries and a half which saw the production of the antique sen, many edicts were issued by the government against the persistent forgery of the national currency.* The penalties of death, forfeiture of property, banishment and exclusion from the clemency extended to ordinary criminals on occasions of rejoicing, testify to the severity with which the Crown regarded the crime of

---

* See Appendix.

counterfeiting, or even the passing of impure coin. It may be that the characters were altered from time to time, in order to guard against counterfeiting, as happened in the case of some Chinese coins, but this plan would not be very effective; indeed, it may be doubted whether it would not render it more difficult for the ignorant peasants and merchants to distinguish between genuine and counterfeit coin. On the other hand, the design may have been altered without any valid reason, for there is sometimes no accounting for the vagaries of officials, even in Japan.

It is likely enough that some of the existing specimens are forgeries of the Wado period, or shortly after it. The classical sen, which we may call the "Kaigen" Wado, was almost certainly, a government coin, as is also the silver Wado, and probably the copper "Ko" or old, Wado. What is known as the "Noge"

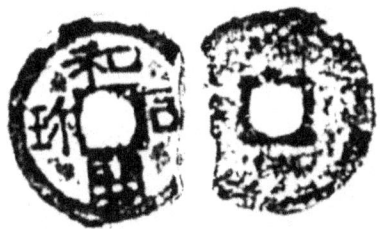

FIG. 8

FIG. 9

Wado, figs. 8 and 9 is so called because the two lower oblique strokes of the left hand part of the character "Wa" (和), are nearly equal in length, while in the ordinary or "Futsu" Wado sen, figs. 1 and 2, the left stroke is much longer than the right one. This left hand part thus resembles the radical or "Hen" called "Noge" (禾), hence the name. The "Noge" Wado is exceedinly rare and many imitations exist. It has the appearance of having been a regular government issue. Figs. 10 and 11 shew the "Hane" (跛) or "hook" Wado, so called from the fact that one or more of the characters has a hook or "Hane" on the lower end of each vertical stroke. It

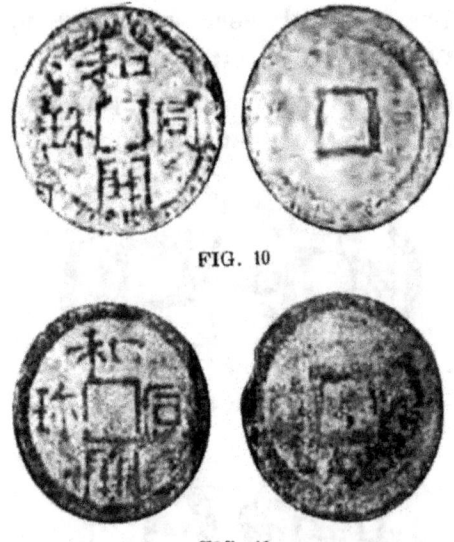

FIG. 10

FIG. 11

is doubtful whether this coin is a regular issue and Mr. Muramatsu looks upon it with severe scepticism. In the work called "Shin Kosei Koho Dzukwan" there is a variety illustrated, called the "Sho Chin" or "Small

Chin" Wado which is scarcely worthy of special mention, but, following this precedent, I give it here, fig. 12. It

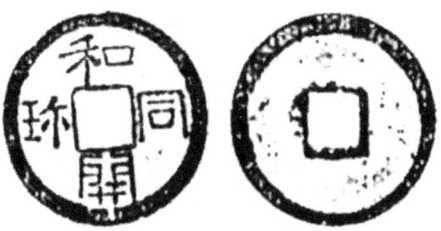

FIG. 12

may be recognised by the fact that an interval separates the right oblique stroke of the character "Ho" (和) from the margin of the central hole. Many such "varieties" exist, the slightest difference in the writing of which even if due to the casting, or some accidental circumstance, may give a certain specimen the patent of nobility in the eye of its possessor, and stamp it as the one and only one of its kind.

There are many genuine specimens of the Wado sen which may be bought for a shilling or two, though specimens like fig. 1 are rare. I have come, however, to regard some of my specimens of this sen as ancient counterfeits, made during the Wado period, or shortly after. These may justly claim to be over a thousand years old; and though we may despise them in our hearts, they are entitled to the outward respect which is paid, even to disreputable age.

Although the silver Wado coin heralded the advent of the copper currency, its circulation was stopped in the eighth month of the second year. This was exactly one year after the copper coin came into circulation.

According to the "Zoku Nihongi," the government had announced in the third month of the 2nd year of Wado, that the ratio of silver to copper would be one to four. The same work states that it was found necessary, as early as the first month of the 2nd year, to issue a prohibition against the "many forgeries" that were being made, that is to say only five months after the copper, and eight months after the silver coin came into being. Whether the silver coin was considered to have done its duty as the forerunner of the copper sen, or whether it was arrested with a view to stop these forgeries, the tempting ratio of one to four being more than honesty, such as it was, could withstand, history does not relate. It is certain, however, that the bimetallists of the day were unable to uphold the sanctity of this fixed ratio against the stern reality of practical economics. From this time forth, until the period of Meiji, copper, in a more or less diluted form, has been the mainstay of the official currency. Some silver and gold coins have been produced, not always for circulation, and those that have been so designed, had probably, as we shall see, a special *raison d'etre*, such as to stimulate foreign trade.

In the 4th year of Wado, the price of rice, or its ratio to copper, was fixed by government edict. Six "sho" or sixty "go" of rice could then be had for one cash or sen, usually called in its unit capacity, the "Mon." At the present day the price for average quality of rice is about one yen for sixty "go." Presuming that the measure called the "go" is the same

THE ANTIQUE COINS.

now as then, the purchasing value of the Wado sen was about a thousand times that of the present day. A Japanese man consumes about five " go " of rice daily, so that he could have lived in the Wado period for twelve days on one sen or mon, with the addition of a few "snacks" of fish and vegetable. At the present time, the wages of a carpenter are about a yen per day. Now the yen is equal to a thousand mon of the smaller sen and five hundred mon of the larger ones, so that he could have provided himself with rice, if we count only five hundred mon to the yen, for sixteen years, on the wages which he receives for one day's labour in the year 1904! At this time, the highest officials in the realm, chiefly princes of the blood, received in one year, 30 "Hiki" of cloth, 100 hanks of silk and the princely salary of 2000 mon, the present equivalent of two yen, while the eighth class were given 1 "Hiki" of cloth and 20 mon per annum, which is equal to one fiftieth of the present yen. As the yen is about the value of two shillings sterling, the latter officials could not have got less than one halfpenny per annum.

The decision to pay these handsome salaries was announced in the tenth month of the fourth year, and at the same time an order appeared offering various grades of official rank to those who had amassed certain amounts of cash, the lowest being five thousand mon, a comfortable fortune in those days. Severe penalties were imposed upon those who borrowed money for this purpose. A concrete instance this, of the rank being "but the guinea stamp"; still, habits of thrift were encouraged, while the government got rid of its surplus stock. This latter object was also furthered by an edict in the 5th year, ordering travellers to use sen instead of commodities to defray the cost of travelling, and in the 6th year it was decreed that no officials could rise above their present grade unless they possessed a sum of 6000 mon. In the 5th year of Yoro the ratio of copper to silver was fixed at twenty-five to one, the value of the silver Wado, it will be remembered, having been one to four of the copper sen.

It would appear that the Wado Kaiho was coined for fifty years after its first appearance, for we read in the Zoku Nihongi, that in the 2nd year of Tempei Hojŏ the Empress Koken gave permission to Shibi Naisho Fujiwara Ason Nakamaro, one of the great Fujiwara family, upon whom she looked with favour, to cast coin for the government. The long continued mintage of this coin probably accounts for the fact that, although the most ancient of the twelve antique coins, it is the least rare of any, and it may also explain the circumstance that there are so many different sizes of this coin.

MAN-NEN TSU-HO
萬年通寶
A.D. 760

In the third month of the fourth year of Tempei Hojŏ, A. D. 760, the Empress Koken having gone into retirement (which afterwards proved to be temporary), three new coins were minted, of copper, silver, and gold respectively. Each coin had a distinct denomination. There is little doubt that the copper coin alone went into general circulation. It is called the "Man-Nen Tsu-Ho"

(萬年通寳), or Current Treasure of Ten Thousand Years. The characters thereon are said to have been written by Kibi Mabi, a scholar and man of genius, who invented the first Japanese system of syllabic writing, known as the Katakana. Mr. Enomoto Bunshiro attributes the production of this coin to extensive forgeries of the Wado sen, which a former edict stated to equal in amount the legal currency. The new coin was issued at the rate of one to ten of those previously in circulation. With the exception of the "Jingo Kai-ho," the third on the list, each new issue of the antique sen was valued at *one* to *ten* of the previous denominations, so that the government, or those interested in the matter, made a huge profit out of the transaction. When a new issue was decided upon, the last specimens of the former one were usually so poor in size and quality, that the new sen was quite superior, and its acceptance was doubtless facilitated by this fact. The possession of money, too, was chiefly limited to the upper classes, or those in the provinces immediately surrounding the capital, who probably found means to recoup themselves for this sudden and rather startling fall in exchange. Still, it is difficult to see how such a measure could avoid producing distress and discontent. We are not told whether, in fixing this exchange of the good new, to the bad old currency, any attempt was made to discriminate between the former government issues and those counterfeits which were the assumed *raison d'etre* of the new coin.

THE ANTIQUE COINS.

The first issue is a large coin with good body and fair workmanship, though not so fine as that of the "Kaigen" Wado sen, figs. 13 and 14. It is called the "Ogata"

FIG. 13

FIG. 14

(大形), or "Large Size" Mannen, and it will be noticed that the dot of the character "Nen" (represented by a short stroke) is placed vertically on the lowest horizontal one. Another variety, fig. 15, known as the "Yoko Ten"

FIG. 15

(横点) or "Horizontal Dot" Mannen, has the dot (Ten) written horizontally (Yoko) between the two lower

THE ANTIQUE COINS.

strokes of the character "Nen" (年); All of the characters differ slightly from those of the first variety, especially the lower one, "Tsu." Figure 16 shews another

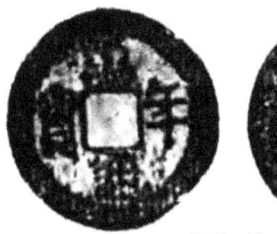

FIG. 16

specimen with a relatively broad rim, and therefore styled the "Kwatsu En" (濶 緣), or Broad-rimmed Mannen. The dot on the character "Nen" is horizontal. Still another kind has a round dot between the two lower strokes of "Nen," and is therefore called the "En Ten" (圓点), or "Round Dot" Mannen fig. 17. In a variety of the latter, fig. 18, the lower strokes of

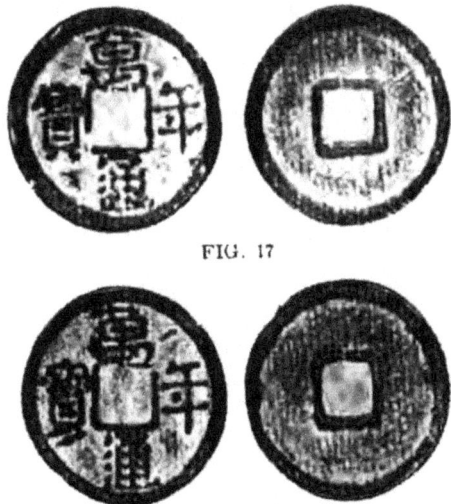

FIG. 17

FIG 18

42   THE ANTIQUE COINS.

"Ho" (寳) both turn to the left. It is open to question whether this is a government coin, or a forgery of the period. Smaller specimens of the Mannen abound, but they do not fall to the dwarf-like dimensions of the other antique sen. The "Currency of Ten Thousand Years" expired before a decade had elapsed, and probably did not have time to undergo further degeneration.

TAI-HEI GEN-HO
大 平 元 寳
A.D. 760

This silver coin, which is called Taihei Gempo, for the sake of euphony, or rather it should be said, for ease of pronunciation, is seen in fig. 19. The only specimen which

FIG. 19.

is recognised by experts as genuine, is in the possession of Mr. Kameoka Seikoku, but there are a few others in the hands of collectors, which are probably of recent origin. That seen in fig. 20 is probably not more than two

FIG. 20.

THE ANTIQUE COINS.

hundred years old. "Tai-Hei Gen-Ho" (大平元寳) reads "Original Treasure of Great Peace." It was cast at the same time as the Mannen sen and was issued at one to ten of the former. It will be remembered that the ratio of copper to silver started, during the first years of Wado, at four to one; then it reached twenty-five to one; now another rate of exchange, namely of ten to one was arbitrarily fixed to correspond with the ratio of the Taihei Gempo to the following coin which was of gold, and which was called the

KAI-KI SHO-HO. This coin fig. 21, was designed to be
開 基 勝 寳 issued with the silver and copper sen
A.D. 760 above-mentioned and to bear the same ratio to the silver coin that it held in regard to the Man-

FIG. 21

nen sen, namely one to ten. Like the Taihei Gempo, it has, with a solitary exception, vanished from human ken, and left a host of conjectures which it would not profit us much to pursue. The one specimen now remaining, is in the possession of the Imperial Household Department, and was exhumed from under the gateway of the Sai-Dai-Ji Temple at Nara, in company with one Taihei Gempo, one silver Wado, and one Mannen Tsuho. In the second year of Jisho, A. D. 1177, according to the book called "Sei-Sui-Ki," Komatsu Naidaijin, a famous minister of the crown, placed 99 pieces of gold under the pillow of his sister, who was the wife of the Emperor, during her accouchement, and prayed for her speedy recovery. It has been assumed that these gold coins were no other than the Kaiki Shoho, but this belief does not rest on any solid foundation, so far as I know. Pieces of gold stamped with their weight were known at that time, and besides it was quite customary to follow the Chinese fashion of using paper substitutes, which were afterwards burned, as an offering to the god. This was an economical plan, and reminds one somewhat of the two persons who undertook to place an equal sum in the coffin of a deceased friend. A, having conscientiously put his amount therein, B signed a cheque for double the amount, and pocketed the change. While we cannot be certain that Komatsu Naidaijin presented the god with a cheque for the 99 coins, it is equally doubtful that he paid it in cash, and it would be unwise to accept the story as a proof that the Kaiki Shoho was current in the twelfth century, or that it had ever been in general circulation. The words 'Kai-Ki Sho-Ho'* (開基勝寳) probably mean "The Initial Foundation of Excelling Treasure." There is no doubt that this coin was intended to be the pioneer of a gold currency, and we may believe that the idea had the approval, and perhaps started in the brain of Kibi Mabi, the most original and learned genius of his time. The

---

* Kaiki is a Buddhist term and now usually refers to the founding of a new temple or sect. The specimen above illustrated is said to be an exact model in gold of the one in the collection of the Household Department, correct even to weight.

THE ANTIQUE COINS.

country was, however, too poor to warrant such an experiment being carried out on a large scale, and it is very probable that only a few specimens came from the mint.

JIN-KO-KAI-HO
神功開寶
A.D. 765

This coin was issued in the first year of Tempei Jingo, A. D. 765. The Empress Koken, who had resigned in favour of the Emperor Junnin, now resumed the throne, while the latter went into exile. On this second assumption of power, she took the name of "Shotoku" (denoting virtue), and the "year name" was changed from Tempei Hoji to Tempei Jingo. The expression "Jingo" is a softening of "Jinko" (神功), which may be rendered "Divine Merit." It is worthy of remark that the slang expression "by jingo," shews the same euphonic softening, being derived from the Basque word "Jinkoa," "God," "the Lord of the High." It has thus the same basic idea as the Chinese "Jin"* or "Shin," "God," "Superior or Exalted Being," and I venture to think that these words may have a common origin, as the Basque language has a close affinity to the Mongol group.

"Jin-Ko Kai-Ho" (神功開寶) is best translated, perhaps as the "New Treasure of Divine Merit." It has been given as the "New Treasure of the period Jingo,"† but this is not correct. Three consecutive periods begin with "Tempei," viz. "Tempei Shoho," "Tempei Hoji," and "Tempei Jingo," and the word "Jingo" of the

---

* Pronounced variously in the Chinese colloquial, shin, through various grades approaching the French "jeune" to the English word "gin." This latter sound is often used in Japanese, especially in compound words.

† "Coins of Japan" by William Bramsen 1880.

latter phrase is written thus, (神護) meaning "Divine Protection," and not thus (神功), like those of the coin in question, which reads "Divine Merit." According to Yoshikawa Iken, this coin was also written by Kibi Mabi. It was circulated at the same value as the Mannen Tsuho, and Mr. Enomoto suggests that its issue was due to a dearth of the latter coinage. The Dai Nihon Kwaheishi, quoting the Zoku Nihongi, says that at this period, the government found that the people were storing up their money and thus causing a scarcity in the currency of the country. This is stated to have been due to the excessively high rate of exchange, those who had amassed a hoard of Wado sen being naturally loath to part with it for one-tenth the amount of a coin, in no respect its superior. This reluctance, and the desire to save, which was doubtless stimulated by the government pronouncement that "the rank is but the guinea stamp," doubtless occasioned the shortage of money in circulation. Be the cause what it may, it is certain that the Jinko Kaiko was issued at the same value as the Mannen Tsuho, and is the only member of the antique group which did not appear at tenfold the value of the preceding issue. In the eighth month of the 3rd year of Hoki, A. D. 772, it was further decreed that the value of all old and new coins would henceforth be the same, as it was found that the people kept the old ones and used only those recently made.

The early Jinko Kaiho is a coin of good size, quite equal in this respect to the two previous sen, but, the size did not remain constant during the thirty

THE ANTIQUE COINS. 47

years of its existence. Probably also, its long run of popularity accounts for the many varieties which are to be found, of which I shall give only the chief. It will be understood that, just as two specimens of English handwriting may resemble each other and yet present points of difference on close inspection, so the inscription of Chinese characters by separate individuals may appear at first sight to be identical, but they are quite easily distinguished by an attentive inspection.

FIG. 22

FIG. 23

If we compare figs. 22 and 23 with 24 and 25 we see that the characters, in the two former "Ko" (功) are not quite similar to that in the two latter. In both, the character "Ko" is made up of two parts, a left and right hand radical. The left hand part in both is the same, except that it is a little shorter and further from the hole in figs. 22 and 23 than in figs. 24 and 25, its upper and lower strokes being longer. This by itself is the character "Ku" (工), meaning toil, and in figs. 22 and 23, its neighbour on the right is the character "To," (刀) meaning a sword. Toil with the sword was, in ancient times, the most laudable occupation, and the combination with its implied deeds of "derring doe," was a significant way of writing "merit." "Ku" and "To", combined therefore mean, merit. Now, in figs. 24 and

FIG. 24

FIG. 25

25 the right hand character is not exactly the same as the right hand radical "To" (刀) in figs. 22 and 23. It will be noticed that the inner vertical stroke of this character projects a little above the horizontal line in figs. 24 and 25 whereas it ends on a level with it in figs. 22 and 23. This makes all the difference in the name and meaning of these two right-hand characters, for the one with

THE ANTIQUE COINS.   49

the projecting stroke is not called "To" (刀) a sword, but
"Riki" (力) strength. This coin is said to have been also
written by Kibi Mabi, and it may have occurred to his
humane intellect, that the combination of strength and
skill was a more worthy way of acquiring "merit"
than expert work with a sword. Although the
reading (功) is recognised as "Ko" on this coin, it is
not the classical and accepted form, but Kibi Mabi,
when he invented the Katakana, departed from ancient
usage in a very decided manner and he may have
made this innovation as a protest against the savage
and uncivilised plan of acquiring merit (工 刀) by
swordmanship.

It will also be seen that the character "Kai" differs
in figs. 22, 23 and 24, 25 in that it is "open," in the former, as we have described it in the later Wado sen, while
it is "closed" in figs. 24, 25 as it occurs in the early Wade
coins. Close inspection will also reveal points of dissimilarity in the characters "Ho" (寳) and "Jin" (神), and
indeed the "To" (刀) and "Riki" (力) also differ in minor
ways. In passing, I may say that anyone desir-
ing to become expert in the fascinating study of
ideographic coins, will do well to study each character
separately and to compare it with the same on other
coins. In Chamberlain's "Introduction to the Study of
Japanese Writing," most of these characters may be
found in very large type, sometimes larger than the
coins themselves, and each detail may thus be easily
impressed on the mind. Without enlarging the scope of
this work beyond reasonable limits, it would be obviously

impossible to point out all the minor differences in the handwriting of these coins, and I shall be content to indicate the main features, leaving the reader to exercise his discrimination in noting the rest, a very useful exercise for the attention. On account of the above-mentioned dissimilarity in the formation of the character "Ko" (功), the coin illustrated in figs. 24 and 25, is known as the "Riki" (力) Jingo. In most of the coins which I have seen, those bearing the "Riki," have a wider margin than those having "To" as a radical. Of this style is the sen given in fig. 26, which is called the

FIG. 26

"Kwatsu En" Jingo, on account of its wide margin. In one very rare variety of the "Riki" Jingo, the character "Riki" is lower and shorter than usual, while the body of "Ho" (寶) is rounded, figs. 27 and 28. It is known

FIG. 27

FIG. 28

as the "Shuku" Riki Jingo, or "Low" Riki Jingo. Another very rare kind is the "Cho Ho" Jingo, or long "Ho" Jingo, fig. 29, the general characters being much the same

FIG. 29

as in figs. 22 and 23, but minor differences will be noticed, and the "Ho" is longer. Another specimen, not very rare, but interesting, is seen in fig. 30 and is called the "Fu

FIG. 30

Riki," or "Non Riki" Jingo, from the fact that though the character "Kai" (開) is closed, and the others also

resemble those of the Riki Jingo, yet it is not a
Riki coin, as the inner vertical line of what would be
Riki, does not project above the horizontal one. In
figs. 1 and 2, plate 5, chapter 3, may be seen a coin of this
denomination which has been struck, not cast. It
cannot have been a government sen and is either a gross
counterfeit of the period, or a later production of the
"Shima Sen" order, to be referred to later on. An
illustration of what is known as the "Tsume" Jingo,
will be found amongst the picture sen, in the last chapter.
The mark on the back is supposed to be the impression
of a thumb-nail after the fashion of certain of the Kaigen
Tsuho sen of China, but its whole appearance betrays
rather the work of the forger's hand.

RYU-HEI EI HO　　In the beginning of the reign of
隆平永寶　the Emperor Kwammu, in the fourth
A.D. 796　　month of the 1st year of Enryaku,
A.D. 782, the government decreed that as things
were sufficiently prosperous, and there was enough
money in circulation, the officials of the mint should be
retired. Eight years later the necessity for a fresh
coinage became evident, and officials were again
appointed to the mint. No definite step, however, seems
to have been taken till the eleventh month of the 15th
year, A.D. 796. An edict then appeared to the effect
that many imitations existed, which were not worthy of
being called current coin, and therefore a new coin would
be introduced, which would be issued at the rate of one to
ten of the old ones. These latter would be removed
from circulation within four years, counting from

the following year. The new coin would be called the "Ryu-Hei El-Ho" (隆平永寶), or Eternal Treasure of Prospering Peace. The delay in issuing this coin may have been due to the scarcity of copper, for a great wave of religious enthusiasm had set in, which found expression in the erection of the gigantic Daibutsu, or statue of Buddha, at Nara in A.D. 750, which used up 868,000 kin* of copper, while thousands of smaller images were erected everywhere between this date and the period of Enryaku. We can be certain that the trend of thought was profoundly modified by the moral precepts of Buddhism which had spread throughout the land. This can be traced even in the decrees which related to purely economical matters. For instance, in the second month of the 16th year of Enryaku, the government announced that it collected taxes in order to assist the people in times of drought, famine or such calamity. "Cash or cloth," it said, "cannot be used as food. It is understood that at the present time the officials are receiving cash in payment of taxes, but they should bear in mind the reason for taxation, and receive cash no longer. There are various classes in the country, however, and those who cannot provide enough grain for the purpose of taxation should be allowed to pay in cash to the extent of not more than one-fourth of the whole tax." The government apparently found that the retention of money in the hands of the people did not facilitate its circulation, for we read (Dai Nihon Kwahei-

---

* About 1,157,000 lbs. avoirdupois, on the supposition that the weight of the Kin has undergone no change.

shi, quoting from the Ruishiu San Dai Kaku) that on
th 23rd day of the ninth month of the 17th year, a
further decree appeared to the effect that the use of coin
is to give general convenience to all alike but that the
officials and farmers in the five provinces* around Kyoto
(the capital), were saving too much money while there
was not sufficient in the city. "This is contrary to our
intention to confer equal benefit on all, and it is strictly
forbidden. All possessed of means must contribute
money and these taxes must be paid in cash. Those
guilty of secreting money will receive the punishment
of lawbreakers, and their property will be divided into
five portions. One fifth will be given to the informant
of the fact, while the remainder will be forfeited to the
government. The provinces of Iga, Omi, Wakasa,
Tamba, and Kii, are exempted from this law."

The early specimens of the "Ryu-Hei Ei-Ho" (隆平
永寶), Prosperous Peace Eternal Treasure, are large and
well finished (fig. 31). Note the relatively small size of the

FIG. 31

character "Ei" (永) in this specimen and consequently
the interval which separates it from the central hole.

---

* The five Provinces or "Go-Ki" were Yamashiro, Yamato, Kawachi, Idzumi, and Settsu.

This is the "Ogata Sho Ei," or Large Model small Ei coin. It may be the first issue. Fig. 32 illustrates a coin of the

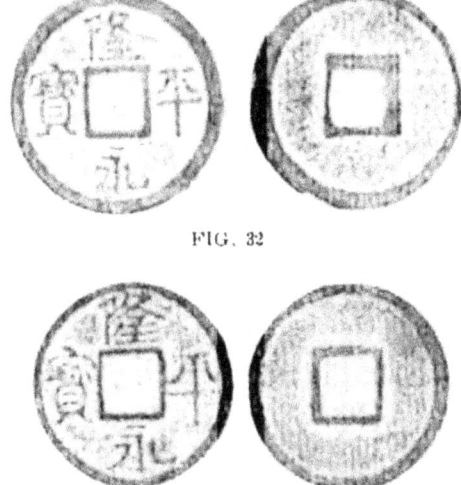

FIG. 32

FIG. 33

same issue as that given in the first volume of the Meiji Shin Sen Sempu, and was probably the finest specimen then known. It is somewhat inferior to fig. 31.

FIG. 34

What may be called the "Futsu" or ordinary Ryuhei, fig. 33, is characterised by the smaller size of the coin and the larger relative size of the character " Ei " (永) Note also the writing of the character "Kei." Fig. 34

shews a neat looking coin, smaller than the above, the character Ei being rather less than in fig. 33.

Various sizes of this coin exist, with varying breadth of rim; but they do not need special description. This coin is said, by Mr. Yoshikawa, in the Wakan Sen-Ii, to have been written by the Emperor Kwammu himself, and it is certainly worthy of such an exalted penman. To my thinking, it is almost the best of the "Jiu Ni Zene," whether in style of writing, material or workmanship. Over a hundred years ago, a large number of these sen were found in the river Horiye at Osaka, and a bridge afterwards built on the spot, has ever since been known as the "Ryuhei" bridge.

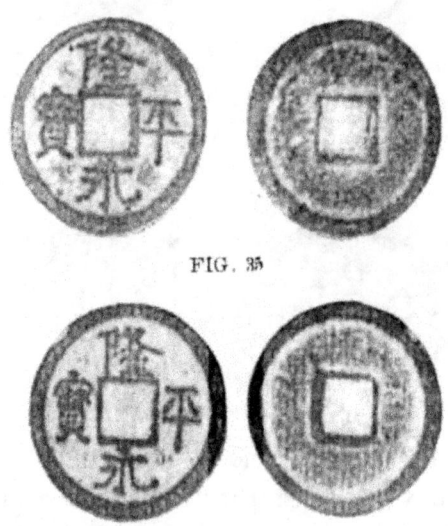

FIG. 35

FIG. 36

The chief variety of this sen is the "Nisui" Ryuhei, figs. 35 and 36. It is so called because the lower of the two horizontal strokes of the character "Ei" (永), instead of

THE ANTIQUE COINS.

simply extending to the left of the vertical stroke, passes also to the right, (永) giving the appearance of the numeral "Ni" (二), which stands for "two." The part of the character below this resembles the character "Sui" (水) "Water," hence the name "Nisui." There are two kinds of the Nisui Ryuhei, the "Dai Ji" (Large Character) fig. 35, and the "Sho Ji" (Small Character) Ryuhei, fig. 36. In another variety the lower horizontal stroke of the "Ei" (永) passes more to the left than is usual and is therefore called the "Cho To Ei" or Long-headed Ei, fig. 37. Yet

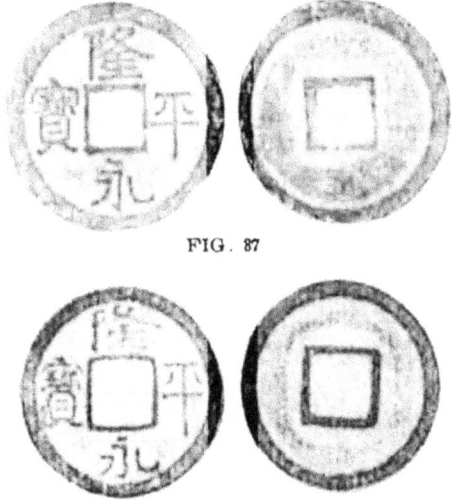

FIG. 87

FIG. 88

another kind is seen in fig. 38, known as the "Cho Hei," or Long Hei, because the vertical line below the two horizontal strokes is longer than the space between them and reaches down to near the margin of the coin.

In the fifth month of the 3rd year of Daido, in the reign of the Emperor Heijo, according to the Nihon

Koki, an edict appeared saying "there are not many coins in circulation amongst the peasants, and therefore they will be permitted to use both old and new sen in order to relieve this want" (at the same rate of exchange?). In the first year of Konin, A. D. 810, and of the reign of the Emperor Saga, it is stated (Nihon Koki and Ruishiu Kokushi) that 1040 "Kwan"* of coin, probably Ryuhei sen, were cast from the copper remaining in the mint. We may presume that this was the last issue of this coin.

FU-JU JIN-HO. 富 壽 神 寶 A.D. 818

In the third month of the 9th year of Konin, the governor of Nagato province was appointed chief director of the Mint, the officials of which were, one director, two inspectors, three accountants, two coiners, one chief moulder and five clerks (Ruishu Kokushi). In the eleventh month of the same year, the "Fu-Ju Jin-Ho" (富壽神寶) pronounced Fuju Jimpo, the Divine Treasure of Wealth and Longevity, appeared—surely a high sounding and felicitous title! It steps forth amid a flourish of "Gekitaku,"† and smiles its benevolent formula upon the world. It is not so large and imposing as those that have gone before, but we hear no reproaches this time about the degenerated state of the currency. What it lacks in size it wins in its message of good-will. "Wealth and long life to you," it says,"if you keep me

---

* The expression "Kwan" probably refers here to 1000 pieces, though it may have been applied in the usual sense of 1000 momme, about 8¼ lbs avoirdupois.

† Or "Hyoshigi", the two pieces of resonant wood which were struck together to call attention to proclamations, etc. They are still used in theatres and advertising processions.

long enough, you will never want for either." We can well imagine that the good wish found its echo in many a wistful heart, and that the chord of superstition awoke to the sentiment. It may even be that the Fuju Jimpo was much sought after and that there was quite a rush for it, notwithstanding its diminished size.

This coin is said to have been inscribed by the Emperor Saga, and by Kukwai, canonised as Kobo Daishi, who "was noted equally as preacher, painter, sculptor, calligraphist and traveller".* He was the founder of the syllabic writing called the Hiragana and is worshipped as the sage of writing. We are told that 5670 Kwan of this coin were cast annually till the 12th year of Konin, (A. D. 821), 3000 Kwan till the 5th year of Tencho (A. D. 828), and 1830 Kwan till the first year of Showa (A. D. 834). The cause of this reduction is said to have been a falling off in the production of copper which seems to have been so serious that the casting of coin from new metal was stopped for a time, while the former issues of Wado, Mannen, Jinko and Ryuhei sen were collected and recast into the form of the Fuju Jimpo. While the primary cause of this deterioration of the national currency is to be traced to a deficiency in the output of copper, the wholesale contribution of coin towards the creation of Buddhist images, bells and religious ornaments, must be regarded as an important factor. The Fuju Jimpo was not destined to carry its message of hope for an indefinite period, for within eighteen years it had to give place to another, and finally, like its forerunners, under-

---
* Chamberlain and Mason's " Handbook to Japan."

went dissolution in order to furnish the material for a diminishing currency. The coin illustrated in fig. 39

FIG. 39.

is, if we may judge by its size, probably of the first issue, and therefore I give it precedence. It bears the characters "Fu-Ju Jin-Ho" (富壽神寶) Wealth, Longevity, Divine Treasure. This specimen is usually called the "Tate Nuki", or "Warp and Woof" Fuju sen, because the central vertical stroke in the character "Ju" (壽), crosses several (five) lines on its passage to the fourth, and longest, horizontal stroke. In other respects this coin closely resembles the "Taiji" or large character sen, fig. 40. In this, however, the vertical stroke

FIG. 40.

extends only to the second horizontal line. The Tate Nuki sen is said to have been written by the Emperor Saga.

The Taiji, is stated by Mr. Yoshikawa to have been

THE ANTIQUE COINS. 61

written by the immortal Kobo Daishi. It is scarcely likely that the Emperor would have been asked to write the inscription for an inferior coin such as the Futsu or common sen, though this is stated by some authorities. It may be that the statement was invented by the Fujiwara who "advised" the throne at the time, in order to add to the popularity of the coin. As however we have no data to judge by, and can not transpose our minds to the scale of intellectuality prevailing at that time, we cannot say what motives governed the actions of officialdom, though we may derive some amusement from such speculations. Like the "Taiji" or large character sen, the Ogata or large sized coin, fig. 41, is a much more

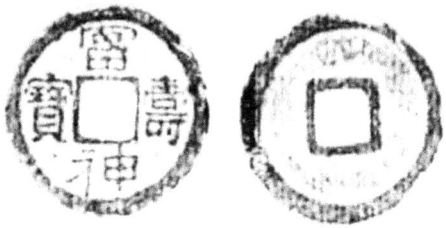

FIG. 41

imposing coin than those that follow, and its claim to represent the first issue is almost as valid as that of the Tatenuki sen though, so far as I have seen, its diameter is less than that of the latter, by about a centimetre. These three coins resemble each other especially in the writing of the character "Fu" (富), meaning wealth. Here we may still discern the roof of the storehouse, with the goods contained therein, the solid guarantee of wealth. In the "Tatenuki" and "Taiji" or "Daiji" Fuju sen, figs. 39 and 40, and in the "Ogata" or "Large Sized" coin fig. 41, there is no dot on the top of the roof to represent the cross section of the ridge pole, nor is there a horizontal line below the roof, such as we find in the ordinary Fuju figs. 42 and 43. It is scarcely necessary to

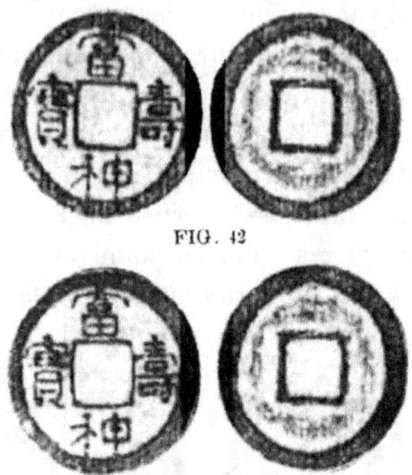

FIG. 42

FIG. 43

add that the characters are larger in the three former coins than in the ordinary Fuju and that minor differences can be seen on close inspection, for instance, the third stroke of "Ju," which joins the margin of the central hole in the case of the smaller sen, the dotlike stroke of the left hand part of "Jin" (神) etc. Another well marked variety is called the "Shimesu" (示) Fuju, figs. 44 and 45 because the lefthand part or radical, of

FIG. 44

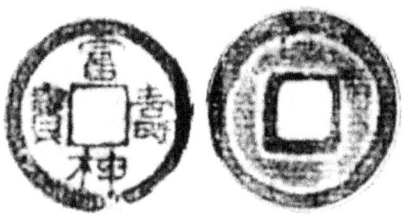

FIG. 45

the character "Jin," (神) exhibits a peculiarity which causes it to resemble the character "Shimesu" (示), meaning to indicate. This consists in the lengthening of the lower horizontal stroke of this radical to the right, after the fashion of the "Nisui" Ryuhei, figs. 35 and 36 The "Ko Sen," or "Large Hole" Fuju, explains itself; and needs no illustration in size it resembles the two previous coins.

SHO-WA SHO-HO.
承和昌寶
A.D. 835

In the first month of the 2nd. year of Showa, the usual decree appeared, attributing the defects in the currency to the "secret counterfeiting by private persons, which undoubedly renders the coinage worthless. To remedy this a new coin shall be issued." This coin was named the "Sho-Wa-Sho-Ho" (承和昌寶) or "Flourishing Treasure of (the period) Showa. According to the Zoku Nihon Koki, the Emperor Nimmei, in a special edict on the occasion of his accession to the throne, thus gave the reason for the change of the period from Tencho to Showa. "I succeeded to the throne of the Peaceful Emperor (his father, then living), and now the time has come to give a new name to the era, thus changing the 11th year of Tencho to the first year of Showa." By way of explanation, he stated that he was following the custom of a thousand Emperors in altering the "Nengo," or year name on their accession and in choosing an auspicious title, in order to have a fortunate commencement to each reign.

Special emphasis seems to be laid on the accession to the "Peaceful Emperor" and we shall probably not be far wrong to translate the expression "Showa," as "Succeeding Peace." The "Ogata" or large sized coin, figs. 46 and 47, is slightly smaller than the Tatenuki or

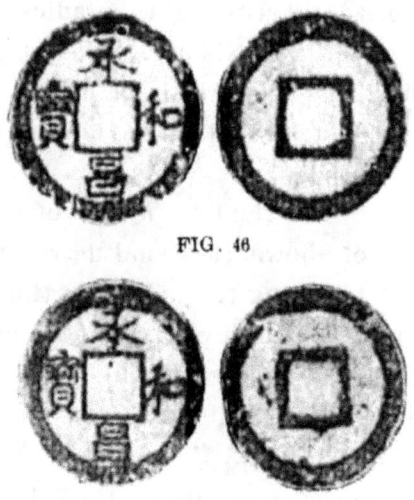

FIG. 46

FIG. 47

Daiji Fuju and the quality of the metal also shews the stigma of degeneration. From the Fuju sen to the end of the twelve antique sen we shall see a gradual deterioration in size and quality, due to the scarcity of copper and the necessity of remelting former issues in order to get material for the national currency. The "Futsu" or common Showa, fig. 48, is much smaller than the "Ogata" sort, and has a narrower rim. The characters of both coins are supposed to have been written by one Sugawara Kiyokimi. It is to be noticed that the two

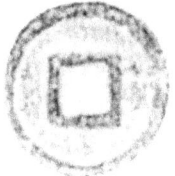

FIG. 18

characters "Sho," on this coin, though having the same sound, are entirely different words, the former meaning "receiving" or " enjoying," (in common use) (承) and the latter, "prosperity," (昌).

This coin was issued at the rate of one to ten of the previous coins, in conformity with the usual rule. About this time there seems to have been a dearth, not only of copper, but also of silver and gold, as several edicts appear against the general use of these articles for ornament, the privilege of doing so being restricted to officials above the 5th grade.

CHO-NEN TAI-HO
長年大寶
A.D. 848.

In the 15th year of Showa, the court astrologer announced that rain was impending, that the year's produce might be ruined and great distress follow, unless special precautions be taken. He advised that prayers be offered up to the great Deities throughout the whole country, for protection against calamity. For this reason, the new period Kasho, namely, Rewarding (or Praising) Good Luck," was initiated. In the tenth month of the 1st year of Kasho, a decree said "Heaven has given good fortune and the "Nengo" (year name) has been altered: if we do not alter our currency, some calamity will surely befall us. The new coin will be named "Chonen Taiho" and will circulate at the rate of one to ten of the old coins." A nice way to bloster up a falling currency! Having just escaped a famine through an appeal to the Gods, and the adroit change of the year name, the people must now propitiate the powers by the sacrifice of their hard earned cash, lest worse things befall them.   In this way the Chonen Taiho came into being; but it did not avert a famine which visited the land in the tenth month of the 2nd year of Kasho.   To relieve this, 500,000 mon were distributed amongst the poor of the capital, but history does not say whether relief was extended to the more remote districts.

The "Cho-Nen Tai-Ho" (長年大寳) or Great Treasure of Many Years, is a dwarf in comparison with the early members of the twelve sen.   Its Ogata or large size variety, fig 49, is but a trifle larger than the ordinary

FIG. 49

issue.   Like the Futsu or ordinary sen, fig. 51, the character "Tai" (大) has a hook above the cross stroke. What is known as the "Taiji" (pronounced "Daiji,") or large character sen, fig. 50, shews a relatively large

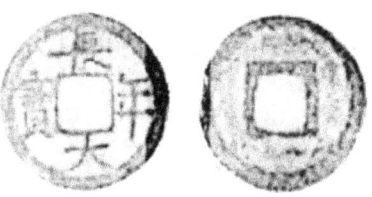

FIG. 50

character in proportion to the size of the coin, which is usually a trifle smaller in diameter than the Ogata coin. The hook of the character "Tai" (大) however, is not quite so marked, and the upper transverse stroke of the character "Nen" (年), is somewhat longer, in the specimens that I have seen, while the body of "Ho" (寳) is wider. The Futsu or common sen, fig. 51, resembles

FIG. 51

the first very closely, a slight difference being observed in the shape of the character "Ho" (寳), and sometimes only in the lower portion of "Cho" (長). Sometimes too, the Taiji variety has a slight hook on the lower end of the vertical stroke of "Nen" (年), which is absent on the other specimens. According to Mr. Yoshikawa in the Waken Sen Ii, these coins were inscribed by the Emperor Nimmei.

68   THE ANTIQUE COINS.

NYO-EKI JIN-HO. This coin was issued in the fourth
饒 益 神 寳 month of the 1st year of Teikwan, A.D.
   A.D. 859.   859, in the reign of the Emperor Se-wa.
It bears the motto "Nyo-Eki Jin-Ho" (饒益神寳)
which may be rendered "Divine Treasure of Abundant Profit." The large or introductory variety is very slightly smaller than the Ogata sen, and is styled the "Daiji" Nyoeki, fig. 52. The Futsu or common sen, fig. 53, is also slightly smaller than

FIG. 52

FIG. 53

the above, and the writing differs from that of the Daiji sen mainly in size and the greater length, in the larger coin, of the left oblique stroke of the left radical (Shimesu) of the character "Jin" (神). There is a slight difference also in the character "Eki" (益), but these characters vary more in point of size than anything else. The character "Jin", in the Futsu, specimens frequently partakes of the "Shimesu" type noticed in the Fuju sen, figs. 44 and 45.   In fig. 54 there is rather an interesting

FIG. 54

FIG. 55

case of faulty alignment, due to careless casting. A rare variety of the "Shimesu" type is seen in fig. 55. Here the character "Jin" (神) is out of alignment, being placed too much to the *right* and the specimen is therefore known as the "Sa Jin" or *left* "Jin" Nyoeki, the coin being thus, and quite properly, considered to be facing the observer. Not withstanding the general inferiority of the Nyoeki, it was placed in circulation at the rate of one to ten of all previous coins.

JO-KWAN EI-HO. The priod of Teikwan (貞観) "Be-
貞 觀 永 寶 holding Chastity," witnessed the pro-
A.D. 870. duction of another chaste coin, which took its name and quality from the era in question. It is called the "Jo-kwan Ei-Ho" (貞觀永寶), or Everlasting Treasure of Teikwan, called in this connection, Jogwan, and it is not too much to say that it is the

meanest effort of the Jiu ni zene. In size it is not the least, but the metal is of very inferior quality, and the characters are so shallow as to be often indecipherable. Fig. 56 is an exceptionally clear specimen.

FIG 56

According to the San Dai Jitsu Roku, considerable difficulty had been experienced, and no wonder, in persuading the long suffering Japanese to take kindly to these latter coins. By an imperial edict the people were accused of refusing, sometimes as many as two or three out of ten and of trusting to their own judgment instead of considering that "small defects do not necessarily interfere with their utility as current coin!" This notice was ordered to be placed on all the highways, and the threat was held out that any one caught refusing such coin would be whipped in court. The injustice of this proceeding is made apparent by the decree published in the first month of the 12th year of Teikwan A.D. 870, to the effect that the coins which were then in circulation were of little or no value, and that a new coin would be minted. The Jogwan Eiho presents no noteworthy variety as regards either size or writing, and is supposed to have been written by Fujiwara no Ujime, an official at the imperial court and a member of that family which controlled the affairs of the country for four hundred years. According to Masatsuna Kuchiki, author of the old but standard work, Kokon Senkwa Kan, there were two kinds of handwriting of this coin, but I have not been able to see a specimen differing from the above.

KWAN-HEI TAI-HO. The interval between the period of 寛平大寶 Teikwan and the first year of Kwanhei A.D. 890. (pronounced Kampei), when the following coin was issued, shews further evidence of the difficulty in gathering supplies of copper. In the 17th year of Teikwan, 875, A.D. the manufacture of copper utensils was prohibited by special decree, and subsequently anxious enquiries were made in various parts of the country, to ascertain if possible the existence of copper. Special envoys were sent to the places favorably spoken of, to make detailed investigations. These efforts met with some slight success, and accordingly, in the fifth month of the first year of Kwanhei, the "Kwanhei (Kwampei) Taiho" (寛平大寶), or Great Treasure of Kwampei "Liberal Peace," was minted. The characters are said to have been written by the Emperor Uda, but chiefly by Sugawara Michizane, afterwards deified as Tenjin.* The Kwampei Taiho continued to be minted for

* "Tenjin is the name under which is apotheothised the great minister and scholar Sugawara no Michizane, who, having fallen a victim to calumny in A. D. 901, was degraded to the post of vice-president of the Dazaifu, or Governor Generalship of the island of Kyushu, at that time a usual form of banishment for illustrious criminals He died in exile A. D. 903, his death being followed by many portents and disasters to his enemies. He is worshipped as the God of Calligraphy, other names for him being Kan Shojo and Temmangu. He is represented in the robes of an ancient court noble, and the temples dedicated to him bear in several places his crest of a conventional plum blossom,—five circles grouped round a smaller one. A recumbent image of a cow frequently adorns the temple grounds, because

18 years, and several varieties are known, of which the following are the chief. Futsu or common Kwampei, fig. 57. Note the difference between the "Kwan" (寛) of

FIG. 57

this coin and the "Kwan" (観) of the previous sen. Note also the careless casting of this specimen, the apparently greater size of this coin being due to this cause. "Kwatsu Dai," or "Broad Tai" sen, fig. 58, is known by the long transverse stoke of the character Tai.

FIG. 58

It is said to have been written by the Emperor Uda. The "En Kwan," or Long "Crown Kwampei," fig. 59, may be recognised by the greater length of the upper horizontal curved stroke of the character "Kwan" (寛). It may be easily identified also by the side strokes of the character "Hei" (平), which are mere dots. Another variety fig. 60,

---

Michizane was wont to ride on a cow in the land of his exile. A plum tree is also often planted near the temple, that having been his favourite tree. Indeed tradition avers that the most beautiful plum tree in his garden at Kyoto, flew after him through the air to Dazaifu, where it is still shewn," 7th edition, page 57, Chamberlain and Mason's "Handbook to Japan."

shews two short vertical strokes below the upper curved line of "Kan," whereas the ordinary sen has only one. The "Kan En Hi," or Empi, the long-tailed Kan, and the

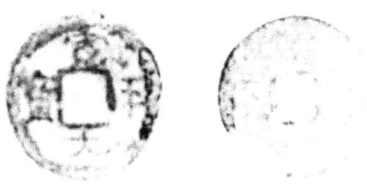

FIG. 59

"Cho Hei" or long Hei are also mentioned, but do not need special notice. It may be taken for granted that this coin which was issued for 18 years, would exhibit slight variations such as the above.

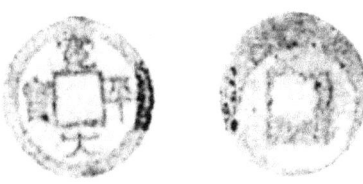

FIG. 60

EN-KI TSU-HO.
延喜通寳
A.D. 907

In the eleventh month of the 3rd year of Engi, "Prolonged Gladness," in the reign of the Emperor Daigo, the Kampei Taiho sen were recast, with doubtless others of various sorts and conditions, and possibly with a leaven of new metal, into the form of the En-Ki Tsu-Ho, (延喜通寳) (pronounced Engi), or "Current Treasure of Prolonged Gladness." Like its predecessors, it was issued at the rate of one to ten and the feelings of "Prolonged Gladness" of those who were compelled to give ten of their sen, bad though they were, for one of these wretched tokens, could probably not be adequately expressed by any language at their command at that time.

The Ogata or large-sized Engi, can only be so called relatively to the other specimens of this denomination, fig. 61. The ordinary sen is shewn in figs. 62 and 63,

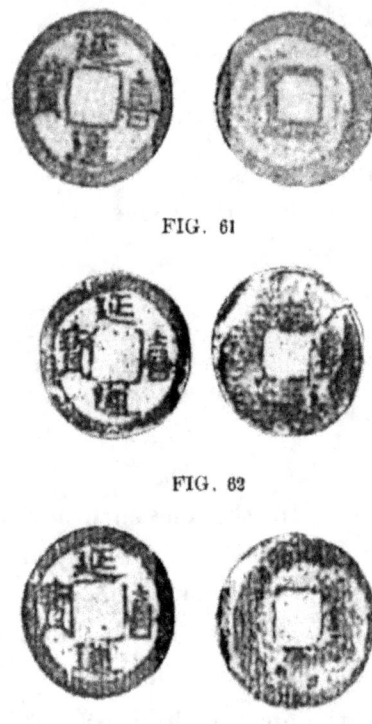

FIG. 61

FIG. 62

FIG. 63

the latter having rather a broad rim. Fig. 64 illustrates another of the same, with a slip in the casting of the reverse.

Owing to the dearth of copper, coins of this and the next issues are to be found having all the appearance of government coin, and which indeed were so, as far as can be known, but the material of which is not bronze but pewter, an alloy of lead with tin, fig. 65.

FIG. 64

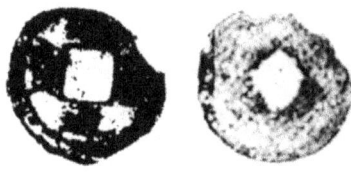

FIG 65

KEN-GEN TAI-HO
乾 元 大 寳
A.D. 958

We come now to the last of the twelve antique sen, namely the Ken-Gen Tai-Ho, (乾元大寳) or Great Treasure of Cosmos.* It was issued in the 2nd year of Tentoku, A.D. 958. According to the Kokon Senkwa Kan, the celebrated scholar Ono Dofu, who is said to have begun seriously to learn the art of writing when over fifty years of age, and one of the Fujiwara, also a noted scribe of the time, were asked to write the characters for this coin. The former however, stated that he could not do so,

---

* "Ken-Kon" Heaven and Earth, are synonymous with "Universe" The word Ken has usually the signification "Heaven," only in this connection. Brinkley, however, in his excellent dictionary, gives it this meaning. Should this word stand by itself for Heaven, then it is quite possible that this coin should be read in a different order from those of the other twelve sen, and that it should read "Ken Tai Gen-Ho" (乾 大 元 寳), the First Treasure of Great Heaven.

owing to age and visual infirmity, as the characters were too small, and the latter was unable to comply with the request as he was in mourning at the time. This double refusal has the air of being more than accidental. Without question, it must have been a more difficult task to write on this dwarfed and degenerate "Great Treasure" than on the ample surface of a Wado or a Ryuhei, but it was not impossible, and the refusal of these two scholars to do so, suggests a sly rebuke. Two others were chosen to compete for this honour and one, Aho Muneyuki by name, was finally selected. There seems to be no Ogata variety of this coin in bronze, though some may be half a millimetre or so larger than others, owing to earlier casting.

See fig. 66, Futsu or common Kengen, about the size of the Engi Tsuho. Like the latter coin, there is a variety made of pewter, the diameter of which is about a millimetre greater than that of the bronze coin, fig. 67.

FIG. 66

FIG. 67

It is not likely that this pewter coin was the first issue. Notwithstanding its large size, its baser constitution would debar it from use as an introductory coin. The refusal of the learned men to write the inscription may be traced rather to the diminutive size of this coin than to its composition. In one variety of it the characters seem to be crowded around the central hole, so that there is a space between them and the margin. This kind is called the "Setsu Kaku" (pronounced Sekkaku,) Kengen, fig. 68.

I may add another variety, fig. 69, in which the

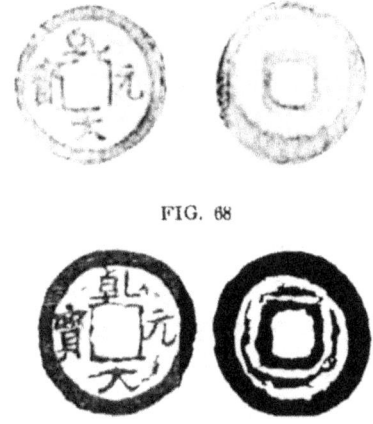

FIG. 68

FIG 69

character "Gen" is written like this, (元), that is to say in the style familiar to some of the Chinese coins, and on the later ones made in Japan in imitation of these. It will be noticed that the left inner stroke of this character meets the transverse line above, instead of joining the right vertical one as in figs. 66, 67 and 68.

A coin resembling this but differing from it in the penmanship, is illustrated in the Waken Sen Ii.

In the preceding remarks, enough has been said to show that the gradual decline in size and quality of the "Jiu Ni Zene," must be attributed primarily to a deficiency in the output of copper and secondarily to the lavish use of the metal in the erection of Buddhist images. Although the edicts which usually preceded the issue of new denominations and fixed the values of new coins at tenfold that of their predecessors, did not emanate from an unbiassed source, there is no doubt that counterfeiting was a common offence. Owing, too, to the dearth of the red metal, the cost of each new coin must have been greater than that of previous issues. Yet, during this period of 250 years, excellent money was being made in China, at moderate cost, so that if Japan had been able to give its value in some other commodity, there would have been little difficulty in importing copper, which could have been coined at a substantial profit. The probability is that Japan was too poor to buy this metal, and had to depend upon her home supplies.

The extortionate price of the new, in relation to the old sen, must be regarded as a species of oppression, initiated by the high, sullenly borne by the middle and probably affecting but little the lower classes, the majority of whom were not likely to come in contact with "hard cash." We may also remember that Japan does not stand alone in the extortionate use of a debased coinage.

III

MEDIÆVAL COINS.

So far as can be known, no coins were made by the government of Japan during the six hundred and odd years that separate the period of Tentoku from the 15th year of Tensho (A.D. 1587). A diminishing remnant of the twelve antique sen persisted during this interval, and we have reason to think that counterfeits of the same were also put into circulation. A series of nondescript coins, too, came into existence, bearing mottoes of the most varied kind, the "Shima" sen, sometimes also called "Bita" sen, though the latter word more fitly applies to forgeries of Chinese, Annamese, Corean and Japanese sen, which competed with the coins imported from the mainland. Though occasionally interdicted, we shall see that Chinese coins were in great demand and were sometimes besought in urgent terms from the great and friendly neighbour of Japan. Thus Chinese coin gradually accumulated, so that there ultimately resulted such an overwhelming preponderance, that it was practically the only currency of Japan. Although I have included this coinage in the category of mediæval sen, it is well to emphasize the fact that Chinese coins were used long after the period of Tensho (A.D. 1573-1591). This period has been taken, as an arbitrary landmark, to divide the mediæval from the modern coins of Japan, as the sen known as

"Tensho Tsuho" (silver), was issued in its 15th year, and is the first reliable government coin to appear since the close of the twelve antique sen. As a matter of fact, the use of Chinese coins continued to extend until the issue of the "Kwanei Tsuho" near the middle of the 17th century, and, though not now regarded as. national currency, they continue in limited use till this day.

Historical reference is made to two coins as having been issued by the government, and, although there is no evidence that these were ever in circulation, I shall mention them here, for the sake of completeness. The first is the "Ken-Kon Tsu-Ho" (乾坤通寶), or "Current Treasure of the Universe." An illustration of this coin is given in the third volume of the "Meiji Shin Sen

FIG. 1

Sempu," fig. 1, which was edited by Mr. Morita; but the specimen from which it is taken wears a very doubtful appearance.

It may, however, have been made as a sample at that period. The "Kokon Senkwa Kan," quoting the "Kemmu Ni Nenki," says that on the 28th day of the third month of the 1st year of Kemmu, in the reign of the Emperor Go Daigo, an imperial decree appeared to

MEDIÆVAL COINS. 81

the effect that from a remote period we have had coins of more than ten different denominations, which appear in our histories (the twelve sen). In more recent times many different coins have been imported from foreign countries and are circulating amongst the common people. Such a proceeding is against good order; to remedy this defect we shall have a new coin which shall be called the "Ken-Kon Tsu-Ho." The author of the "Kokon Senkwa Kan" says that the coin, *which he had never seen*, was said to be a large one, like the Mannen sen, and he thinks that this may be true, for it was specially designed to displace the "bad sen." This coin certainly did not go into circulation, though probably some samples were made and submitted to the government. In later years, it was customary for private individuals, as well as officials of the mint, to submit experimental, or "Shiken" sen to the authorities for approval, and many such are still in existence, as will be seen later on. Still, it cannot be doubted that if this coin had gone into circulation, it could not have completely disappeared within the six hundred years that separates the period of Kemmu from the present time.

The Emperor Go Daigo seems to have been one of the few sovereigns who earnestly claimed the temporal power which was his nominal prerogative. After being compelled to retire, he succeeded in regaining authority for three short years, between A.D. 1333 and 1336. In A.D. 1334, the Ken-Kon Tsu-Ho was authorised to appear, but the troubles of the unfortunate ruler began to recrudescence in that year, and doubtless prevented the carrying out of this worthy design.

It may conduce to a clearer comprehension of the matter, and throw light on the *raison d'etre* of the "Shima" and other non-official coins, if I give here the briefest outline of Japanese historical events, during the Middle Ages.

Even as far back as the Wado period, the Fujiwara family had risen to a degree of dignity and power which overshadowed the throne and controlled its occupants to such an extent that this relation has been spoken of as a "proprietorship." We have indications of this relationship, in the close intimacy of one Fujiwara with the Empress Koken, and in the writing of the Wado, Jogwan and Kengen sen by others of this family. They became advisers, then dictators and finally the *de facto* sovereigns of their country, allied by close marriage ties to the throne, yet standing aloof in order to enjoy the privilege of real power which was denied to the sacred person of the Emperor. "For a period of four hundred years," says Murray, "from A.D. 645 to 1050, they monopolized nearly all the important offices in the government. The wives and concubines of the feeble emperors were all taken from its inexhaustible repertoire. The men of the family, among whom were always some of administrative ability, found it a task of no great difficulty to rule the Emperor, who was supposed to be divinely inspired to rule the empire, especially when he was usually a boy whose mother, wife and court favorites were all supplied from the Fujiwara family. This kind of life and environment could not fail to produce on the successive emperors a sadly demoralising effect." The Fujiwara in turn were ousted from their monopoly by the rise of the military family of Taira, about the middle of the 11th century. The long established custom of controlling the throne from the vantage-ground of military force, did not lapse, so that Japanese history continued with few interruptions, to resemble a kind of chess in which the combatants fought for the control of the king, without the intention of taking his life or occupying his nominal position. Sometimes, too, each side had its own king who, as a penalty of greatness, was bound to follow the "advice" of the power that hoisted him on the throne. Yet, with all this lawless turmoil and bloodshed, it was seldom that outward respect was lacking to the throne, and no one dared to arrogate to himself the title of Emperor, save those who had a right to it by descent. European history is not without cases of a parallel kind, that is to say, attempts to assume the power of royalty under the guise of loyalty to the throne. Even at the present day, in monarchial countries at least, the blood royal is regarded by the public as something apart from that of the commonality, in virtue of its succession through a long line of ancestors; in the past there have been but few instances in Europe where persons of other than royal descent have attempted to seize the crown. In Japan moreover, where the cult of Shinto, the profound veneration, and even worship, of ancestors is deep-rooted in the soil of prehistoric antiquity, in this country where the Emperors, the Sons of Heaven, claim lineal descent from the godlike beings of forgotten ages, it is not surprising that no one has had the temerity to commit such sacrilege. We thus have the spectacle of the usurper assuming control of the state and ruling it with an iron hand, yet barred by popular and even personal convictions from the throne itself. The sacred person of the Emperor was held inviolate, while his exalted position was supposed to exempt him from the task of ruling the common herd. In conformity to this conventional idea, which seems to have been actually accepted by the majority of the Mikados themselves, there were occasions when the throne was voluntarily vacated in order that the resigning Emperor might have a more controlling influence over the affairs of state.

From the beginning of the eleventh century, the power of the Fujiwara began to pale before the military prowess of the Taira and Minamoto clans and from the middle of this century till the end of the twelfth, the history of Japan was practically a sanguinary see-saw between these later rivals. First one and then the other came up, the supremacy of the latter ending with the life of the great Yoritomo, whose younger brother, the still more famous and romantic Yoshitsune, had previously been slain, or at least had disappeared, after incurring the jealousy of the elder. The Minamoto family was then succeeded by that of the Hojo, who have been held up to execration. "It is the fashion," says James Murdoch, in his "History of Japan," "to declaim upon the miseries of Japan under the rule of the Hojo; but as a

MEDIÆVAL COINS.

sober matter of fact, the administration of the Hojo during the first century of their unobtrusive yet vigorous supremacy was one of the best that Japan has ever known." It was one of them who routed the Mongol invaders in A.D.1281, and it was the dissolute profligacy alone of the succeeding thirty years that led to the downfall of this family. Then it was that the Emperor Go Daigo, with his generals Kusunoki Masashige and Nitta Yoshisada, succeeded in overthrowing this regency in a fierce battle at Kamakura in A.D. 1333. Ashikaga Takauji, who had captured the stronghold of Rokuhara in Kyoto, on behalf of his royal master, now turned upon him, and by intrigue and force drove him from power and set up a rival prince of the blood in his stead. The Emperor Go Daigo was not, strictly speaking, deposed, but his authority was defied and his rival, upheld by the Ashikaga interest, controlled the main finances of the country. Thus the "Kenkon Tsuho" was never coined. Thus also the dynasty was split into two branches, though united fifty six years later by the diplomacy of the third Ashikaga Shogun, Yoshimitsu, "the ablest of all the fourteen successors of Ashikaga Takauji, the founder of the line" (Murdoch). The Ashikaga family occupied the position of Shogun for two hundred and thirty seven years, during which time they managed, after a fashion, to keep the belligerent daimyos from deposing them, though, latterly at least, they did not govern the country in the sense of maintaining law and order in the provinces. Towards the end of their rule, the country was torn by the continual feuds of the warring daimyos, so that a state of general anarchy prevailed. It was not until the overthrow of the Ashikaga shogunate by Nobunaga in 1573, that anything like a genuine central authority existed. This latter general did not assume the name of shogun, though he wielded all the power pertaining to the rank. A great man in himself, he was one of three, the forerunner and uplifter of the renowned Hideyoshi, "Taiko Sama," who rose from a humble station to the highest rank outside the throne. He was succeeded by the sagacious if unscrupulous Iyeyasu, the founder of the Tokugawa shogunate.

During the Ashikaga shogunate, in the period of Choroku, A.D. 1457-58, while the emperor Go Hanazono was on the throne and Ashikaga Yoshimasa was in power, a coin called the "Cho-roku Tsu-ho" (長祿通寳) was said to have been made. There are two, perhaps three, specimens in existence of a coin bearing this inscription, but they do not look like government coins. We cannot, of course, answer for the products of those rude times, and opinions are divided as to whether these are experimental or "Shiken" sen cast during the Choroku period. In any case it is exceedingly unlikely that the Choroku Tsuho went into circulation. It is practically impossible that this coin could have so nearly disappeared had it been in use so late as A.D. 1457. The early works on Japanese numismatics refer to this coin as a historical fact, but were unable to show any specimens. That is to say, about two centuries ago this coin was quite unknown, so that it must have become extinct within a period of three

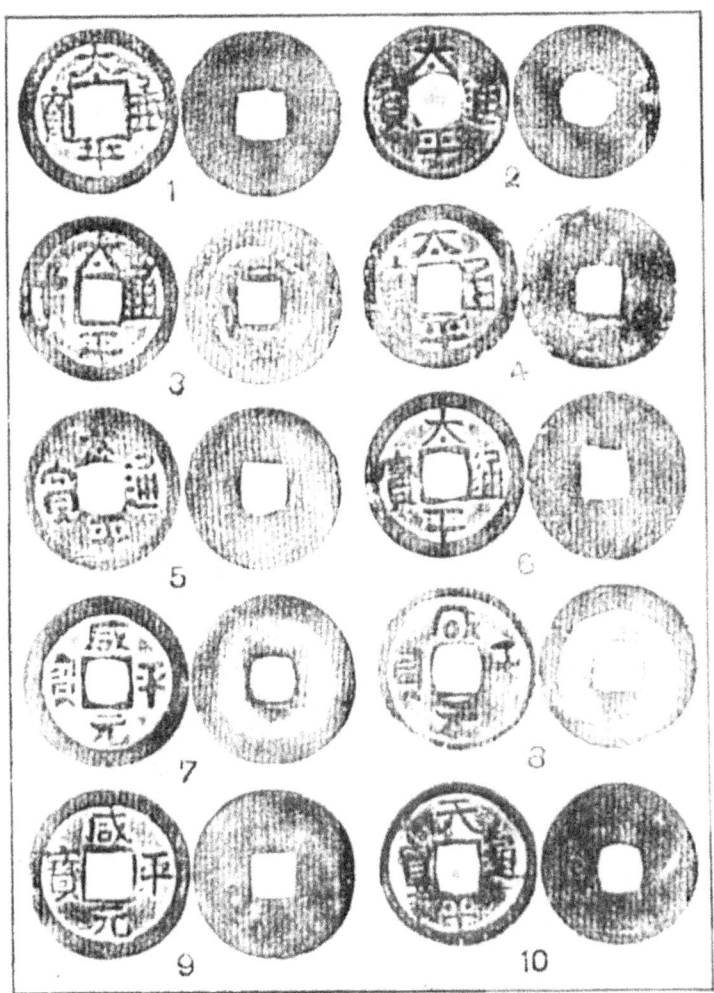

PLATE 1.—SHIMA SEN

hundred years. The coin illustrated in fig. 2, which is in the possession of Mr. Morita, may be a "Shiken"

 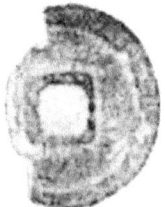

FIG. 2

sen or experimental sen, cast for the purpose of obtaining official sanction for its manufacture.

We come now to the consideration of the "Shima" sen, those marvellous attempts at coin-making which are typical of the self-confidence inherent in the Japanese. The word "Shima," an "Island" is a kind of nickname intended to denote that these coins are in a class by themselves. That they stand alone and are not to be mistaken for the everyday, commonplace sen, is evident to anyone who glances at the following plates.

There are several hundreds known, and though the mottoes are not so varied, there are many grades of eccentricity in the matter of style, material and workmanship. They have a fascination all their own. They are the gypsies of the race of sen. Their origin is wrapped in mystery. For many years they were supposed to have migrated from China, or Annam. So far as I have been able to enquire, however, nothing quite like them is found in China or Annam, and in the former country, at least, the supply of coin has usually been sufficient to discourage a demand for such poverty-stricken emblems of currency. It is possible that they are "Brummagem" coin, specially manufactured in China during the middle ages for "export only"; but I do not think so. There is no positive evidence of their Japanese origin, but their uncouth make, their usually attenuated proportions and frequently their inconsequent or meaningless inscriptions, mark them out as the rude product of troublous times. There is something pathetic, too, in many of these mottoes. While the shabby look of these coins betoken "hard times," their legends seem to breathe the "sigh of the weary." They speak of peace which their owners could scarcely know. Thus the motto "Tai-Hei" (太平), "Great Peace," is found in many various kinds of handwriting (Plate 1, Nos. 1, 2, 3, 4, 5 and 6); "Kan-Hei" (咸平), "Universal Peace" (Plate 1, Nos. 7 and 8); "Ten-Hei," (天平), "Heavenly Peace" (Plate 1, No. 10) "Jun-Hei," (順平) "Orderly Peace" (Plate 3, No. 9); "Ji-Hei" (治平), "Tranquil Peace" (Plate 3, No. 3); these and other lucky or hopeful sentiments are to be found on nearly all the legible "Shima" sen.

In some of these coins the writing is "Hidari Moji," that is to say, "Left-hand Character," not in the sense of having been written by the left hand, but the character appears as if one were looking at it in a mirror, the left stroke being on the right, and *vice versa*, *e.g.* (Plate 2, Nos. 8 and 10). This is the natural result of writing on the mould, used for the casting, in the ordinary manner, instead of in the reverse way. I am

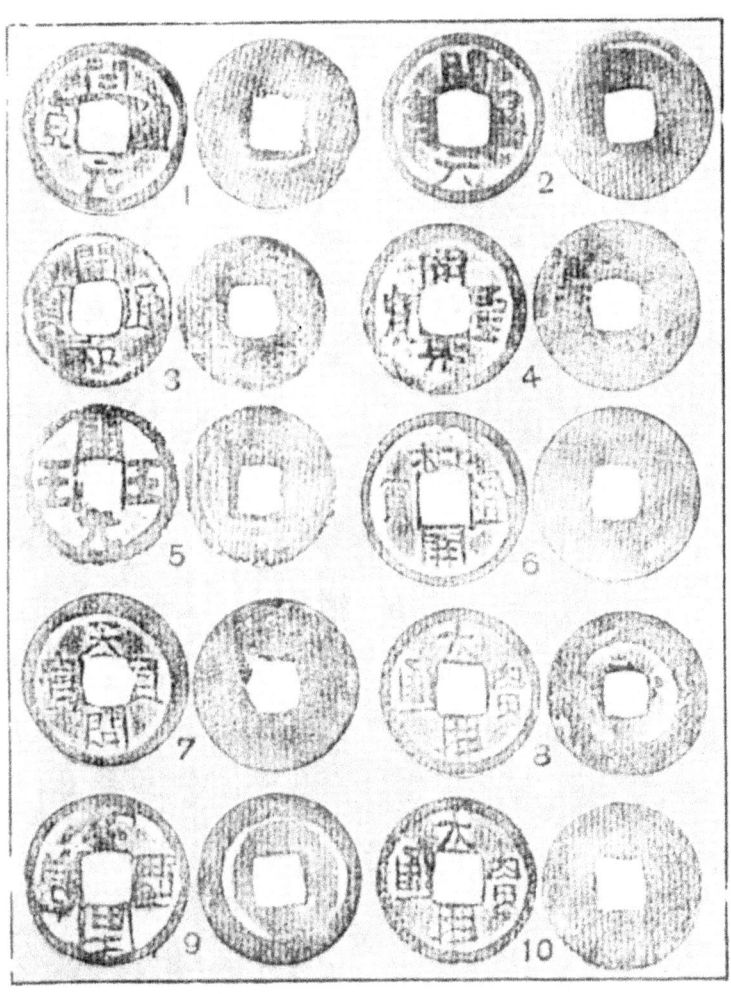

PLATE 2.—SHIMA SEN.

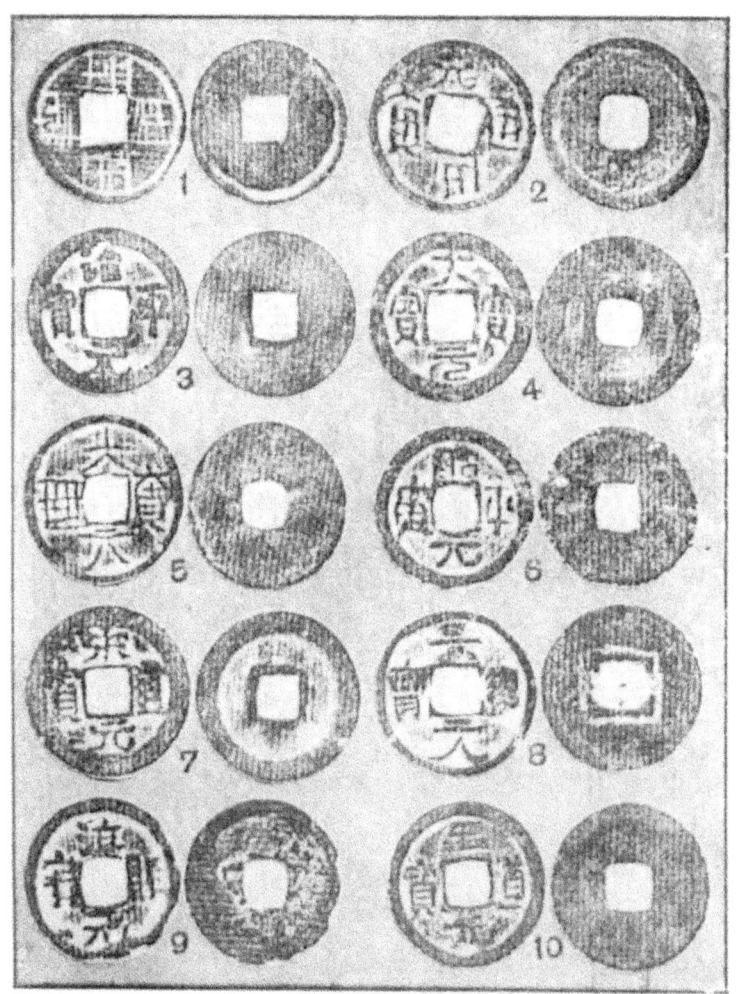

PLATE 3.—SHIMA SEN.

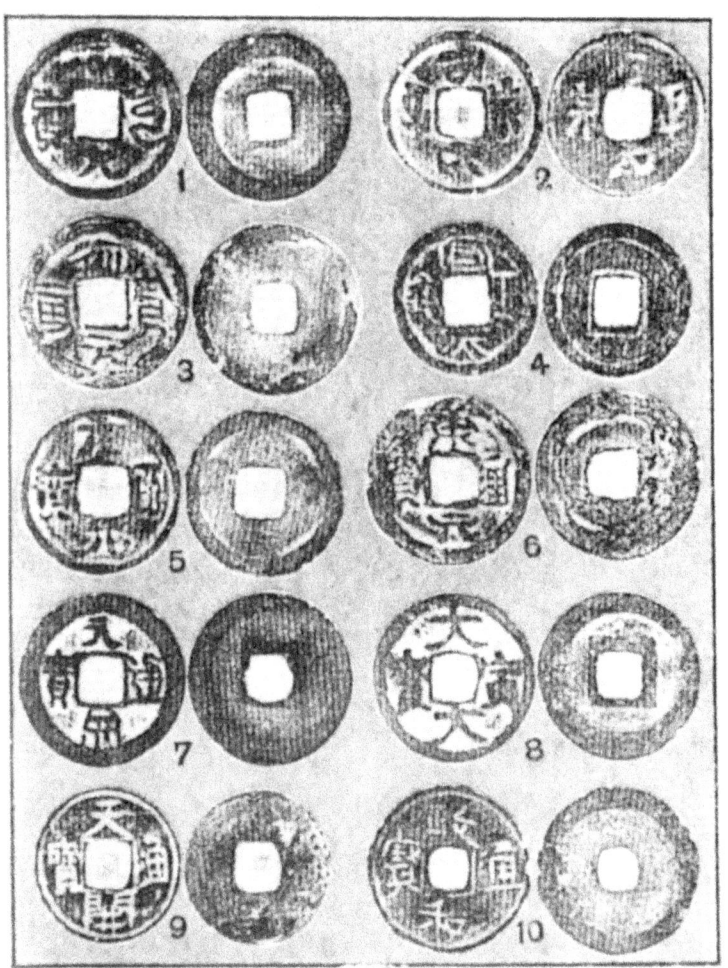

PLATE 4.—SHIMA SEN

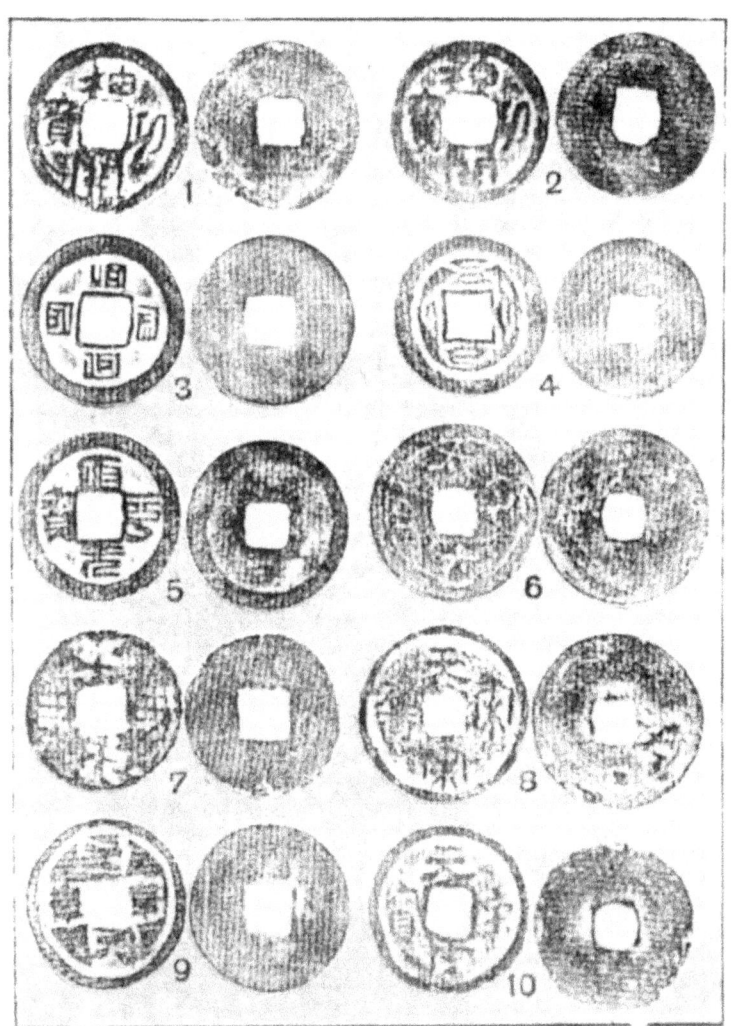

PLATE 5.—SHIMA SEN.

informed by Mr. Muramatsu that this "Hidari Moji" is quite characteristic, being found on the coins of no other country. Many of these Shima sen are struck, not cast, and in some the inscriptions are in intaglio, e.g., Plate 3, No. 1; Plate 4, Nos. 2, 9 and 10; Plate 5, No. 6. In others again, the characters are either illegible, incomprehensible, or, when read together, have no rational meaning. Some of them would seem to have been made by illiterate persons. Quite a number have evidently been taken from the Chinese sen, which were prevalent in Japan during the middle ages. In few instances has this copying extended to all the characters, as in the case of the "Tai-Hei Tsu-Ho" (太平通寶), Plate 1. In most cases one character has been altered, occasionally two, and rarely only the sequence is changed. The following will illustrate this:

"Gen-Kai Tsu-Ho" from "Kai-Gen Tsu-Ho" Plate 3, No. 2
"Ten-Kai Tsu-Ho" from "Kai-Gen Tsu-Ho" Plate 2, No. 7
"Kai-Gen Sei-Ho" from "Kai-Gen Tsu-Ho" Plate 2, No. 4
"Tai-Kai Tsu-Ho" from "Kai-Gen Tsu-Ho" Plate 2, No. 8
"Kai-Gen O-O" from "Kai-Gen Tsu-Ho" Plate 2, No. 5
"Jun-Gen Sho-Ho" from "Jun-Kwa Gen-Ho" Plate 3, No. 9

Our old friend, the Wado sen, also came in for its share of this kind of flattery, viz:

"Wa-Kai Tsu-Ho" (和開通寶), from "Wa-Do Kai-Ho" (和同開珎) (Plate 2, No. 6). Truly, the Shima sen furnish food for reflection.

During the middle ages, and for some centuries later, the currency of Japan, however, was mainly upheld by the coins imported from China. The general superiority of their material and workmanship, the high character, as a rule, of the writing, the veneration held for things Chinese, and above all their moderate cost, placed them beyond competition as a medium of exchange. The scarcity of copper in Japan, which discouraged the minting of government coins, seems to have lasted during the whole of the intervening period between the Kengen and Tensho issues. We are told that in the time of the Emperor Shirakawa (A.D. 1075-1086), three thousand images of Buddha were made, but that copper was so scarce that Chinese coins had to be imported, an instance surely of religious enthusiasm bordering on reckless improvidence. There is ample evidence that this influx of Chinese sen was not regarded with favour by all the rulers of Japan. The sentiment against foreign coin is shewn in the terms of the previously mentioned decree of the Emperor Go Daigo (P. 81), and it may be traced in various other edicts. On the 4th day of the seventh month of the 4th year of Kenkyu (A.D. 1191), it was decreed "From this date, do not allow the coins of the So dynasty to circulate." As the coins of the So dynasty of China (A.D. 963-1273), furnished the great bulk of the Japanese currency, it is evident that, had this decree been carried out, the country would have been practically without a circulating medium. The ostensible reason was that the Japanese currency had depreciated since the Kampei sen was issued and the country had become permeated with foreign coin. It may be ungracious to hint that possibly some official had a sordid motive behind this preposterous ebullition of

MEDIÆVAL COINS.

patriotism. At any rate, it is difficult to see how such a measure could improve matters, in the absence of any attempt to renew the national currency. No such attempt was made till a hundred and fifty years later, and this, as we have seen, did not succeed, so that the currency of China flourished for many centuries in Japan. Even to this day, the average Japanese or European resident in the country, has a loose and careless idea that the sen, or "cash," which he sometimes sees floating around, are specimens of Japanese money, whereas the fact is that there is usually a fair proportion of Chinese coins in a handful of this money. The following list shows the Chinese coins in use during the mediæval period:

Kaigen Tsuho
Kengen Juho
Shutsu Genho
Tokoku Tsuho
Shotsn Genho
Taihei Tsuho
Junkwa Genho
Shido Genho
Kanhei Genho
Keitoku Genho
Shofu Genho
Shofu Tsuho
Tenki Tsuho
Tensei Genho
Meido Genho
Keiyu Genho
Kwoso Tsuho
Shiwa Genho
Shiwa Tsuho
Kayu Genho
Jihei Tsuho
Jihei Genho
Kine Genho
Genho Tsuho

Genyu Tsuho
Shosei Genho
Genfu Tsuho
Seiso Genho
Daikwan Tsuho
Seiwa Genho
Senwa Tsuho
Kenen Tsuho
Shoko Tsuho
Junki Genho
Shoki Genho
Keigen Tsuho
Kaitai Tsuho
Kaiki Tsuho
Kajo Tsuho
Taiso Genho
Shojo Tsuho
Tanhei Genho
Kaki Tsuho
Junyu Genho
Kwoso Genho
Kaikei Tsuho
Keijo Genho
Kanjun Genho

92 MEDIÆVAL COINS.

The Kai-Gen Tsu-Ho, although the oldest of the common Chinese sen, dating as it does 87 years before the Wado period, is very frequently found and its antiquity lends it interest. There is a Chinese coin of much later date which had a somewhat dramatic entry into the country, and which so won its way into favour by its sterling worth that it received official recognition, and was actually used as a standard of equivalence for a time. Though not properly speaking a Japanese coin, yet it was adopted by and, one might say, naturalised in the land, and is therefore worthy of special mention. It is called the "Ei-Raku Tsu-Ho" (永樂通寶), or "Current

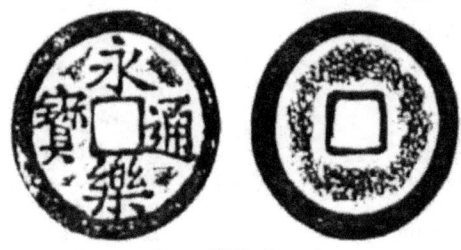

FIG. 3

Treasure of Ei Raku" (Everlasting Happiness) fig. 3. It was cast during the Min Dynasty, in the 10th year of Eiraku, which corresponds to the 19th year of the Japanese period, Oyei, A.D. 1412. For the following information, I am indebted to an interesting note by Mr. J. H. Wigmore, which is well worth quoting in full.[*]
"In the 10th year of Oyei (1403), says the story, the greatest typhoon ever known in Japan drove a Chinese ship to Misaki village in Izu, now Soshu. Ashikaga Mitsukane, in command of the Kwanto, sent three

---

[*] Transactions of the Asiatic Society of Japan.

high officers to Misaki to see the ship. The people of the ship told the story of how they were driven out of their course, and requested a harbour. Five or six kwan of Eirakusen† were found on board; and on hearing of this, 'Mitsukane' sent word to Kyoto to Yoshimitsu, the Inkyo Shogun, and Yoshimochi, his son, the Shogun, to ask what should be done; Mitsukage was told to decide for himself. So he confiscated the ship's cargo, and, after provisioning the crew with miso, salt, fuel and rice, sent them back to China. The author of Denyeu does not credit this story, for he says (1) the 10th year of Oyei, when this incident is said to have happened, was only the first year of Eiraku in China, and the Eiraku sen was not coined until the 9th year of Eiraku, or about 1413, the 19th year of Oyei; (2) the ex-Shogun Yoshimitsu died on the 15th of Oyei; (3) Mitsukane died in the 17th of Oyei, so neither of them could ever have seen an Eiraku sen, nor could one have been imported in the 10th year of Oyei. This may all be, and yet the story may have a framework of truth." It is generally admitted that a Chinese junk, with a cargo of Eiraku coin got ashore in this neighbourhood (Sagami), possibly in the 20th year of Oyei, and that the authorities robbed her, taking care, however, to provision her for the return voyage, which we may be sure was not delayed longer than necessary. The Eiraku Tsuho, though introduced to Japan in this

---

† "Five or six Kwan" (5—6 thousand?) seems to be too small an estimate. On the other hand, I find in the "Kokan Senkwa Kan" a statement that then were one hundred. "Man" Kwan, literally a thousand millions! It may, however, be taken to mean only that there was a vast amount of this coin on board.

violent manner, may have been subsequently sent over from China in greater amount, for it is one of the commonest of the Chinese coins to be found in Japan. Though not so large as the earlier antique sen, it greatly exceeds in size the eight later ones of this group, and is of infinitely superior finish. Following Mr. Wigmore's excellent resumé from the "Denyen Jikata-Kigen," "Towards the latter half of the 16th century, the Eiraku sen had begun to displace the ordinary money (akusen, bad money) in the Kwanto. In 1573, Hojo Ujiyasu* conquered that region, and soon afterwards he called a meeting of some of the chief lords of the region and submitted a proposition prohibiting the use of any money except Eiraku sen. His reasons were: (1) the Eiraku sen was of much better quality; (2) disputes about media of payment must be stopped; (3) such a measure would stimulate trade. His views met with favour, and the law was passed." (Incidentally, this method of passing it raises questions of great interest). "Thereafter" says the chronicler, "all bad money in every Machi, Gun, Sho, Go, Mura, and Sato was collected and sent to the Kamigata (or Kyoto region); from this time bad money was called 'Kyotosen' (or Kyosen). In 1590 Tokugawa gained the mastery in the Kwanto, and (in some unexplained manner) the kyosen came partly into use again and its ratio to the Eiraku sen was fixed at 4 to 1. But disputes again rose, and a law was passed more than once prohibiting the use of the Eiraku sen except for the payment of taxes. The reason for this was

---

* Not a descendant of the other great Hojo family mentioned on page 84.

said to be a dream of Ieyasu; for one night in his castle at Sumpu (now Shizuoka) he dreamed that he was changing his castle, and on telling this to Honda, an official, the latter interpreted it as meaning that the money should be changed. Perhaps Honda had a stock of Kyosen which he was anxious to put upon the market. This account differs slightly from that of the authorities cited by the learned author (1) in regard to the time when the rate 4 to 1 was fixed; (2) in regard to the time when the term Kyosen came into use. But my purpose in mentioning it is to call attention to the important connection between the Eirakusen and the history of land tenure. Under Yoritomo there came the final step in the process of commuting the old labour and commodity taxes into money. From this time (the middle of the 12th century) until Ieyasu, the principal taxes ("ta" and "hata") were paid in money. Kwan being the unit of coinage, the amount due from a given piece of land was called the Kwandaka. It is probable that the amount of Kwandaka was determined in the beginning by the amount of land producing sufficient to support one horseman for the lord's service. Now when the Eirakusen came into use, the value of the Kwandaka came to be often expressed in the terms of the Eirakusen. When so expressed, the term Eidaka was used. The income of the samurai was paid in Eirakusen and the term Eidaka was thus forced into being. Ordinary taxes were senno; taxes paid in Eirakusen were Eino. The use of Eidaka apparently began about the time that Hojo Ujiyasu made Eirakusen the sole lawful medium."

From the fact that this coin received official sanction to be used as the sole currency of the eight considerable provinces called the Kwanto, it must have existed in sufficient amount for this purpose, and, as we have seen, its present numbers shew that this was so. We are scarcely, however, entitled to regard it as a government coin. Hojo Ujiyasu had possessed himself of the Kwanto by force, near the end of the Ashikaga shogunate, and until beaten by Hideyoshi, his brother Ujimasa held the strongest and best provinces of the country. Still he did not attempt to give the Eiraku sen a national distribution, and had not the authority to do so if he desired it. So far as his authority extended, this coin was officially recognized, and we must therefore admit it as a local government coin. I am not aware to what extent it was sanctioned by Hideyoshi, but the position seems to have been something like this. Hojo Ujiyasu collected it in the Kwanto and excluded the other sen, Shima, Chinese, and Bita sen. Under Hideyoshi, who defeated the Hojo and succeeded in controlling the whole country, a redistribution took place, the inferior sen flowed back to the Kwanto, to the great disappointment of its population, while the Eiraku filtered slowly out to the surrounding country. Owing probably to its superior excellence, it was admitted, under Ieyasu, for payment of taxes, even when debarred from general circulation. By this means it was gathered into the government coffers.

In plate 7, are illustrated what are known as the Eiraku "Ban," or "Numbered" sen, each having a

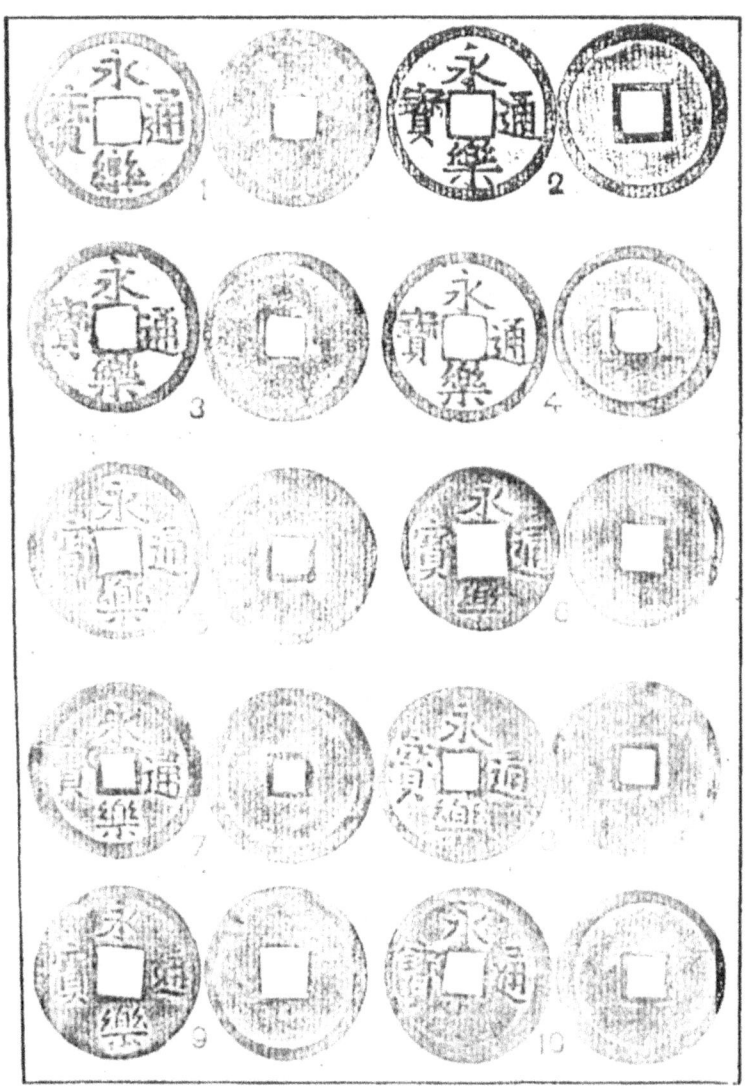

PLATE 6.—EIRAKU SEN.

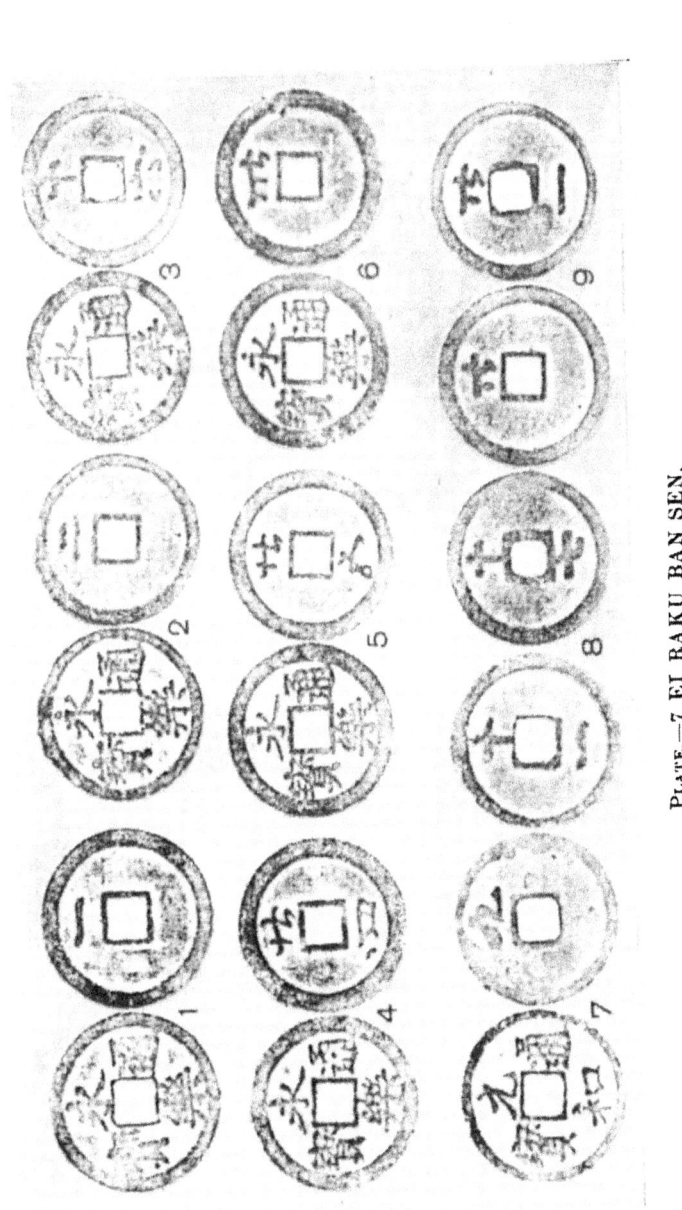

PLATE.—7 EI RAKU BAN SEN.
Nos. 1 to 6 Inclusive. GENNA BAN SEN, Nos. 7, 8 and 9.

number on the reverse. They are not to be regarded as government coin, but may have been cast for official inspection, though not sanctioned for circulation.

Plate 6 shows a number of gold and silver Eiraku sen from my collection. These might have been appropriately placed in chapter 4, where they are referred to, but may be inserted here for the sake of comparison.

Fig. 4 shows a gold coin with the government crest,

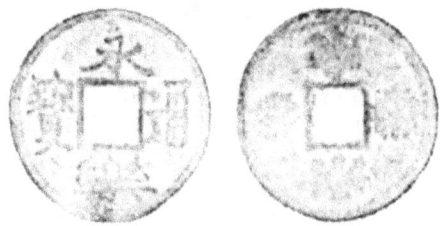

FIG. 4.

not very distinct, that is to say the "Kiri" leaf and flower. (Paulownia Imperialis)

Many counterfeits of the Eiraku sen were made in Japan, but these are easily detected, and come under the heading of Bita, or bad sen. Fig. 5. which, together with

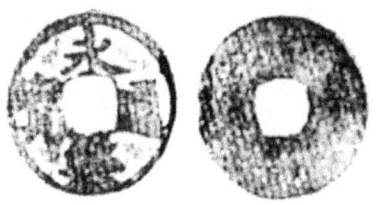

FIG. 5.

the Shima sen and probably the Chinese coins, other than the Eiraku, were designated in contradistinction to this

MEDIÆVAL COINS.

desirable sen, Kyosen (Kyoto sen). The Bita sen include other forgeries than those of the Eiraku; also probably the various kinds of "bad sen," such as small sized, cut or defaced sen, cracked, broken coins and those made with very inferior metal, such as lead, figs. 6, 7 and 8.

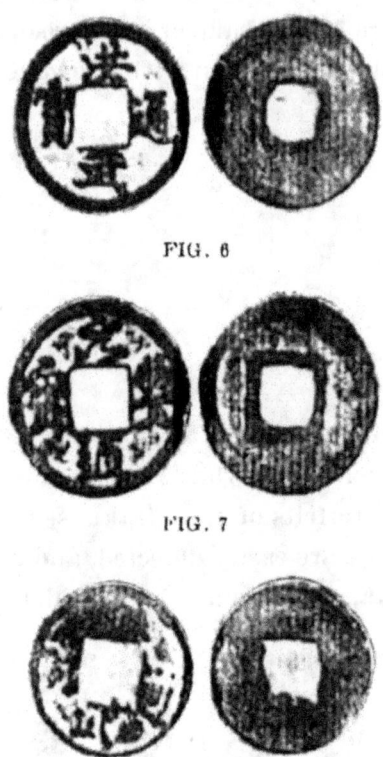

FIG. 6

FIG. 7

FIG. 8

The class Bita sen, most likely included what are now known to collectors as Shima sen, but from the above description, no one is likely to confuse the inferior imitations of Chinese or other coins, or any of the host of infirm, deformed or senile sen, with the coins which are like an island in their isolated peculiarities. The Bita sen are the result of accident or evil design, the "Shima" or "Island" sen seem "poor but honest", though decidedly eccentric. A few of them are of fairly good dimensions, and may have formed the circulating medium of a daimyo's realm.

IV

FROM TENSHO TO MEIJI.

The death of Nobunaga in 1582 left Hideyoshi master of the political situation. It is true that he had several rivals and had to walk warily, but he was without a peer in the combined arts of statecraft and strategy. Tokugawa Ieyasu alone, the founder of the dynasty of Shoguns which ruled from the death of Hideyoshi till the present era of Meiji, might have coped with him. As it was, he ventured to oppose Hideyoshi by force; but his extreme caution, the distance of his base from the capital, and the failure of his allies to give effective support, led to the collapse of this opposition. The two redoubtable warriors thereupon concluded a pact whereby Ieyasu gave his support to Hideyoshi during the lifetime of the latter, while preparing the way for his own ambitious schemes.

The personality of Hideyoshi dominates Japanese history. Born two years after Nobunaga and the same time before Ieyasu, there was nothing in his plebeian descent, his diminutive figure or homely features to encourage advancement amongst the proud and great. He rose by merit alone, an almost impossible feat in those days. It is true that Nobunaga deserved success, if only for discerning in a humble laquay the genius of incomparable strategy, and applying it to his service. We may say that the elevation of Hideyoshi became indispensible to the fortunes of his patron, so that, in spite of the scowls of the aristocracy, he attained a position second only to that of Nobunaga himself. On his death, the claims of his infant grandson were temporarily upheld by Hideyoshi, who was thus enabled to consolidate his authority, after which they received scant consideration. During this period he set himself to conquer the outstanding Daimyos and directed his famous expedition against the House of Shimadzu of Satsuma, A.D. 1587, which resulted in the defeat of this powerful enemy.

TEN-SHO TSU-HO It was in this year that the coin
A.D. 1587 called "Ten-Sho Tsu-Ho," or "Current Treasure of Tensho," (Heavenly Rectitude) was minted, figs. 1, 2, 3, 4, and 5. This coin was of silver. According to the works called "San Kwa Zui" and "Wakan

FIG. 1

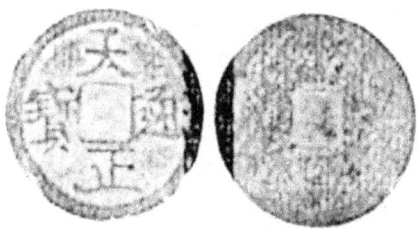

FIG. 2

Sen Ii," both a silver and copper coin were issued, but the few copper specimens in existence are generally admitted to be copies of the silver coin. It is quite certain that, had the copper sen been in circulation, it could not have disappeared completely. The silver coin was so roughly made that the author of the "Kokon Senkwa Kan" refused to admit that it was a government coin. If we consider, however, that the art of coining had been neglected for centuries, and that silver requires great care in casting, we need not wonder at the lack of finish in this coin. It is quite possible too, that it was cast in haste, like the silver Wado, as it was intended to supplement the war chest of Hideyoshi.

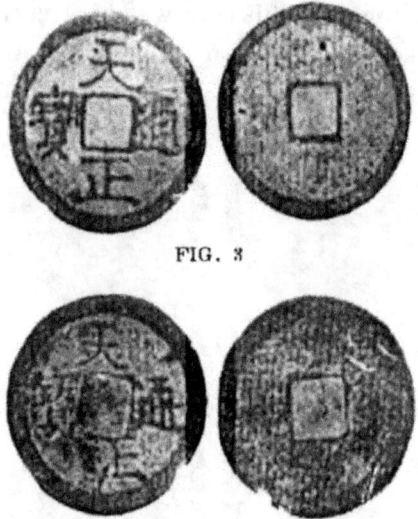

FIG. 3

FIG. 4

It is said that the inscription was written by the Emperor Go Yozei. If so, the motive of Hideyoshi in thus securing evidence of the Imperial approval is not far to seek, as this coin was identified with the expedition against one of the most powerful and haughty princes of the realm. The fact that the Tensho Tsuho was bestowed upon those warriors who excelled in courage and conduct, lends also significance to the statement that it was written by the Emperor. It will be noticed that the characters "Ten-Sho Tsu-ho," are not read in a circular fashion, as in the antique sen, but from above downwards and from (the reader's) right to left. From this coin onwards, the characters are always read in the same sequence.* There are several varieties of it. That shewn in fig. 4 is called the "Kin" Tensho, as it is supposed to be a copy of a "Kin sen" or gold coin. The coin does not exist, but is said to have been specially inscribed by the Mikado. I take this to be a mere surmise. It is apparent that the Tensho Tsuho has been copied from the renowned "Eiraku Tsuho,"

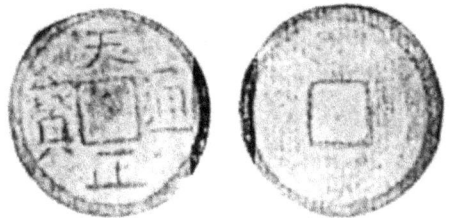

FIG. 5

page 92. That shewn in fig. 5 is an exception and is probably of later design. Here the body of the character "Ho" (寳) is large and square and the alignment of the characters "Tensho" indicates that they were originally "written for the part," whereas those

---
* As the reader can thus easily identify the characters, they will henceforth be omitted from the text, except where specially called for.

in figs. 1 and 4, prove that they were impressed on the mould of the "Tane sen" after the coin had been shaped thereon.

BUN-ROKU TSU-HO In the first year of Bunroku, **A.D. 1588** "Magnificent Gift," or "Splendid Official Emolument," A.D. 1592, the silver coin called "Bun-Roku Tsu-Ho" or "Current Treasure of Bunroku" was

FIG. 6

minted. Armed with the Imperial sanction, we may be sure that Hideyoshi neglected no means, however trivial, to attract and retain all who had an axe to grind, and few, whether lord or samurai, were proof against the attractions of "Bunroku." Though it is known that many of the high born held him in secret contempt, his tactful combination of the open hand and the "mailed fist," earned him the devoted services of the many who had something to gain or keep. Two years previous to the issue of this coin, Hojo Ujimasa, who from his proud and giddy height as commander of the Kwanto had challenged Hideyoshi to combat, and met a grievous fall. The outstanding opposition of the Daimyos collapsed, and it remained with Hideyoshi to reward the faithful with "Splendid Official Emoluments," which he did with no niggard hand. Like the Tensho Tsuho, this coin was not intended for circulation. It was probably designed for use in the invasion of Corea, which began in the year in which the coin was cast. Like the Tensho sen also, it is coarsely

FIG. 7

made. There are two kinds of handwriting, figs. 6 and 7. A copper coin is spoken of; but does not exist. Forgeries are shewn by dealers, however, to tempt the uninitiated. The gold and silver Eiraku sen shewn in plate 6, chapter 3, are reputed to have been designed by Hideyoshi as rewards to his officers; and though not current coin, they came into limited use, possibly at their bullion value. In one of these, plate 3, chap. 3, No 1, it will be seen that the characters "Tsu" and "Ho" have a great resemblance to those of the Tensho Tsuho seen in fig. 5. In this case, the Eiraku sen has been copied from the Tensho Tsuho, instead of the reverse, and this specimen is therefore of unusual interest.

The Corean war, designed by Hideyoshi as a step towards the invasion of China, dragged on in victorious but fruitless battles against the forces of these countries, and was finally ended by the death of the great "Taiko," who quietly breathed his last on the morning of the 16th September, 1598. Such matters do not properly

FROM TENSHO TO MEIJI.

fall within the scope of this work, but it may conduce to a better understanding of the origin of some of the following coins, if I quote from Murdoch the following passage: "Ieyasu was summoned to the Taiko's sickroom, and there the dying ruler told him that after his death, there would be great wars, and that only he (Ieyasu) could keep the empire tranquil. 'I therefore,' Hideyoshi proceeded, 'bequeath the whole country to you, and trust that you will expend all your strength in governing it. My son Hideyori is still young. I beg that you will look after him. When he is grown up, I leave it to you to decide whether he shall be my successor or not."

KEI-CHO TSU-HO "The Current Treasure of Keicho,"
A.D. 1606 was cast in the 11th year of Keicho

FIG. 8

"Rejoicing Continually" (1606). It was made of silver and copper and both these metals were in circulation, though the copper, or bronze coin, was issued in much greater amount, and was the principal currency. The silver coin is getting quite rare. The "Tsu" and "Ho" of the Keicho coin are taken from the Eiraku sen, while the "Kei" (慶) and "Cho" (長) have been added according to the method previously mentioned. Several varieties are known. Fig. 8 shews the ordinary or "Futsu" Keicho. Note the likeness of the "Tsuho"

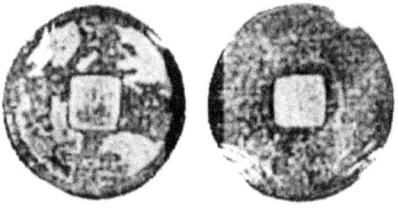

FIG. 9

to that on the Eiraku sen. In fig. 9 the true silver coin is seen. Fig. 10 illustrates the "Ho Cho Sei" or stroke on the head of "Ho," added to disguise the likeness to the Eiraku sen. There are other kinds

FIG. 10

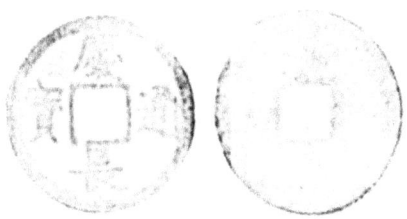

FIG. 11

mentioned in the books, viz. "Shoji," or small letter Keicho, fig. 11, "Shinsho" a name for a certain square style of writing, and the silver coin written in the "Tensho" style of character. This latter name (as will be seen by the characters) does not refer to the period of that name but to one of the various styles of writing. The three latter varieties have been placed here for the sake of continuity; but they were not in current use at any time, and ought properly to be classed with the "Shiken" (test or trial) sen. The "'Tensho," as opposed to the true silver coin, may be reckoned as a "Raku" or fancy sen, probably not even deserving a place amongst the "Shiken" sen. Some writers distinguish a "Taiji," or large character variety, but the distinction is trivial.

The Keicho Tsuho was coined ostensibly in order to have a substitute for the Eiraku sen, which seems to have provoked much dissension by its superiority to the "Bita" sen. If the object was to make a coin of inferior grade to the Eiraku sen, the Keicho Tsuho is a decided success. At the time of its debut, the celebrated pilot Will Adams, was enjoying the confidence of the Shogun Hidetada; his father Ieyasu, who had retired in 1603, but who still practically managed the affairs of the country, ardently espoused the cause of learning and the arts.

GEN-WA TSU-HO In 1615, the first year of Genwa **A.D. 1615** (pronounced "Genna") "the Commencement of Concord," the coin called "Gen-Wa Tsu-Ho," or Current Treasure of Genwa, was issued. The period of Genwa was established to celebrate the peace which followed the defeat of the party whose object was to put Toyotomi Hideyori, the son of Taiko Hideyoshi, in the place usurped by Tokugawa Ieyasu. Another attempt was made in the summer of the first year of Genwa, but met with no success. It may be worth while to dwell for a moment on the cause of this outbreak in favour of Hideyori, as it has a bearing on one of the most interesting coins of Japan, namely the universal "Bun" sen of the Kwanei period. This coin was made from the metal composing the huge image, or "Daibutsu," which Ieyasu had induced Hideyori and his mother to erect, together with temples and other buildings, in order it is said, to exhaust his resources. At the last moment, however, when the ceremony of consecration had already commenced, the great multitude which had gathered, not only from the capital, but surrounding provinces, were astounded to learn that the ceremony had been prohibited by Ieyasu.* His cunning plan of humiliating Hideyori, on the pretence of having been slighted by an obscure inscription on the great bell, precipitated the conflict above referred to, if it was not the sole cause of it. In extenuation, however, it may be said that Ieyasu, who had reached the age of seventy-three, knew that the rival powers were only waiting for his decease, and decided to strike the final blow while his presence could encourage his friends and dismay his enemies. He accomplished his object, and the Tokugawa family occupied the shogunate till the present era of Meiji.

* "It afterwards became known that Ieyasu had taken umbrage at the wording of the inscription on the great bell, into which the characters forming his name were introduced, by way of mockery, as he pretended to think, in the phrase "Kokka anko", "May the state be peaceful and prosperous" [Ka and Ko being the Chinese for Ie and Yasu], while in another sentence which ran "On the east it welcomes the bright moon, and on the west bids farewell to the setting sun", he chose to discover a comparison of himself to the lesser, and of Hideyori to the greater Luminary, from which he then inferred an intention on the part of Hideyori to attempt his destruction." Chamberlain and Mason's "Handbook of Japan" 5th Chapter, Page 370.

FROM TENSHO TO MEIJI.

Ieyasu died in the year following his triumph, in the second year of Genwa, A.D. 1616.

FIG. 12

The "Gen-Wa Tsuho" or "Current treasure of Genwa A. D. 1615, fig. 12, is a copper coin, of better finish and design than the Keicho Tsuho. We can still trace the influence of the Eiraku sen in the style of the characters "Tsu" and "Ho," though they have probably not been directly transferred to it, as in the case of the Keicho coin. On the reverse it bears the Japanese numeral 1. This might be supposed to refer to the first year of Genwa in which it was issued, but it seems rather to have been intended to indicate its value, which was one mon or sen. Fig. 13 illustrates a

FIG. 13

variety which, from its comparative rarity, is probably a "shiken" or "mihon" sen (trial or sample sen). It is lighter in colour than the "Tsuyo" or circulating sen, but can scarcely be called a brass coin. The characters all differ slightly from those on the ordinary sen, especially those of "Gen" (元) and "Wa" (和). Besides these, there are what are known as the "Ban" or numeral sen, each having a number on the back, Plate 7 Chapter 3. Nos. 7, 8 and 9. They are made of the same metal as fig 13, and are rare. It was not unusual in China to number the coins on the reverse according to the year of the period in which they were made; but this can scarcely have been the intention in this case, for the period of Genwa extended for only nine years, while the illustrations shew not only the number 8 on the back, but also 10 and 20. Another set (we cannot say series) for consecutive numbers have not been found, is made of silver. Pewter sets also exist, but are of no special interest. These coins, which were probably made in the government mint are, as already stated of the nature of "Shiken" sen; and the numbers on the back were probably affixed for the purpose of inspection only.

KWAN-EI TSU-HO The period of Kwanei, or Permanent
A.D. 1624 Liberality, began in 1624 and lasted for twenty years. The throne was occupied by the Emperor Go Mizu No-O till the 6th year, then by the Empress Meisei till its close, while the Shogun Iemitsu, grandson of Ieyasu, administered the affairs of the realm. In the 3rd year of this period the "Kwan-Ei Tsu-Ho or Current Treasure of Kwanei" was minted. The idea of this coin is said to have originated in a dream of Iemitsu which was interpreted by the priest Tenkwai as a call

for the institution of a new coinage. It proved so acceptable that it continued to be issued till the 6th year of Ansei, 1859, that is to say, for two hundred and thirty-three years. A currency which lasted for such a time and so nearly bridges over the interval between the feudal age and modern enlightenment, must have been deserving of the popularity which it won. It is an excellent coin, as issued from the government mint, and even many of the varieties made in the provinces are good specimens of the minter's art, though some form an exception to this statement. We may also make an exception in the case of the Kwanei *iron* sen, made in the provinces from 1769 onwards, which are naturally very inferior. Including the varieties made in different parts of the country, many of which were not acknowledged by the government, and taking into consideration slight differences in character, size, design, nature and quality of metal used in their composition, there are over a thousands kinds of Kwanei sen recognised by connoisseurs. I possess some three hundred varieties; and it would be an easy matter to double the number. To experts in Japanese calligraphy, a full collection of these sen may be a matter of interest, there being Japanese collectors who devote themselves entirely to it. Except in a few instances, where special interest attaches to a specimen, I propose to give only such as can be readily distinguished from one another.

The first Kwanei Tsuho coins were made in the province of Mito, an ancient centre of classical learning

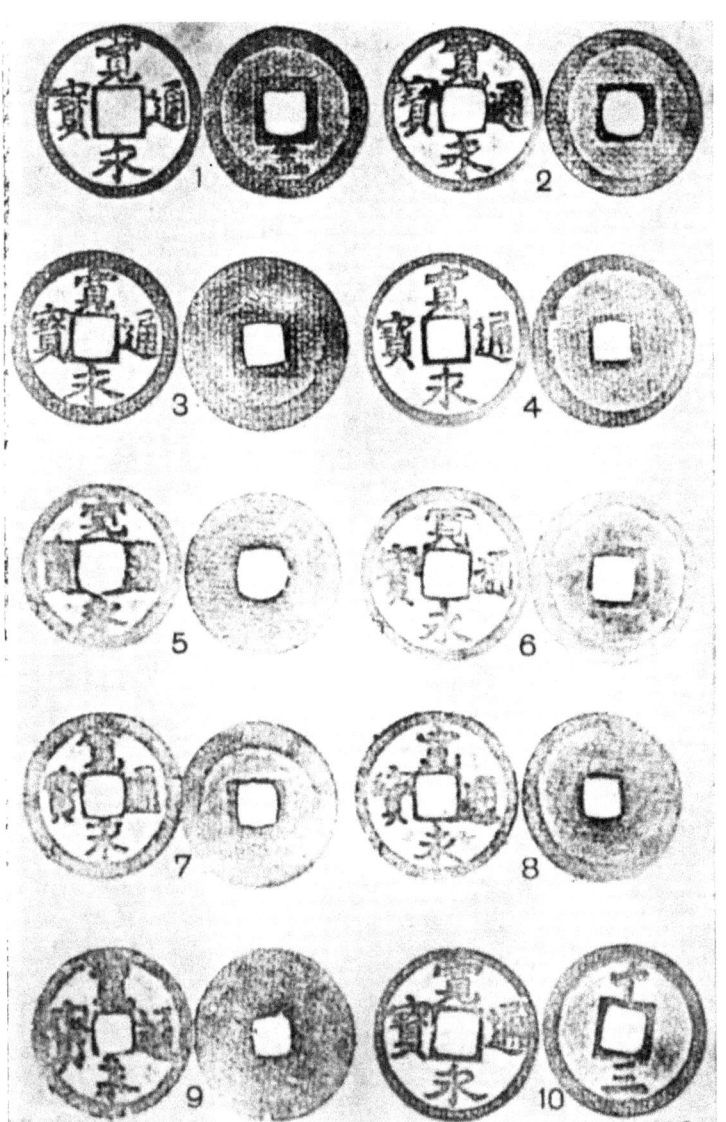

PLATE 1.—EARLY SEN.
"KWANEI TSUHO."

and famous for the number and variety of the coins which it produced, not only for provincial but for general circulation. They are inferior in many respects to the later sen, and may always be recognized by the fact that the "Ei" (永), is written in the "Nisui" (二水) style already noticed in the Ryūhei Eiho sen, (page 56), figs. 35 and 36. From the 13th year of Kwanei onwards, this coin became the established government currency, an order having appeared in that year to the effect that it would in future be minted in Tokyo, the seat of the Shogun, and at Sakamoto, in the province of Omi, which adjoins that of the Imperial capital. It was further forbidden to cast it in any other place. Other decrees relating to this coin appeared from time to time.

The order limiting the coinage of this sen to Tokyo and Sakamoto fell into abeyance, and legitimate centres of minting, as well as private foundries, sprung up over the land. There are three or four specimens all which distinctly bear witness to their origin from previous currencies. Of these I may mention the "Kaigen" "Te" or hand, Plate 1., No. 5, the "Eiraku" No. 6, the "Taihei," No. 7, and the "Genna" hand (writing) No. 8. In these cases the "Tsu-Ho" has been taken by direct transference from China coins. They are not common, No. 5 being very rare. This is the coin which was one of the main actors in the incident illustrated in the frontispiece. The first Kwanei Tsuho, of reliable date, is illustrated in fig. 14. It was cast in Mito, Hitachi Province, in the 3rd year of Kwanei, 1626. On the obverse, the character "Ei" (永), is seen to be of the "Nisui" type, while the reverse

FIG. 14

bears the Japanese numeral for three(三), which evidently refers to the 3rd year of Kwanei. Figs. 15, 16 and 17 are without numbers on the reverse and were also cast in

FIG. 15

FIG. 16

Mito. According to the "Shin Sen Kwanei Sempu," fig. 14 represents the first Kwanei sen minted in the

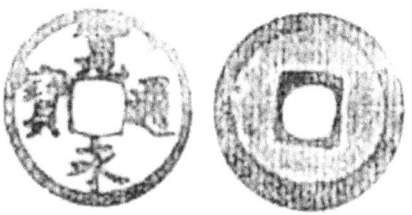

FIG. 17

country; but this statement may be questioned. It seems to me that any of them might have been the first attempts at making the Kwanei Tsuho, though they were probably not considered good enough for the

FIG. 18

new circulation. In fig. 18, the "Nisui" style is seen with a dot or star on the back. ("Hai Mon Sen," or

FIG. 19

Back Star Character), also made in Mito. In the 13th year of Kwanei this mint also produced a coin, fig. 19, with the Japanese numeral for 13 on the back and with the character "Ei" written also in the "Nisui" style." It is rare, and was probably a shiken or trial sen sent in for government approbation. This appears to have been refused, for we find that the Kwanei sen were issued in this year from the Asakusa mint in Tokyo.

FIG. 20

In fig. 20, the first coin made in the latter mint appears without the Nisui character, but with a dot on

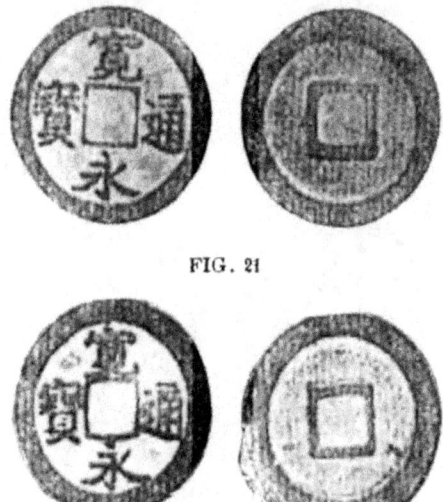

FIG. 21

FIG. 22

the back. It was issued in the 13th year of Kwanei. There were several varieties of this sen fig. 21, "Mu Hai" or "No Star," and fig. 22, "Kyo Sen" or "Small Hole", which appear to be of excellent quality and design, but for some reason or another this mint did not retain its monopoly of manufacture, and the edict above mentioned appears to have reference to the establishment of a purely government mint at Shiba, which, with the mint at Sakamoto, in the province of Omi, were thenceforth decreed to be the only legitimate sources of the national currency. This decree was rescinded, or at least disregarded, even in the year of its promulgation. The coin shown in fig. 23

FIG 23

is also from the Asakusa mint. It is known as the "Sekkaku" Asakusa sen, because the characters are crowded around the central hole, like those of the Kengen Taiho in Chapter 2, fig. 68, p. 77. To numismatists some interest attaches to the series of sen issued from the Asakusa mint called "Ban" or "Number" sen, though not properly speaking coins of the realm. Whether they were intended as trial sen, or whether they were meant for fancy sen, the Asakusa mint being the source of many such coins, one cannot say. The fact however, that these sen were also made in the official government mint at Shiba, may indicate that they were designed for official inspection, with the intention possibly of casting fresh coin each year and placing the date of each on the reverse, after the fashion of some of the Chinese cash. Such sets are very rare, practically unobtainable indeed, and consequently there are many forgeries. Those illustrated in plates 2 and 3, are good specimens, thirteen out of the sixteen being from the Asakusa and three from the Shiba mint, namely, Nos. 2, 4 and 10. A close inspection of the latter, will enable any one to detect the variations in the characters from those of the remaining thirteen numbers, the difference in breadth of the body of "Ho" being specially obvious. No. 17 shews an ordinary sen from the Asakusa and No. 18 a corresponding one from the Shiba mint. The "Shiba Shin Sen Za" or New Sen Mint at Shiba, was established in the 13th year of Kwanei, and the sen emanating therefrom were of fine quality and

FIG. 24 T

workmanship. Fig. 24 shews one of these sen, a trifle larger than the "Tsuyo" or circulating sen, for it represents what is known to collectors as a "Tane" sen. The "Tane" sen have already been described, but the

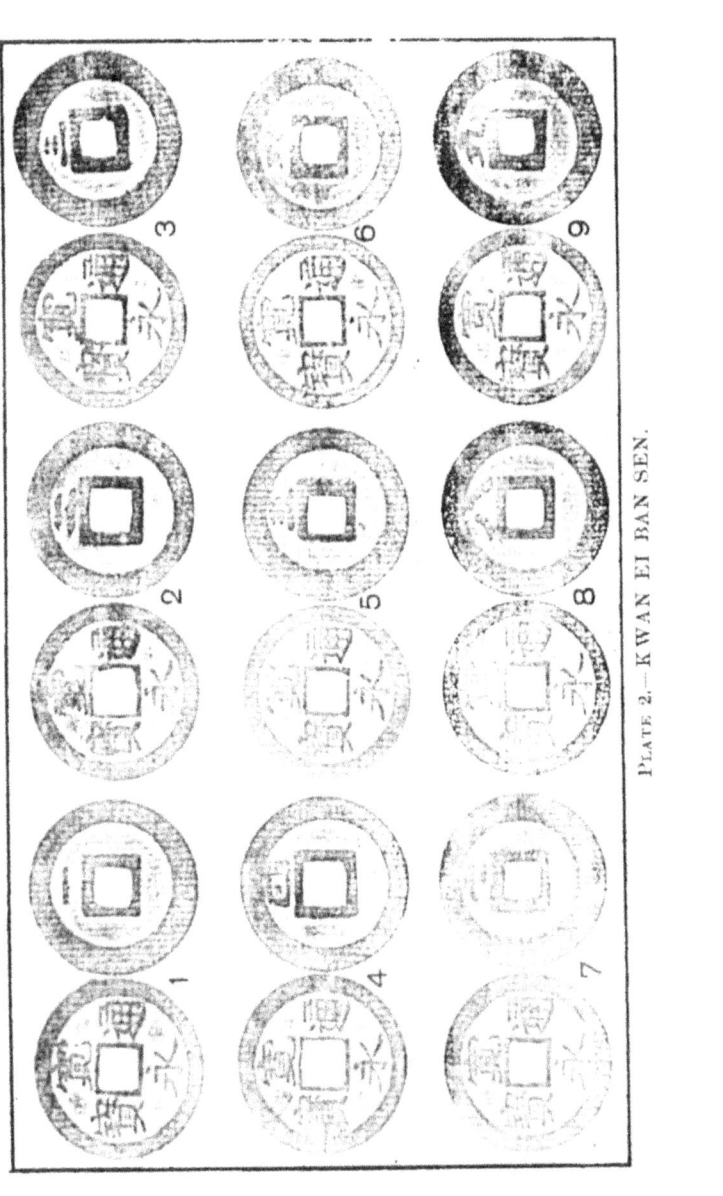

PLATE 2.—KWAN EI BAN SEN.

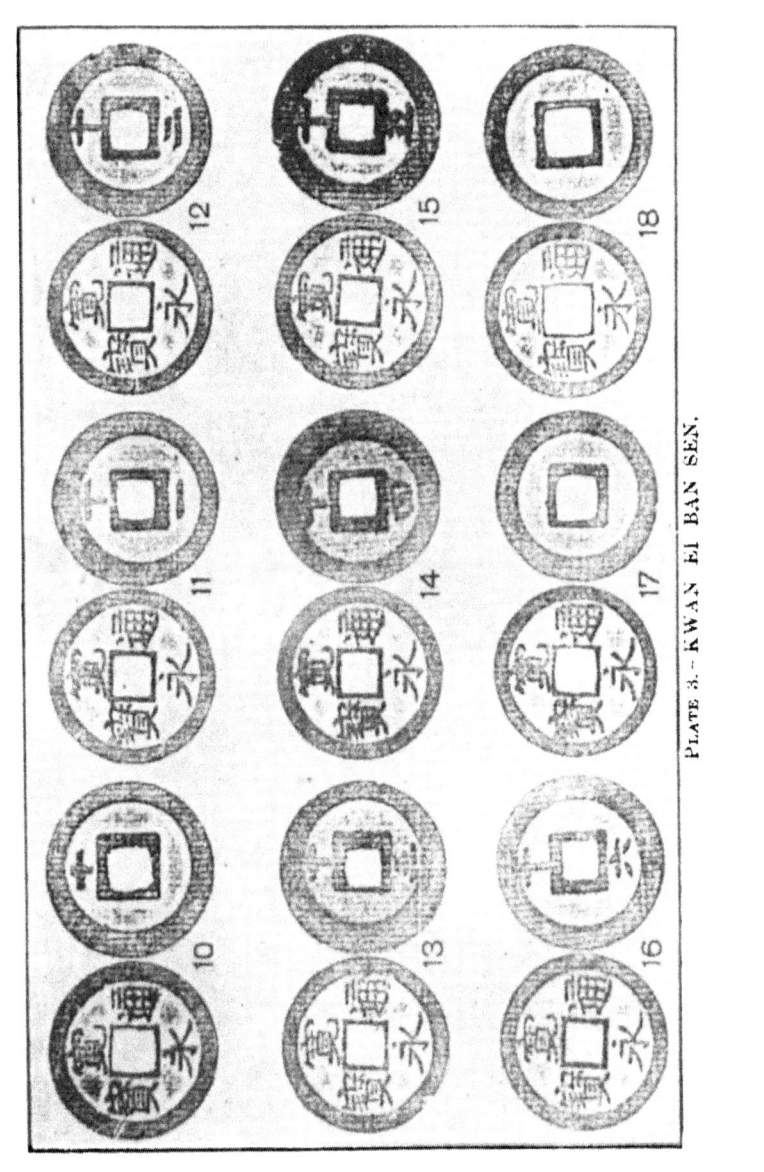

PLATE 3.—KWAN EI BAN SEN.

reader may be again reminded that a "Tane," sen is one which is used to make the impression on the clay moulds into which the metal is poured to make coin. They are therefore of the best and clearest design and are much in demand, being also rarer than the ordinary sen. The "Tane" sen of the Shiba mint is far from

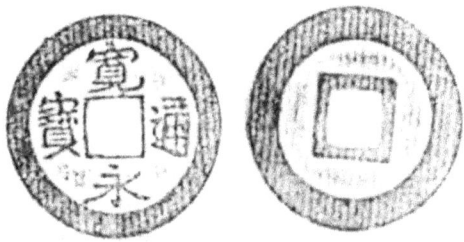

FIG. 25 T

common and that shown in fig. 25 is an exceptionally large and fine specimen.

The sen illustrated in fig. 26, is also a Tane sen,

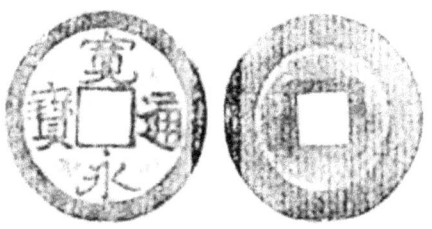

FIG. 26 T

which I shall indicate in the following pages by the capital letter (T). It was made in Sakamoto, Omi Province according to the before-mentioned edict, in the 13th year of Kwanei.

In the same year moreover, this sen was cast in Nara, fig. 27, Matsumoto, Yoshida, and the of Ashi-arai and Koya in Soroga province, besides other places which are not exactly ascertained. That of Ashi-arai is illustrated in fig. 28; the some-

FIG. 27

FIG. 28

what curved lines around the central hole render its identification easy.

In the 8th year of Kwambun, 1668, there was cast at the village of Kameido, in the outskirts of Tokyo, a Kwanei sen known as the "Bun" sen, from the character of that name (文), meaning "Learning," "Literary Composition," which is inscribed on the reverse, figs. 29 and 30. This sen was made from the fragments of the Daibutsu, or great image of Buddha, erected by Hideyori, and the consecration of which was so rudely interrupted by Ieyasu in the year 1614. In 1662 both the temple and the image were destroyed by an earthquake, and it is said that Matsudaira Nobutsuna, a noted statesman, sensibly suggested that it could be put to good use

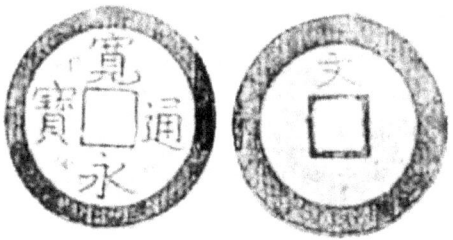

FIG. 29 T

FIG. 30

by converting it into coin, whereas its temple covering always stood in need of repair and was a source of great expense. The Emperor Reigen is said then to have issued a proclamation saying that in the time of the Emperor Seisho (of the Shu dynasty of China,) the Buddhist images were destroyed, and coin made in their stead; a government edict stated that Buddha teaches the good way to the people, but that these copper images are certainly not Buddha, whose chief doctrine is to benefit the people, etc. The character "Bun" on the reverse of this coin, is the same as that of Kwanbun, and is no doubt intended to signify the period in which it was made, the other character "Kwan" being on the obverse of the coin. It has been said that the "Bun" was placed on the back of this sen on account of its having been made by Bun Zaemon, a person of great wealth, who is stated to have made coin at the Kameido mint. This is not, however, the general opinion.

The Bun sen is very plentiful; indeed, one can hardly look at a handful of sen without seeing one, but it is less common than it was ten years ago, and will soon be rare. There are two reasons for this. The first is that the metal contains a very small proportion of gold and probably silver; the other, that it has come from the body of the Daibutsu. It has thus a saving grace in the esteem of those who worship Nicotiana, for they who have the stem of their *kiseru* or pipe made of this metal may burn and inhale the incense all day long without fear of the canker which threatens the devotee of the fragrant weed. Here surely, does comedy follow on the heels of tragedy! Yet what a history might one of these humble sen unfold, were it capable of transferring its experience to ourselves! It may be that part of it was first handled by man in the Wado period and that it may have undergone the most varied metamorphoses through members of the antique sen, and others besides, ere it was cast by some devotee, trying to follow the Good Way, into the furnace (whence it mingled with other and nobler metals) its individuality merged at last in the Daibutsu, the image of the Great Teacher. Then the solemn triumph, turned in a moment to less than nothing, to gall, to unholy chagin, at the word of a scheming mortal! Then the catastrophe, the melting pot once more, the smooth shining Bun sen, personification of Mammon! To be a pipe mouthpiece, beloved of its owner, is truly a better fate!

FIG. 31

There are about half a dozen kinds of this sen, which are easy to recognise, amongst which is the "Shimaya" sen, fig. 31, which may be distinguished from the others by the top of the character "Tsu" (通). It was made in Kameido during the period of Kwan-

FIG. 32

bun, along with another sen which has the same face, but in which the character Bun is lacking on the reverse, fig. 32. These two coins were made by an establishment having the trade name "Shimaya". I must not forget to mention a coin, illustrated in fig. 33, which, though more or less of a freak and probably not intended for circulation, has an interest all its own, for it is the last of the Bun sen and was literally made from the dregs of the melted Daibutsu. It is called the "Tori-

FIG. 33

Sumi" sen, such is the inscription, in a running hand on the back of this coin, but to read it the coin must be looked at in a mirror for, like some of the Shima sen, it is written in reverse. The phrase "Tori-Sumi," "Gathered Ending" implies that the residue was removed for the purpose of making this coin. Its metal is not so good as that of the ordinary Bun sen, as it really represents the dregs, or nearly so, of the molten metal. It is by no means common, although forgeries abound. At the

FIG. 34

ancient capital, Kyoto, in the 4th year of Genroku, A.D. 1691, the coin illustrated in fig. 34 was minted. In fig. 35 and 36 are seen coins with the character "Sa" (佐) on the reverse, and fig. 37 another with the same, in a

FROM TENSHO TO MEIJI.

FIG. 35

FIG. 36

FIG. 37

different hand. They were all made in the province of Sado (hence the "Sa"), in the town of Aikawa, but at different periods. While it is my aim to treat these Kwanei sen in chronological order, it will simplify the task of understanding them if such similar coins are considered together, the time relation being of less importance than that of similarity. That shewn in fig. 35 was cast in the 4th year of Shotoku, A.D. 1774, while fig. 36 was made in the 11th year of Kyoho, A.D. 1726.

There are several varieties which space does not allow us to consider.

That seen in fig. 37 was issued in the first and only year of Manen, 1860, over a hundred and thirty years later than the former and as a current coin, was made of iron.

The next coin can easily be recognised by the upward tail of the side stroke of the character Ei, fig. 38. In this also, as in most of the Kwanei sen,

FIG. 38 T

FIG 39 T

several varieties can be distinguished. It was made at Namba, in the province of Settsu, from the 13th to the 15th year of Kyoho, 1728-1730. The sen exhibited in fig. 40, bears the character "Sen" (仙) a Hermit (see him approaching the mountain peak) on the reverse.

FROM TENSHO TO MEIJI. 127

FIG. 40 T

This is the first character of Sendai, at which place it was minted (Ishi-No-Maki), in the province of Mutsu from the 13th to the 17th years of Kyoho, 1728-1732. Fig. 41 represents one with a different top to the charac-

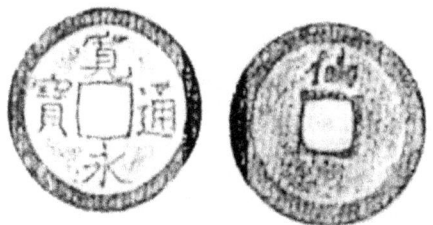

FIG. 41

ter "Tsu" (通), and other slight variations.

In the first year of Gembun, 1736, the coin seen in fig. 42 was cast at Jiu-Man-Tsubo, Fukugawa, Tokyo, and bears on the reverse the Japanese numeral for "Jiu"

FIG. 42 T

(✝) 10, in allusion to the first syllable in the name of its birthplace. Note that the left leg, so to speak, of the character Kwan (寛), springs from the lower horizontal stroke, rather than from the body of the character while the right leg, or tail extends upwards to a much greater degree than in any of the preceding coins. The dot of Ei, too, is formed of an angular stroke, and the character "Ho" has quite a jaunty air. All the characters of this sen are different from those of the earlier Kwanei coins. These points are emphasised, as it was at this mint that the first iron sen was made, though a few iron coins are cast on the lines of some of the previous ones. In fig. 43 is seen a similar coin, though the numeral "Jiu" is not on the reverse, but on the margin of the obverse.

FIG. 43

FIG. 44

Fig. 44 does not differ from fig. 43, except in the size of the cross (Jiu) on the margin of the obverse.

As usual there are several varieties one of which,

FIG. 45

fig. 45, is characterised by the absence of the indicating character "Jiu" (十). In fig. 46 we see the character

FIG. 46 T

"Ko" or "Sho" (小) on the reverse to shew that this coin was made at the village of Ko-uma in the province of Musashi. This was in the first year of Gembun, 1736.

The following coin, fig. 47, was made in the province of Kii in the 1st year of Gembun, 1736. The long upward tail of the "Kwan" and the large central rim,

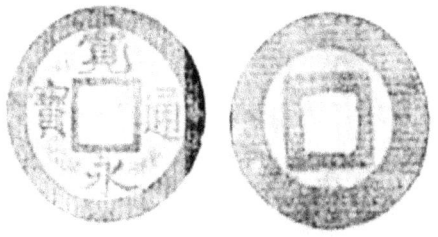

FIG. 47 T

serve to distinguish it. Fig. 48 shews a Kwanei sen from Onagigawa, Tokyo, made in the second year of Gembun. The character on the reverse is that of

FIG. 48 T

"Kawa" (川), a river (with its banks and the water between), after the "Kawa" of the word Onagigawa. Instead of being cast on the back, the corresponding coin

FIG. 49

shewn in fig. 49, is stamped on the margin of the obverse, with this character. In fig. 50 it is twice stamped. Fig. 51 shews a sen minted at the village of Fushimi in the province of Yamashiro, the 1st year of

FIG. 50

(Gembun, A. D. 1736; the width of the rim on the reverse will attract attention.

The coin illustrated in fig. 52, is peculiar in regard to the rim of the central hole, which nearly meets the

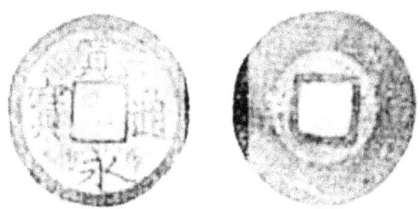

FIG. 51

outer rim. It was made in the third year of Gembun, 1738, and its coinage lasted till the first year of Kwampo, 1741. It was produced in the village of Kashima, in the province of Settsu. One or two varieties were made.

FIG. 52 T

A number of the Kwanei sen have the character "Gen or "Gan" (元) signifying beginning or commencement, on the reverse. Of these I shall give only two; the first, fig. 53, being larger than the second, fig. 54, though the characters are much the same. These sen were cast at Takatsu, city of Osaka, in the province of Settsu, in the first year, or commencement, "Gen" (元) of Kwampo, 1741, hence the character on the reverse.

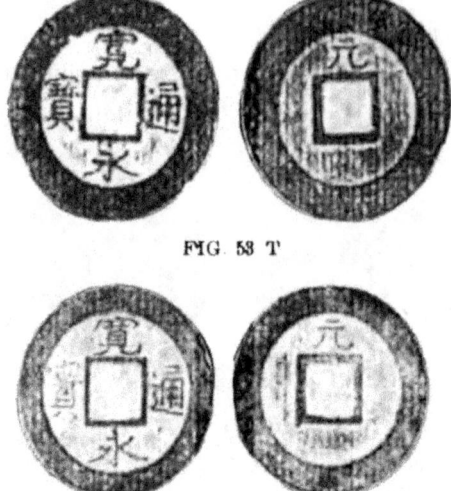

FIG. 53 T

FIG. 54 T

There was a coin, fig 55, made in the village of Ashio, Shimotsuke province, in the 2nd year of Kwampo, 1742, which bears the character "Soku" or "Ashi" (足) a word which means foot, and is applied in the ordinary colloquial to coin, as mentioned in the first chapter.

FIG. 55 T

The Japanese numeral for one (一), on the back of the two following sen (figs. 56 and 57), also refers to their place of coinage, which was at Ichi-No-Sei in Kii province. They were also cast in the second year of

FROM TENSHO TO MEIJI.

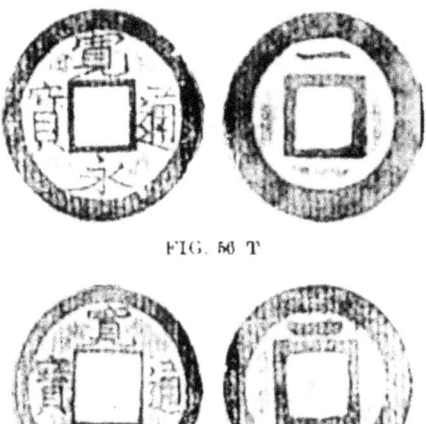

FIG. 56 T

FIG. 57 T

Kwampo. It will be observed that not only do these coins differ in size, and in the thickness of the stroke "Ichi," or one, but that the characters on the obverse are very different in style and size. Fig. 58 represents

FIG. 58 T

another of this kind, in which the face characters resemble those of fig. 56, but the numeral "Ichi" is stamped in two circles on its margin, instead of being cast on the reverse. This mint also produced sen with face characters as in fig. 57, but without the numeral on the reverse.

134 FROM TENSHO TO MEIJI.

Nagasaki comes next on the list, with a rather inferior coin having the character "Cho" or "Naga" (長) meaning "long," cast on the reverse, fig. 59. It was made in the second year of Meiwa, 1765. Fig. 60 shews a

FIG. 59 T

FIG. 60

"Haha" or "Mother" sen from which the Tane sen are cast. In the latter year also, an iron coin was issued from the village of Iida. Two varieties, with the long upward pointed tail stroke of "Kwan", and sharp points on the

FIG. 61 T

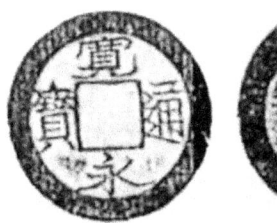

FIG. 62 T

"Ho" are shewn in figs. in 61 and 62. Another iron coin was minted in the first year of Gembun 1736, fig. 63, and from the 4th to the 6th year of Meiwa, 1767-1769, at Fushimi, Yamashiro province. The "Tane" sen of the latter, is an attractive coin, with its solid plain characters and wide rims on the reverse, fig. 63 A.

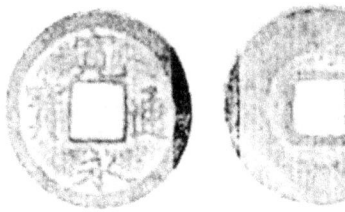

FIG. 63 T

FIG. 63 A. T

Copper must have again been getting scarce, for about this time many iron coins were made in various parts of the country. At Ishinomaki, Sendai, in the province of Mutsu, an iron sen with the character "Sen" (千), a thousand, to mark its origin from Sendai, was issued from the 6th to the 8th year of Meiwa, 1769-1771,

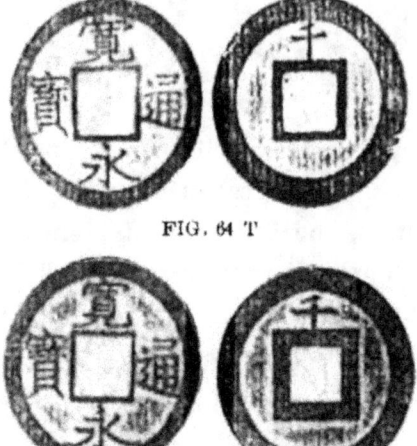

FIG. 64 T

FIG. 65 T

figs. 64 and 65. A reference to fig. 41 will shew that two distinct characters have been used to indicate Sendai, one (仙) for the copper and the other (千) for the iron sen. From the 6th to the 8th year of Meiwa also, an iron sen was cast at the village of Kizaki, in the district of Kuji, province of Hitachi. It has the character "Ku" or Kyu (久) on the reverse, fig. 66. The top of the

FIG. 66 T

FROM TENSHO TO MEIJI.

FIG. 67 T

"Tsu" (通), is triangular; some of them have the characters "Kyu Ni" on the reverse, fig. 67. The latter is the Japanese numeral for two, but the two characters read "Ku-Ni," or "Ku-Ji".* This specimen is larger and better than the copper Tane sen and I therefore use it for illustration. It was no doubt an iron Tane sen. From the 6th year of Ansei, 1859, to some time in Keio, 1865-67, an iron coin was made in Asakusa, Tokyo.

FIG. 68 T

The characters are not unlike those of the Shiba sen, shewn in fig. 24, but the whole coin is somewhat less imposing fig. 68. It so closely resembles the iron coin

---

* It is a moot point as to whether the characters "Kyu or (Ku) Ni refer to the District Kuji only, or whether the "Ni" can be intended to indicate the second issue, of which the coin appears to be a sample. "Ni" is occasionally pronounced "Ji," and the combination may thus be intended for "Kuji." On the other hand it is just possible that, as this coin was a later issue of fig. 66 it may have been minted in the 2nd year of Bunkyu, and that these words have reference to the date of its issue.

138   *FROM TENSHO TO MEIJI.*

which was cast in the Kameido mint from the 2nd year of Kwampo, 1742, that one illustration will serve for both.

During the first year of Ansei also, a copper sen was issued from Mito with "To" (ト) on the back. Two

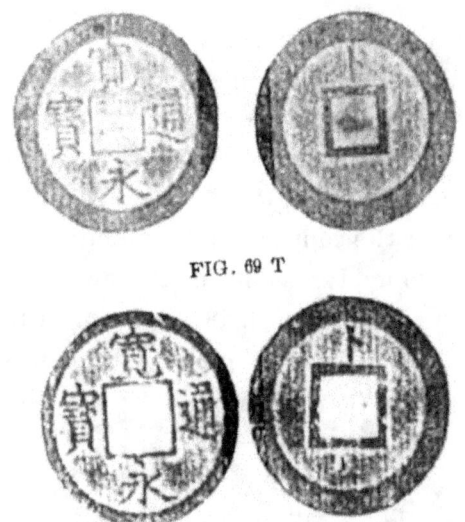

FIG. 69 T

FIG. 70 T

kinds are seen in figs. 69 and 70, one having a wide and the other a narrow rim. At Nambu in the province of Mutsu, a small coin, fig. 71, was made both in copper and iron, probably after A.D. 1860. The first copper

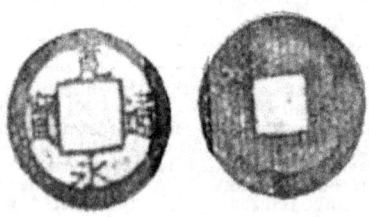

FIG 71

FROM TENSHO TO MEIJI.

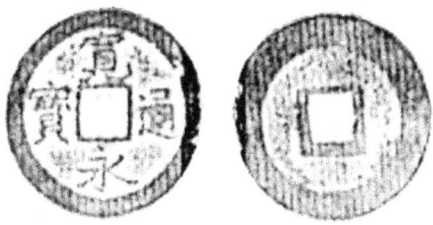

FIG. 72

mine of Akita also produced a copper Kwanei sen, fig. 72, in addition to those mentioned in Chapter 5. At the shrine of Aki (the Autumn shrine of Suwa Jinja) various Kwanei coins were stamped, fig. 73, to celebrate the erection of the temple.*

FIG 73

We now come to the "Nami" or "wave" sen, the reverses of which explain their title. The "Wave" design represents water in motion and further illustrates the similarity between this idea and that embodied in our word "Currency" (see page 22). They were also known as "Shi Mon" (四文), or four mon sen, their nominal value being one to four of the ordinary sen.

---

* The God is Take-mina-gata-tomo-no-mikoto while his spouse is Mai-no-zasaka-no-tome-no-mikoto. At Shima-no-Suwa, there are two shrines devoted to these dieties, one known as the Autumn (Aki) Jinoa while the other is the Spring (Haru) Jinja. The male deity, was ages ago, a supporter of the dynasty which was founded by Jimmu Tenno, though he perished in the attempt to uphold his political opinions. These divinities are said to change their abode twice yearly from the Autumn to the Spring shrine and *vice versa*. It was at the Autumn or Aki shrine that the coins were stamped. They are shewn here merely as curiosities.

There are many kinds, but we must be content with a few of the most prominent varieties.

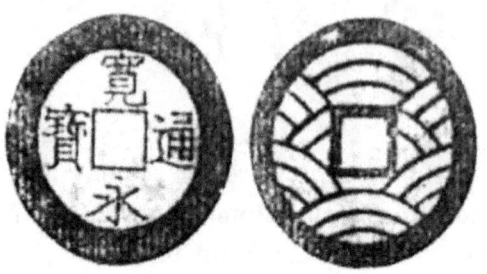

FIG. 74 T

In fig. 74 we see the "Ni Jiu Ichi Nami", or Twenty-one Wave sen, there being several subvarieties. They were minted from the 5th to the 6th year of Meiwa 1768-1769, at Kameido, and are fine specimens of the minter's art. Figs. 75, and 75 A, illustrate another

FIG. 75 T

FIG. 75-A T

"Nami" sen, the "Jiu Ichi Nami" sen, or that with eleven waves. Properly speaking there are only ten waves; the third from the bottom is interrupted by the central hole. Many varieties of this latter coin, were made in several places from the 6th year of Meiwa, 1769 onwards, some of iron. It will be noticed that the top of the character "Tsu" differs in the "eleven" and "twenty-two" wave sen; in the former it is almost a triangle, while in the latter it is rectangular except in some coins with distinguishing characters on the back. Some of these coins have not only waves, but characters on the reverse which I shall briefly mention. Fig. 76 is

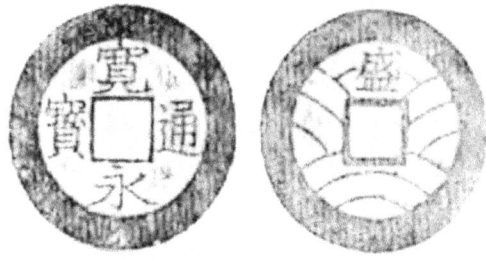

FIG. 76 T.

the Tane sen of an iron issue, cast in Morioka, province of Mutsu, in the single year of the period Manen. On the

FIG. 77 T.

reverse it bears the character "Mori" (盛), to indicate its origin in Morioka.

Fig. 77 has the character "Sen" (千), a thousand, on the back, the mark of an iron coin made in Sendai; it was also made in Manen, 1860.

FIG. 78 T

Fig. 78, shews another iron coin with the syllabic letter "To" (ト) on the reverse. It was made in Mito, in the 2nd year of Kei-O, 1866.

Yet another iron sen, with the letter "I" (イ) on the reverse was made at Tsu in the province of Ise, fig. 79.

FIG. 79 T

In the town of Aidzu, Iwashiro province, during the 2nd year of Kei-O, an iron sen with the syllabic letter, or "Kana" called "No" on the reverse was minted, fig. 80.

FROM TENSHO TO MEIJI.

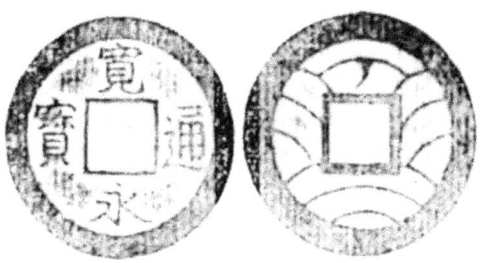

FIG. 80 T

It has been suggested that this letter is an abbreviated form of "A" (ア), and that it has reference to the town Aidzu.

Another with the letter "A" (ア) is said to have been cast at Hiroshima, Aki province, in what year no one knows. The place of mintage is not even positively known, some authorities maintaining that it was made in the foregoing town of Aidzu, and that it was from this coin that the abbreviation of the letter "A" was conceived for the sake of appearance. There were several iron coins of the "Eleven Wave" kind, cast at Yamagata in the province of Dewa, at various dates. Figs. 81 and 82 shew both the eleven and twenty-one wave

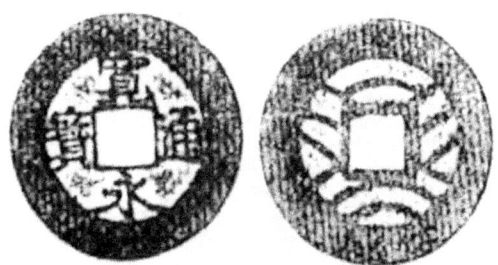

FIG. 81 .T

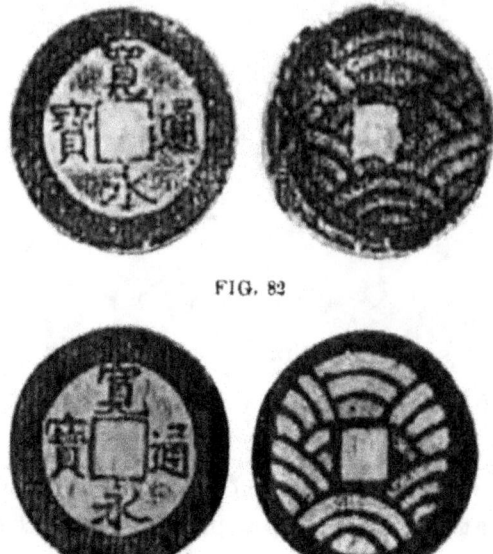

FIG. 82

FIG. 83 T

varieties. The latter is rare; still more so is the brass coin shewn in fig. 83 from the same mint.

Certain large and handsome Kwanei sen called "Go Yo" sen (lit. Honourable Use, meaning, in this case, "for the service of the government") were cast under authority, for the purpose of paying the workmen engaged in the repairs of the great temples at Nikko.

FIG. 84

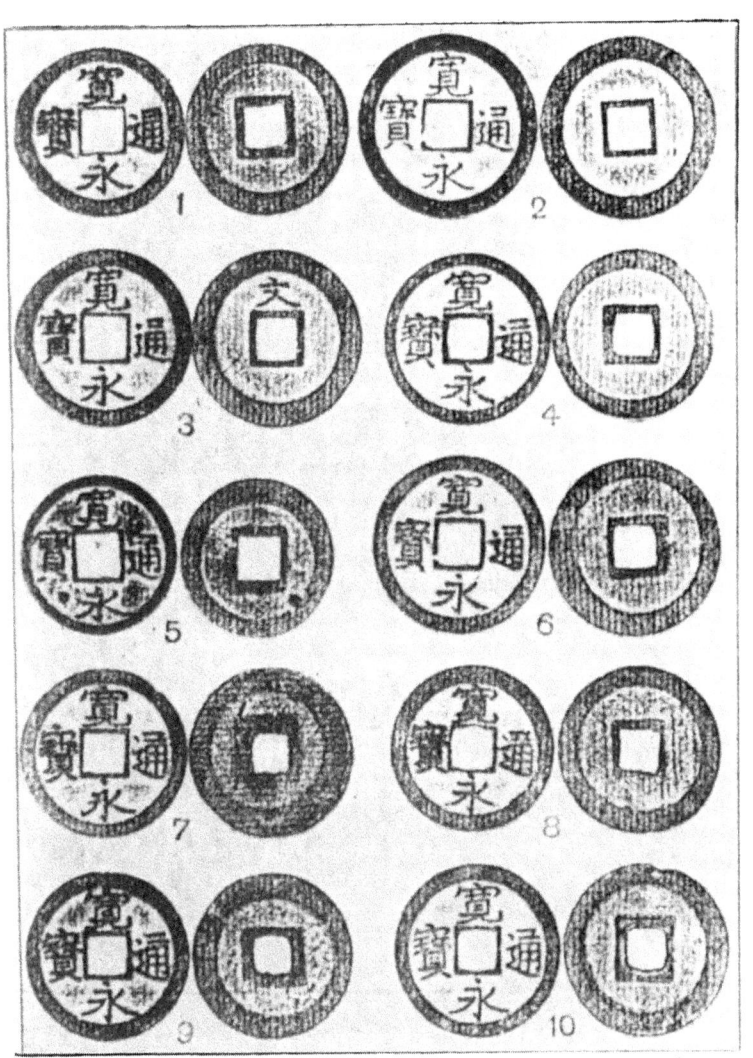

PLATE 4.—KWAN EI SILVER AND GOLD SEN. (Not current Coin.)

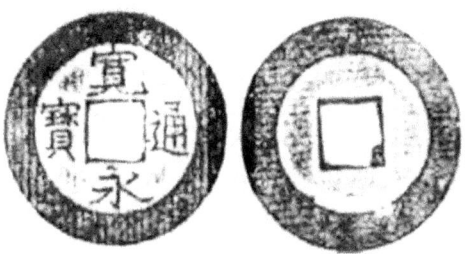

FIG. 85

There are several varieties, of which I give a few examples. They are occasionally called "Ogata" or large-sized "Kwanei" sen. Figs. 84 and 85 were made at Asakusa during the Shotoku period, 1711-15. What is

FIG. 86

FIG. 87

known as the Osaka Namba Go Yo sen is shewn in figs. 86 and 87. In Plate 4 may be seen some of the Kwanei gold and silver sen cast since the time of Iemitsu. A few of them were issued as rewards, and one or two were "Haha" or mother sen; most however were in private use as gifts.

HO-EI TSU-HO. 寶永通寶 A.D. This coin was minted in the 4th year of Ho-Ei, the year of the last eruption of Mount Fuji, which resulted in the prominence on the south side of the mountain called, after the period, Hoei-san; on this occasion the ashes are said to have covered some parts of Tokyo, about 60 miles distant, to the depth of six inches.

FIG. 88

The "Ho-Ei Tsu-Ho" or "Current Treasure of Hoei" (Eternal Treasure), is a large coin, of 37 M.M.

FIG. 89.—Silver Haha Sen.

diameter. Fig. 89 shews a "Haha" or mother sen from my collection, probably unique, made of silver, the parent of the Tane sen, fig. 90. This latter speci-

FIG. 90 T

men is a trifle larger and thicker than the common sen.

The reverse of the Hoei Tsuho has the characters "Ei Kyu Sei Yo" cast on the wide margin, in the same order as those on the face. They read "For the Everlasting Use of the World," a sentiment which was not realized. In the case of the "Tsuyo" or current sen, fig. 88, the additional character "Chin," meaning precious, is struck on the margin.

The Hoei Tsuho was issued at the value of one to ten of the ordinary Kwanei Tsuho but its inconvenient size, and still more, the fact that it was not intrinsically worth this amount, rendered it far from popular. Notwithstanding special edicts to secure its circulation and threats of condign punishment if it were refused, it did not make headway and was withdrawn in the 6th year of the same period, 1709.

FROM TENSHO TO MEIJI.

FIG. 91

Fig. 91, represents a coin which is known as the "Ni Ji", or "Two Character" Hoei. The obverse has only the two characters "Ho-Ei;" the reverse is the same as the ordinary coin. In this specimen, the characters on the back are not distinct. It is rough but rare, and is a Shiken sen, pure and simple, as it was not permitted to go into circulation.

TEN-HO TSU-HO (Pronounced Tempo Tsuho.) This coin A.D. 1835. was first made at Hashiba, Tokyo, or Yedo

FIG. 92 —Haba Sen.

FROM TENSHO TO MEIJI.

as it was formerly called, by order of the Tokugawa government to enable it, it is said, to replenish its exhausted coffers. It is a large oblong coin, fig. 92, and bears on the obverse the characters "Ten-Ho Tsu-Ho" "Current Treasure of Tempo" (Preservation of Heaven), and on the reverse, above the hole, "To Hyaku", "value a hundred" (Mon). Below it there is a curious figure, a signature, it would seem, but of whom no one knows; surely that of some government or mint official. It may be that the oval form of the Tempo sen was intended to suggest the gold "koban", which it was designed to ultimately entice into the vaults of the Tokugawa family. Like most of the Japanese sen, the rim surrounding the hole is narrower on the face than on the back. It is also somewhat larger in front than behind. On either side of the edge, in the case of the current coins only, there is stamped something like a star, or perhaps a cherry blossom, such as appears on some of the rectangular coins. According to the "Dai Nihon Kwaheishi", which was issued by the Finance Department, and probably contains exact information on questions relating to modern coins, the composition of this coin, as first issued was, copper 78%, lead 12% and tin 10%. Though its nominal value was one to a hundred Kwanei sen (Mon), it is very unlikely that it actually sold for that amount. The above authority states that its price at first was 30 to a ryo of former coin, this probably representing 1000 mon, so that its actual value, on this computation would be 1 to 33⅓. This was in the 6th year of Tempo 1835, when it was first minted. It continued to be coined in several places, such as Fukagawa, Honjo in Tokyo, and Osaka. It is possible that the rare provincial shiken sen, of Morioka, Chikuzen and Tosa were only made to cover the secret manufacture of the Tempo coin in these places, a coin which could be used for general use being of greater value than one restricted to a certain locality. These coins are very similar to the Tempo Tsuho in shape and design and were approved by government for local circulation. They are so scarce, however, that they could not have been current coin and I can think of no better reason for their origin than the above. At any rate it is quite certain that the Tempo coin was made in other times and places than those of its first issue, there being more than twenty varieties, whose differences are only perceptible to those who have made such matters a special study. During the period of Ansei, (1854-59), the value of this coin fell to 60 to

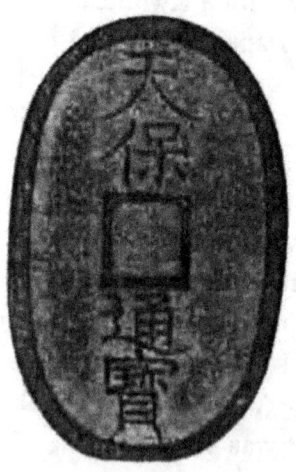 

FIG. 93 T

the ryo, and after the year of Manen, 1860, to a hundred, which would reduce it to 1 to 10. Since the Meiji era it has further depreciated to 125 to the Yen, which is 1 to 8 Mon. On account of this depreciation of the Tempo coin, it has come to be a favourite way of describing a person who is foolish or wanting in intelligence by calling him "Tempo". Fig. 92, shews a mother sen, from which the Tane sen is cast; fig. 93 shews the Tane sen, slightly smaller. The ordinary "Tsuyo", or current coin, is a little less in diameter and is stamped on the margin as above stated.

BUN-KYU EI-HO This is the last copper sen of the
A. D. 1863 Tokugawa Shogunate and was issued in the second month of the 3rd year of Bunkyu, 1863. It bears the characters "Bun-Kyu Ei-Ho", Everlasting

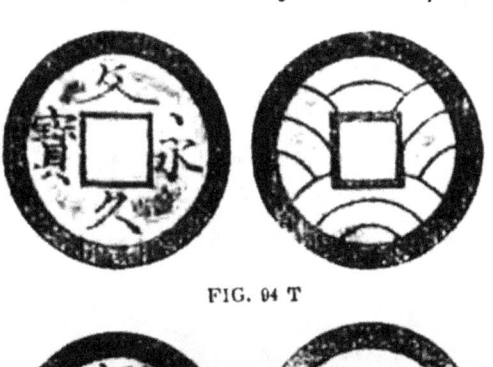

FIG. 94 T

FIG. 95 T

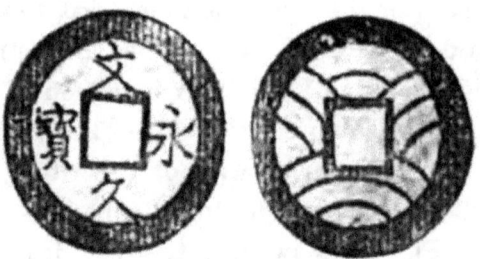

FIG. 96

Treasure of "Bunkyu" (Culture Continued) figs. 94, 95, and 96. All the Bunkyu sen have eleven waves on the reverse.

There are three styles of writing, viz. the "Shinsho" said to be by Matsudaira Shungaku, the "Gyosho" by Itakura Shuwo no Kami and the Sosho by Ogasawara Dzusho no Kami. It will be noticed that in the coins of the "Gyosho" style, fig. 94, the character "Ho" is written in the usual manner, whereas in those of the "Sosho", fig. 95, it is as much abbreviated as in the Wado coin (page 24), but in a different way.* The "Shinsho" writing, fig. 96, differs from the "Gyosho" slightly in the character "Ho", but mainly in the style of "Bun",

FIG. 97

* With the exception of the contracted form of Ho (Chin, 寳) found on the Wado coin, the various writings of this character found on the Chinese and Japanese coins, will be seen in the appendix.

in which the upper vertical stroke comes down to the middle of the horizontal one, being placed otherwise in

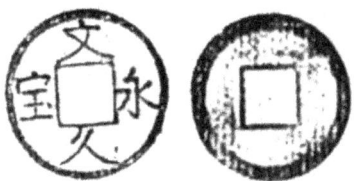

FIG. 98

the first two varieties. Closer observation will also reveal points of difference in the writing of "Ei" and "Kyu"; but these need not detain us here. The Tane sen, figs. 94 and 95, are larger than fig. 96, which illustrates one of the ordinary current sen. Without waves on the reverse, figs. 97 and 98, are examples of Shiken or experimental sen of this denomination and of course were never put into circulation. An iron coin, is occasionally

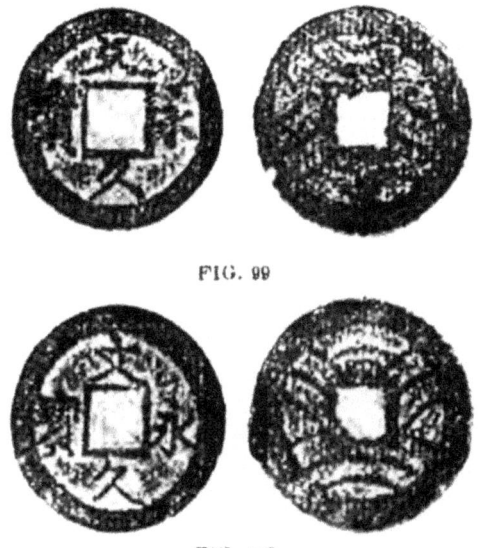

FIG. 99

FIG. 100

seen, of which figs. 99 and 100 are samples, written in the "Gyosho" and "Shinsho" styles. They are not official sen, but sneaked into partial circulation. The total amount of Bunkyu sen issued since their initation, has been computed at 891,515,631,—a detailed calculation indeed, but which may be not far from the truth. It was issued at the rate of one to four of the former coins, Kwanei, Chinese, etc., but its value has declined since the commencement of Meiji to $1\frac{1}{2}$ rin, and it is now worth no more than any of its former competitors.

Many of the Bunkyu Eiho shew variations in the casting and size of the "waves" and characters, but these are of so trivial a character that they do not call for special notice.

V.

PROVINCIAL COINS.

There are now eighty-five provinces in Japan, exclusive of Formosa, but there have been less and more. "At various times" says Murdoch, "Japan had been portioned out into provinces; and about the beginning of the seventh century we hear of as many as one hundred and eighty provincial governors. However, if not before the time of Kwammu, at all events within a century after his death, we meet with that division of the Empire into sixty-six provinces and two islands, which continued down to the date of the Revolution of 1868. At the date of the first appearance of Europeans in Japan these provinces were mostly geographical expressions. Originally however, they had been administrative units, and as such they continued to be down to the thirteenth century."

By the expression "Provincial Coins" one would naturally understand that they have been cast, issued and sanctioned for use only in the provinces to which they are credited. This title, though in common use, is rather misleading, inasmuch as the majority of these coins were not designed for circulation in any one province. Most of them were intended for even more restricted use, such as a Daimyo's fief, or occasionally some insignificant locality which was out of touch with the government currency. Even in places less remote, the dearth of currency or the exigencies of trade, have often led to the straying away of these coins from their place of origin, and their consequent use in other parts of the country. It has happened too, that, as in the case of the later Luchuan coins, they have been made in one province for use in another, and have a right to the name of the latter by adoption only, not by birth. If one uses the title "Provincial Coins," as a means of distinguishing them from those issued directly under the central authority, one may, with the above reservations, do so without impropriety.

It is not always easy to ascertain the exact date at which some of these provincial coins have been made and I have thought it better on the whole, to treat them rather from the geographical than from the historical standpoint, so I shall begin in the South and deal with the various kinds in the order of latitude.

FORMOSA. There is a set of nine sen, which are supposed to have been made at Nagasaki and by some are believed to be imitations of Chinese coins, as stated in the "Sen O Sempu." They are illustrated in the "Wakan Sen Ii," and the author inclines to the belief that they were made at Nagasaki, as they include one with the Kwanei inscription. This however does not by any means prove their Japanese origin, for this very coin has been imitated on quite a large scale, not only in China, but in Annam. Illustrations of such may be seen at the end of the seventh chapter.

On the 14th day of the 7th month of the 2nd year of Manji, 1659, permission was granted to the people of Nagasaki to make coin for the purpose of trading with foreigners. It was expressly stipulated, however, that

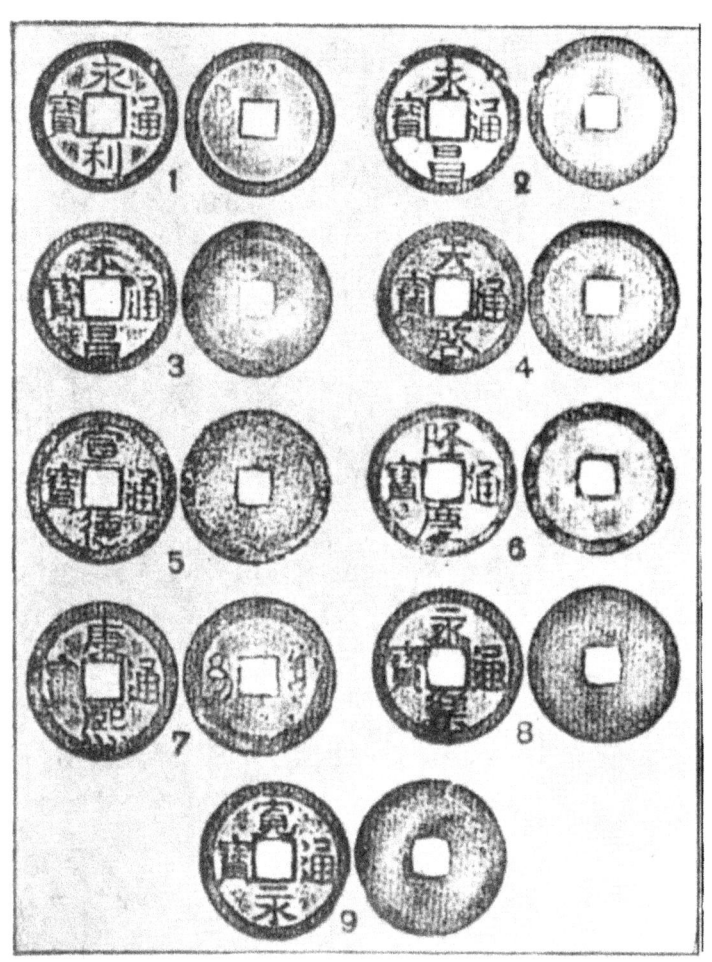

PLATE I.—EI RI TE SEN.

any inscription could be used except that of "Kwanei Tsuho," and it is very unlikely that this express prohibition would have been disregarded. On the whole we may conclude that there is no evidence that they were made in Nagasaki. Mr. Muramatsu suggests that they may have been made in Formosa by the Chinese officials there, and as the writing resembles that on the Chinese coins, I venture to give them a "local habitation" in the latest (up to date) and most southern possession of Dai Nippon. These coins are known to collectors as the "Ei Ri Te" sen, or those written in the hand (Te) of the first on the list viz. the "Ei-Ri Tsu-Ho," plate. 1

Fig. 1. " Ei-Ri Tsu-Ho " "Current Treasure of Everlasting Profit"
Fig. 2. " Ei-Sho Tsu-Ho " " Current Treasure of Eternal Prosperity "
Fig. 3. " Tai-sho Tsu-Ho " " Current Treasure of Quiet Prosperity "
Fig. 4. " Ten-Kei Tsu-Ho " " Current Treasure of Heavens Unfolding "
Fig. 5. "Sen-Toku Tsu-Ho" " Current Treasure of Widespread Virtue "
Fig. 6. "Ryu-Kei Tsu-Ho" " Current Treasure of Prospering Gladness"
Fig. 7. "Ko-Ki Tsu-Ho" " Current Treasure of Peaceful Enlightenment"
Fig. 8. "Ei-Raku Tsu-Ho" " Current Treasure of Everlasting Joy "
Fig. 9. "Kwan-Ei Tsu-Ho" " Current Treasure of Lasting Magnanimity"

It will be understood that the currency of Formosa, prior to its annexation by Japan, was almost exclusively Chinese.

THE LUCHU ISLANDS. There are four well-known copper coins accredited to this little kingdom, now united to the Japanese Empire. There are two others, one of which is not absolutely authenticated, but is of greater age than the rest and forms such an interesting subject for speculation, that I am tempted to enlarge upon it to a greater extent than it may be held to deserve. It has usually been supposed to be a Chinese coin. I was struck however with the likeness which it bears to two of the Luchuan coins and find that the learned author of the "Kokon Senkwa Kan" thought that it might belong to these Islands.

This coin, called the Kinsei Empo, or "Round Treasure of the Kin Dynasty," or of the "Golden Age," resembles the Chinese coins "Shoryu Gempo" and "Taitei Tsuho," in the writing of the character "Ho." A glance at fig. 1 will shew that this writing is quite distinctive.

FIG. 1

It suggests the idea that this coin was copied from the above Chinese coins; the peculiar fishtail like appearance is found on very few of the Chinese coins, the only other example that I know of prior to these being the "Taikwan Tsuho" A.D. 1107-10. I do not mean to say that the writing of the "Ho" is identical, but that the likeness was sufficiently striking to suggest my looking up the origin of these coins. The "Shoryu Gempo" was issued in the second year of Shoryu, A.D. 1157. The "Taitei Tsuho" was, I found, issued in 1177, during the Kin dynasty (Kin Sei). At first sight this might seem to corroborate the idea that the "Kin Sei Empo" was a coin of the Kin dynasty. Further, the author of the

PROVINCIAL COINS. 159

Kokon Senkwa Kan says, "Unnu Somei refers to a book written by Senno Ryusai which says that the first emperor of the Kin dynasty, named Tai So, caused the Kin Sei Empo to be minted, but Unno says that on reading the history of the Kin dynasty he found that over forty years had elapsed between the second year of Shoryo, A.D. 1157, and the date of issue of this coin, which he thought too long an interval to be correct. I imagine him to mean that this would place the date of issue of the "Kin Sei Empo" at about 1200 A.D (1157 plus 43), whereas there can be little doubt that Tai So, the first Emperor, or King, of the Kin dynasty died in the fifth year of Senna (Chinese notation), that is to say A.D. 1123. It follows therefore that if this coin were modelled on the lines of either the "Shoryu Gempo," or the "Taitei Tsuho" (1157 and 1177), it could not have been issued by the Emperor Tai So. It is certainly an old coin; the *sabi* on fig. 2, can scarcely be less than

FIG. 2

five centuries old. Now the resemblance which it bears to two well-known Luchuan coins, figs. 3 and 5 is so close, with regard to quality of material, design, especially noticeable on the reverse sides, and the round central hole, that it is difficult to resist the conclusion that it was cast in or for use in that country. On the other hand it is, with the exception of the similarity in the character "Ho" (寳), so utterly different from the coins of China, that I am disposed to place it amongst the currency of the Luchus. I am the more inclined to do this, as Professor Chamberlain in Vol. 5, No. 4 of the Geographical Journal, states, in his description of the Luchus, that Japanese money sometimes used in the Luchu Islands was always carefully kept out of sight when the Chinese officials were by to see. From this we may infer that a coin, such as the 'Kin Sei Empo" with its suggestion of a Chinese origin, would probably have been a useful addition to the diplomatic "properties" in the flirtation play which kept this little country aloof from either Japan or China and preserved its independence for so many centuries. While it is not possible to fix an accurate date for this coin, I think that we shall not be far wrong if we place it about the thirteenth century.

The two following coins are known to be Luchuan currency and, as above stated, they have a close family resemblance to the "Kin Sei Empo." The first, called

 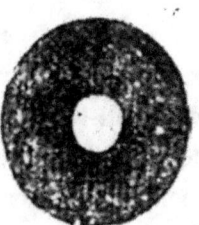

FIG. 3

PROVINCIAL COINS.

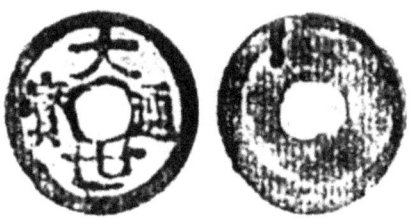

FIG. 4

"Tai Sei Tsuho," or "Current Treasure of Taisei" figs. 3, and 4, is like the others, a roughly made coin. The characters "Tsu" and "Ho" are taken from the "Eiraku Tsuho" sen. Like the "Kinsei," the central hole is round, with a square rim. It was cast between A.D. 1444 and 1460, under king Shotaikyu, who assumed the regal title of Taisei. He died in the latter year and his third son Shotoku took the name Seiko. During the reign of the latter, the second coin, called the "Sei-Ko" Tsuho was minted. Like the former, it takes the "Tsu" and "Ho" from the Eiraku Tsuho. The characters "Ei" and "Raku" were effaced from a good specimen of this coin, which was then pressed on to the clay mould; the new characters "Sei" and "Ko" were then also impressed on the clay. In this manner only can one account for the irregular disposition of these latter characters.

FIG. 5

FIG. 6

There are two writings. In the former, fig. 5, the lower stroke of the character "Sei," forms a right angle with the left vertical stroke. The upper character is too much to the left, while the lower is placed to the right. In fig. 6 the opposite is the case. The top character Sei (世) being to the right, while the lower one Ko (高) is to the left.

An interval of four hundred years separates this coin from the next of which there is any knowledge. This is the "Ryu-Kyu Tsu-Ho," fig. 7, or "Current Treasure of

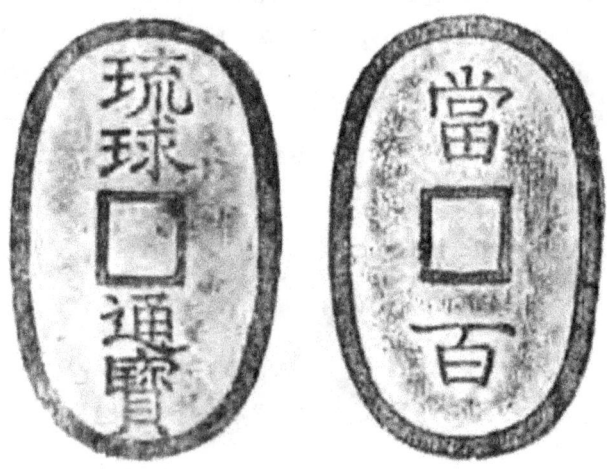

FIG. 7

Rykyu" (Luchu). This may be translated, if somewhat freely, as shining gems and jewels, quite an apt title for this group of islands. It was made at Tempozan, Kagoshima, in the first year of Bunkyu, and was valued at a hundred mon, though its price declined to 88 mon. Dr. Enomoto says that is was originally intended for trading purposes with the Luchus, but became so common in the islands that it was adopted as their currency. It has the oblong shape of the Tempo sen, being just a trifle smaller. It is not quite so well finished as the Tempo, but it is by no means as inferior coin. It is said to have been inscribed by one Matsuoka Judayu. On the obverse it bears the characters "Ryukyu Tsuho," in the same order as on the Tempo coin. On the reverse it has "To," meaning "Value" and "Hundred," written above and below the central hole. The hole is not smaller on the reverse side than

FIG. 8

on the obverse, as in the Tempo coin, and the peculiar signature which distinguishes the Tempo sen is absent. There is a variety, fig. 8, in which the characters are somewhat smaller. I have not seen the "Tane" sen of this coin. The ordinary coins have the "kana" "Sa" (サ), the first syllable of "Satsuma," stamped on the edge to indicate their origin.

In the second year of Bunkyu, 1862, a large and hand-

FIG. 9

Plate 2.—HATOME SEN
LUCHU ISLANDS.

some round coin, fig. 9, with "Ryu-Kyu Tsu-Ho", written in the "Tensho"* style, was cast in the same place. There were fewer of these coins minted than of the oblong ones. On the reverse, written in the same style as the face, are the characters "Han" and "Shu." They refer to the value "Han Shu," or "Half a Shu." The "Shu" was the $1/16$ part of a ryo, so that this coin was supposed to be the equal in value to the $1/32$ of a ryo, that is to say, about 31 mon. Its real value however quickly declined to the $1/64$ of a ryo, so that it was only worth $15\frac{1}{2}$ mon. The current coin has also the edge struck with the character "Sa."

I ought to mention the peculiar coin called "Hatome sen" or "Pigeon eye" sen, plate 2, which were probably in use in the Luchus about 150 or 200 years ago. The "Kisho Hyakuen" says that they were valued at ten to one Japanese mon. A hundred pieces were strung together, the connecting string being sealed and stamped by the King. This was probably a dignified way of getting a "squeeze" on the business done. The coins, if such they may be called, are not stamped, so that the official seal on the string was not altogether superfluous.

KAJIKI. The coins from this mint are amongst the most numerous of the provincial sen, plates 3 and 4. They consist mainly of imitations of Chinese sen, and it is not always easy to distinguish them from the corresponding replica of the province of Mito. The Kajiki sen were made in the village of that name, in the province of

---
* One of the archaic forms of writing.

Osumi, between the periods of Tensho (1573), and Genroku (1688). The provinces of Osumi, Satsuma, and Hyuga, comprising the southern and greater part of the island of Kyushu, were ruled by the Daimyos of Satsuma. Until the time of Hideyoshi they were practically Kings, their authority being only nominally controlled by the central government. The wild and mountainous region that had to be traversed and the absence of proper roads, together with the fierce character of the inhabitants, rendered it difficult to control the Prince of Satsuma, who boasted descent from the great Yoritomo. Even when, after repeated victories, the stronghold of Kagoshima was almost within his grasp, the redoubtable Hideyoshi found it prudent to make easy terms with his enemy. The coins which were made, probably about this time, at Kajiki, were no doubt intended for local use, but it was thought unwise to use inscriptions which might be regarded as infringing on the prerogative of the Emperor or Shogun. For this reason Chinese coin, which was then in general use, was chosen as models for the Satsuma coinage. Whether this was done with the tacit consent of the Government it is impossible to say. This imitation of Chinese coin would render it no easy matter to bring home a charge of minting coin, and of thus foisting a quarrel upon the rulers of Satsuma at some inconvenient moment.

One of the most interesting of these coins is the imitation of the "Ko-Bu Tsu-Ho" of China. In an interesting respect, however, it differs from the Chinese coin and may be identified by the characters on the reverse.

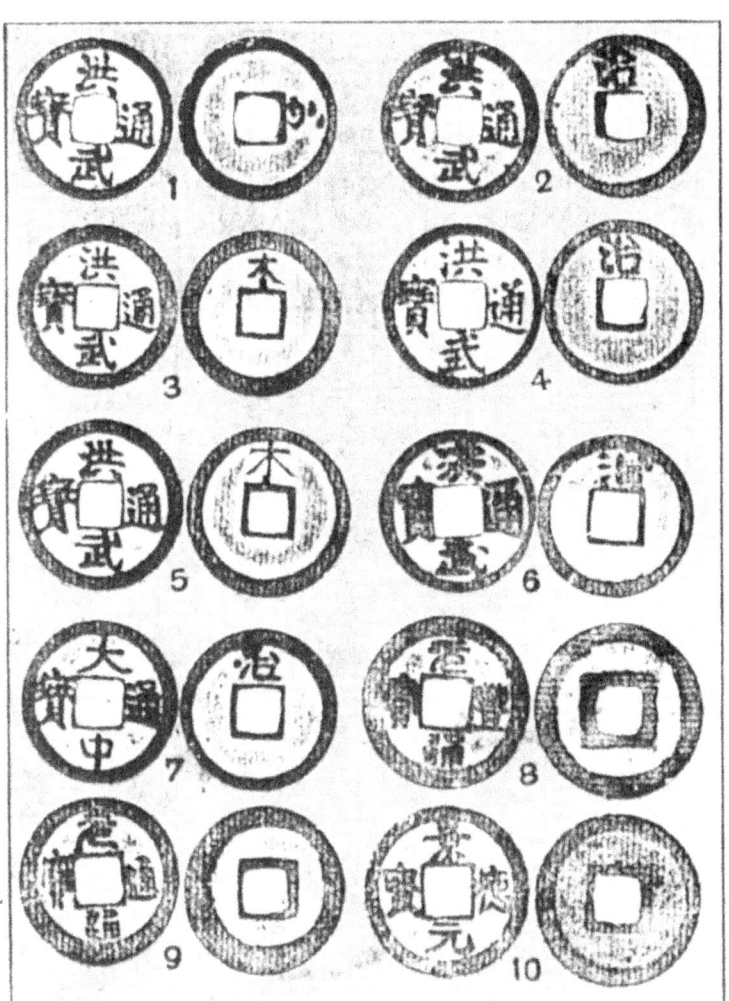

PLATE 3.—KAJIKI SEN.

These read respectively, "Ka" (加), plate 3, No. 1; "Ji" No. 2 (治) and "Ki" (木), No. 3, thus collectively spelling "Ka-Ji-Ki," the name of the village at which they were made. The "Kobu Tsuho" from which they were copied sometimes also has characters on the reverse, but they are different from the above, so that it was possible for the Daimyo of Satsuma to recognise his own coinage, without betraying it to the officials of the government. It would appear that there were very few of the "Ka" (加) coins made, as they are very rare. Those with "Ki" (木) are also scarce, but less so than the former. The "Ji" (治) coins are quite plentiful. No. 5 shews a coin with the character "Ki" written in large hand. In No. 4 the left part of "Bu" (武) resembles the character "Tsuchi." There is a rather rare variety, No. 6, having the character "Ji" on the reverse, but in which the uppermost stroke of the character "Bu" (武), crosses the long right vertical stroke, and thus creates a resemblance, somewhat fanciful, to the "Tasuki," or band, crossed in front of the loose dress of the Japanese, in order to keep back the flowing sleeves when engaged in work. It is essentially a device for household use, but was also employed during the practice of fencing and other pursuits. Another uncommon variety is seen in No. 7. Here the reverse also bears the character "Ji," but the obverse is copied from the "Tai-Chu Tsu-Ho" of China. This motto reads "Current Treasure of Taichu" (Great Centre), the original being a coin of the commencing Min dynasty.

The following list will enable the reader to identify the sen made at Kajiki. I would remark however that those sen resemble the coins made at Mito so closely that uncertainty must prevail with regard to some of them.

PLATE 3.

No. 1 Kobu Tsuho	No. 6 Kobu Tsuho
2 " "	7 Taichu Tsuho
3 " "	8 Genbo Tsuho
4 " "	9 Gentsu Tsuho
5 " "	10 Kentoku Gempo

PLATE 4.

No. 1 Kine Gempo	No. 5 Genho Tsuho
2 Jihei Gempo	6 Genho Tsuho
3 Genfu Tsuho	7 Seiso Gempo
4 Genfu Tsuho	8 Genfu Tsuho

It is said that coins were made at Nagasaki in order to facilitate commercial relations with the Portugese and Duteh traders there. It is possible, as stated by Murdoch, that the gold "Oban" were made for that purpose, but I cannot find any authentic record of it. There was a local paper currency here as elsewhere, and though such does not fall within the scope of this work, I give an illustration of one which has been included in some standard works on coins, plate 5. Here the design of a coin called "To-Kwan Tsu-Ho" has been stamped on a strip of stout paper, the back bearing the inscription "Cho Ki" (Nagasaki) "To Kwan Yaku Sho," or "Nagasaki Foreign House (trading firm) Government Office". There is a fictitious representation of this in metal, made probably about a century ago.

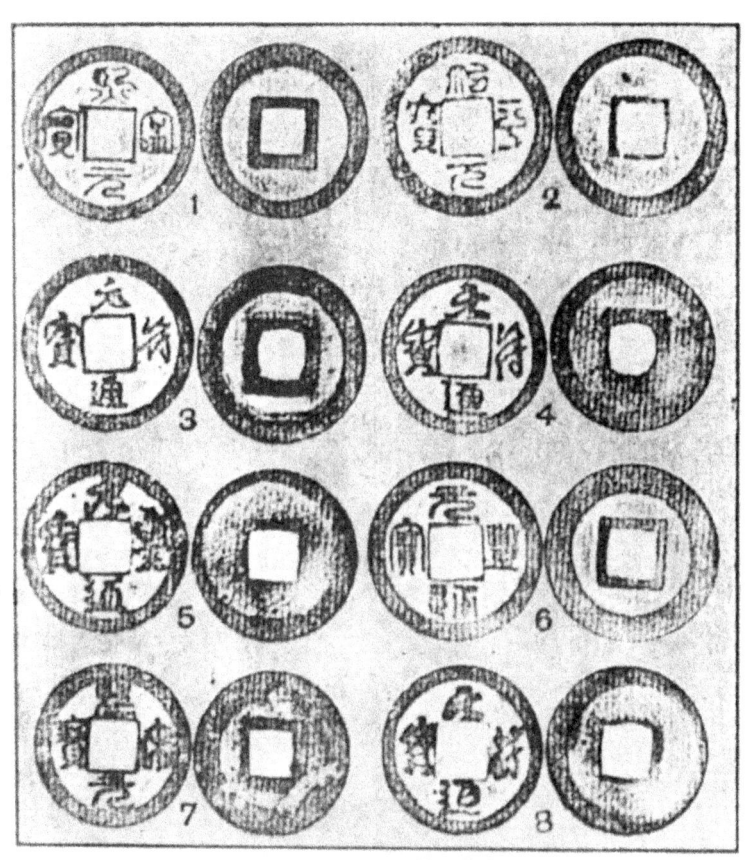

PLATE 4.—KAJIKI SEN.

長崎唐館役所

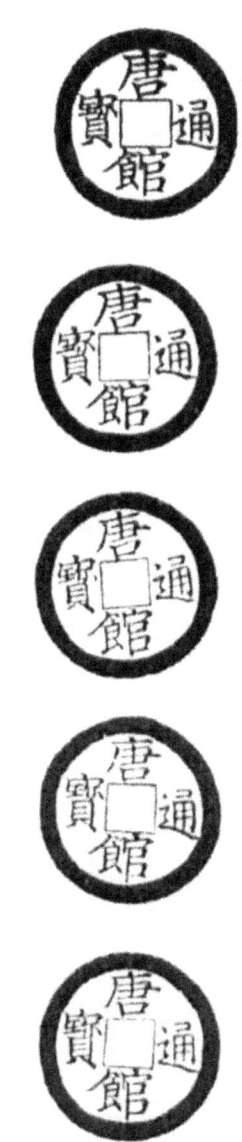

PLATE 5.—TO KWAN TSUHO.

PROVINCIAL COINS.   169

CHIKUZEN A coin resembling the Tempo sen was made in the province of Chikuzen, bearing on the face, fig. 10,

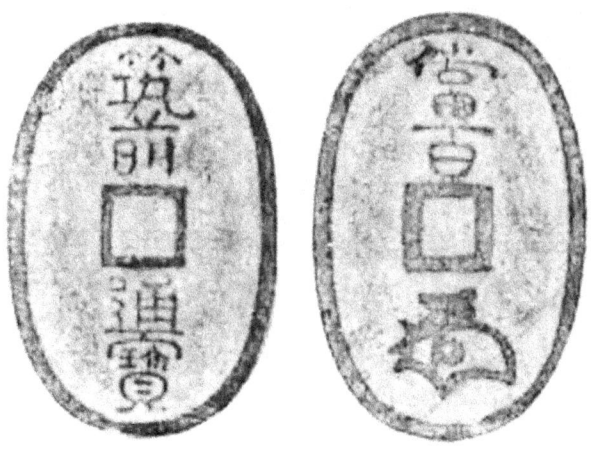

FIG. 10

in the Tensho style, the words "Chiku-Zen Tsu-Ho," and on the reverse "To Hyaku," that is, "Value a Hundred." Below the central hole there is a signature, somewhat like that of the Tempo sen. There is no record of its having been in circulation and it is probably only a "Shiken" (sample) sen, as it is rare.

TOSA Quite as rare as the above are the coins which were made in the province of Tosa, believed to have been cast during the period of Keio, A.D. 1865-67. There are reputed to have existed six round and six oblong coins, bearing different values on the reverse. It is also stated that there was an iron sen, value one mon, but I have not seen it. I am able to show two rare specimens from my collection, figs.

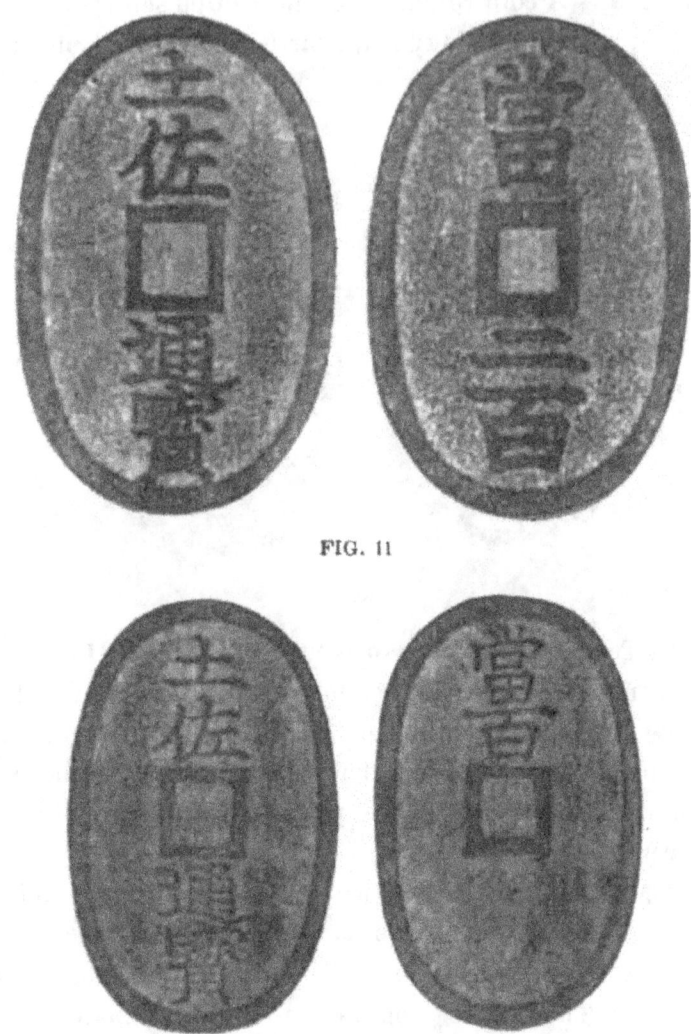

FIG. 11

FIG. 12

11 and 12. The first is a very large coin, with the characters "To-Sa Tsu-Ho" on the obverse. Above the square hole on the reverse is "To," "Value" and below, "Ni Hyaku," "Two Hundred." The other coin is smaller, a fraction

less than the Tempo sen, and the words "Value, a Hundred" (mon), are written above the hole on the reverse. Mr. Enomoto also states, in the "Journal for Discussion of Japanese Coins" that there are two other coins of the Tosa mintage, one like a "Nami" sen on the reverse, the other of oblong form: from the illustration in this journal, the latter is about 54 mm. long and 32 mm. in breadth. The round sen has the same inscription on the obverse as the other Tosa coins; the oblong kind bears the characters "To-Shu Kwan-Ken" or "Official bond of Tosa or (Toshu)." On the reverse are the characters "Go Momme" meaning "Five Momme" by weight.

The "Wakan Sen Ii" gives a list of sen which were minted at Kashima, in the province of Settsu, in the 3rd year of Genbun, 1739. The list consists mainly of "Ei" or picture sen, and in chapter 7 some of these will be treated under this heading.

Iron coins were also made at Kashima, not for provincial, but for general use.

MITO. There is little doubt that some of the Mito sen were made before the period of Kwanei. These are said to have been minted under the Daimyos of the Gamo family, though this statement is open to doubt. As we have seen, some Kwanei sen were also made in this place, or its neighbourhood. None of the Mito provincial coins bear the names of Japanese year periods, though those of China are plentiful. The writing of these, and their general make-up have been severely criticised by Narushima Ryohoku; but this adverse verdict cannot be properly applied to all these sen, some of which are excellent specimens of penmanship, and of by no means inferior finish.

The following list of Mito sen is illustrated in plates 5 and 6; the numbers given below enable the collector to identify the separate coins. There are many others, but these are representative.

PLATE 6.

No. 1 Genho Tsuho	No. 6 Genho Tsuho
2 Kayu Tsuho	7 " "
3 Shosei Gempo	8 " "
4 Genyu Tsuho	9 " "
5 Shofu Tsuho	10 Seiwa Tsuho

PLATE 7.

No. 1 Genyu Tsuho	No. 6 Genyu Tsuho
2 " "	7 Gensei Gempo
3 " "	8 Shofu Gempo
4 " "	9 Tensei Gempo
5 " "	10 Genho Tsuho

KANRAGORI. In the district of Kanra, province of Joshiu, leaden certificates which may be styled coin, were issued by two or three persons of affluence, bearing the values 24 and 16 Mon, figs. 13, 14 and 15.

FIG. 13

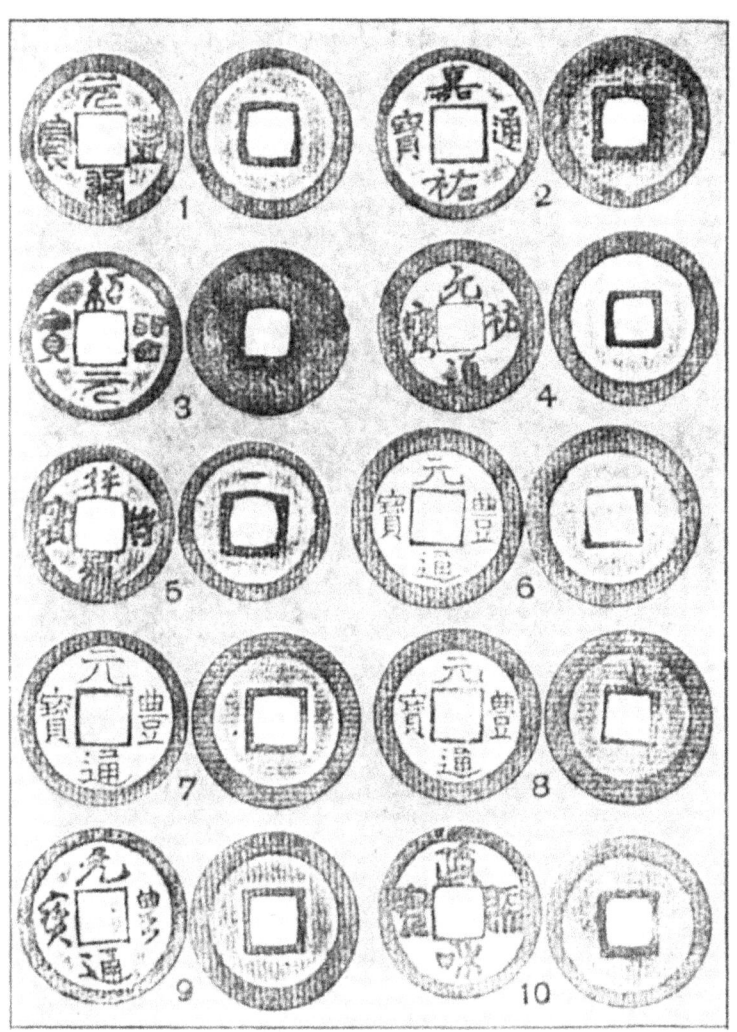

PLATE 6.—MITO SEN.

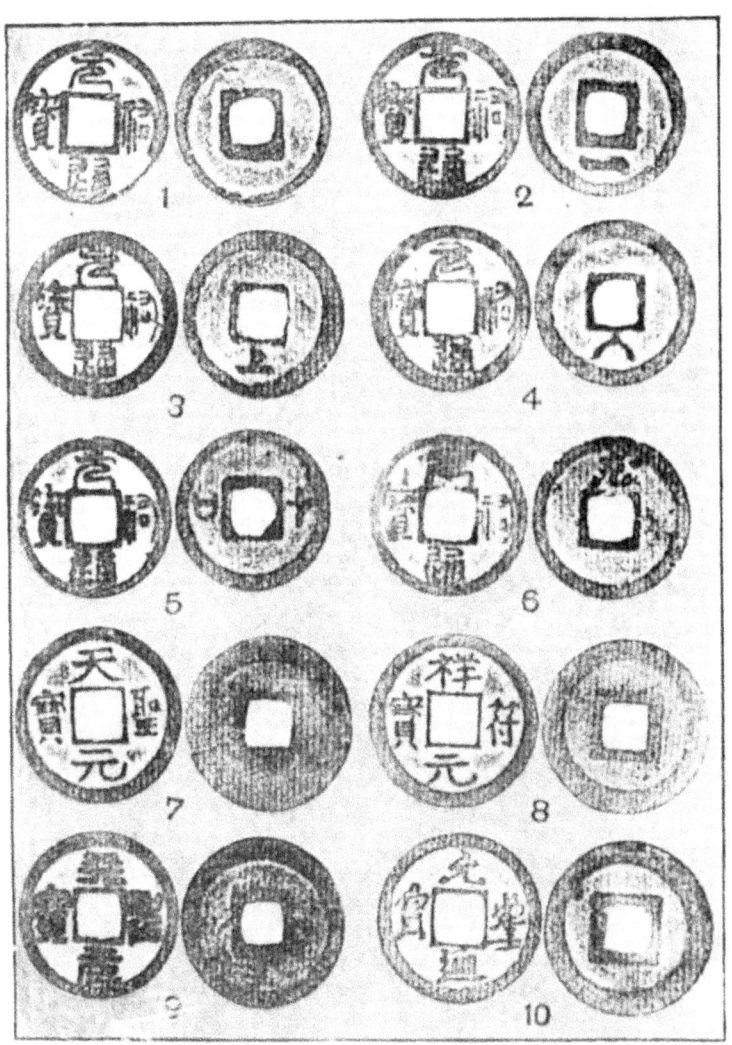

PLATE 7.—MITO SEN.

PROVINCIAL COINS. 173

FIG. 14

FIG. 15

These medals were redeemable at their face value on the guarantee of these men, whose reputation was no doubt of a substantial kind amongst the people of this secluded district. They were in a sense metallic bank notes, issued to cover the deficiency of coin in a place so difficult of access. This kind of money was called the "Usui Toge Kitte Sen", or "Ticket Sen of the Usui Pass." Fig. 13, bears on the face "Ni Jiu Shi Mon", value 24 Mon, and the names Yoshi Ichi and Hori Kichi; fig. 15, has "Jiu Roku Mon", "Sixteen Mon" and the same names; fig. 14, has "Atai, Ni Jiu Shi Mon" on the face, and on the reverse the trade mark "Kane

Jo" with star (Hoshi) and the named Toyohiko. The thick edge of this coin is represented by the figure between the face and back.

AIDZU. In the 4th month of the first year of Genji, 1864, Matsudaira Hige-No Kami, the Daimyo of Aizu, asked permission to circulate the following coin, fig. 16 T.

FIG. 16 T

Permission was granted, or, as it is otherwise stated, the Tokugawa Government agreed to buy it to use as current coin in this district. On the obverse it has "Haku Do Sen' "White, or (Light coloured) Copper Sen." On the reverse, there is "To Ni Hyaku Mon", "Value Two Hundred Mon." The word "Ni" is in the written form. This coin is commonly supposed to be only a private attempt at coin making, or a fancy sen; but Mr. Muramatsu has found a document relating to it which clearly proves its title to be regarded as a provincial coin.

YONEZAWA. Two leaden coins, one square and the other oblong, were made probably just before the period of Meiji. Fig. 17 bears the characters "Atai Ni Hyaku" on one side, and "San Jiu Shi Momme" on the other.

FIG. 17

The other, fig. 18, has the same, with the addition of "Sei San Kyoku," Board of Occupation, on one side. About this time the Samurai or warrior class found their occupation gone and were in many cases reduced to great distress. A society was formed under local government supervision to give them aid, and this coin was given

176   PROVINCIAL COINS.

FIG. 18

to the samurai of the district in order to enable them to get the necessaries of life.

SENDAI.   The square coin of Sendai, figs. 19 and 20, is an

PROVINCIAL COINS.

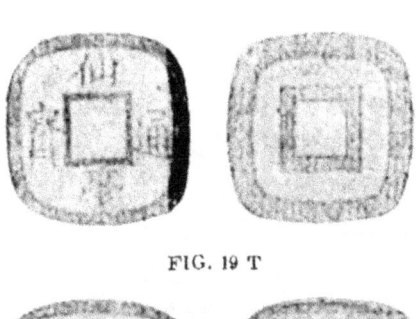

FIG. 19 T

FIG. 20 T

Iron sen, minted at Ishinomaki, Mutsu province, between the 4th and 8th years of Temmei, 1784-88. It bears the characters "Sen-Dai Tsu-Ho" Current Treasure of Sendai. Three hundred and eight thousand Kwan, over three hundred million, were issued. The coin was so bad that, according to Mr. Enomoto, there was a saying that if they were carried in a bag for one day, it would be torn and out of a hundred two or three would be broken. The use of this coin was strictly prohibited out-

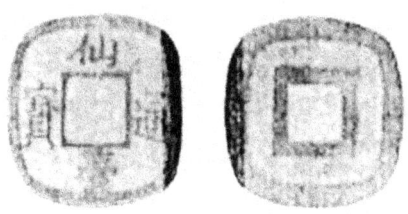

FIG. 21 T

178 PROVINCIAL COINS.

side of Mutsu province. As the figures are taken from a Tane sen, they are presentable, but the iron coin is very

FIG. 22

PROVINCIAL COINS.

poor. Fig 21, also a tane sen, is smaller; but the characters are beautifully clear.

HOSOKURA. This huge coin fig. 22, was made of lead, and was used only in the neighbourhood of that mining centre, in the province of Rikuzen. Sendai is now in this province, Mutsu having been divided up into lesser territories. On the obverse, it has "To-Hyaku Hoso-Kura" and on the reverse, a signature mark. It was so heavy and inconvenient to carry, that a small one, exchangeable at the rate of ten to one of the large, was made. On the face it has the inscription "Gen-Ko-Ri-Tei" in archaic character, while on the reverse is the word "Kayeru" meaning "Exchange." I have not seen the latter and believe that it was not issued.

MORIOKA. This is an oblong coin, like the Tempo, and may be only a Shiken sen fig. 23. The face has the

FIG. 23

characters "Mori-Oka Do-Zan" and the back, "Hyaku Mon Tsu-Yo," "Morioka Copper Mine Current Use at a Hundred Mon. It was made at the above mine, but it is surmised that there was an intention to give it a wider circulation than its name would imply. It is rare, and probably never went into circulation at all.

AKITA. The "Nami" or wave sen of the Ugo province, were made at the Aniyama Copper Mine, Akita, in the 2nd year of Bunyu, 1862. What we may call the face, fig. 24, has twenty-one waves roughly cast in intaglio

FIG. 24

as the sign of currency, while the back simply has the inverted character "Aki" for Akita. At the outset, it was valued at 100 mon, but it was not at all popular and its value depreciated to such an extent that it was deemed advisable to have a change. The coin, shewn in fig. 25, was probably a "shiken," or trial sen, designed with the object of providing something less crude and uncouth. However it was not used. A brilliant, if whimsical, notion was carried out, namely, to enlarge the coin and model it after the favourite sword-guard of the

PROVINCIAL COINS.   181

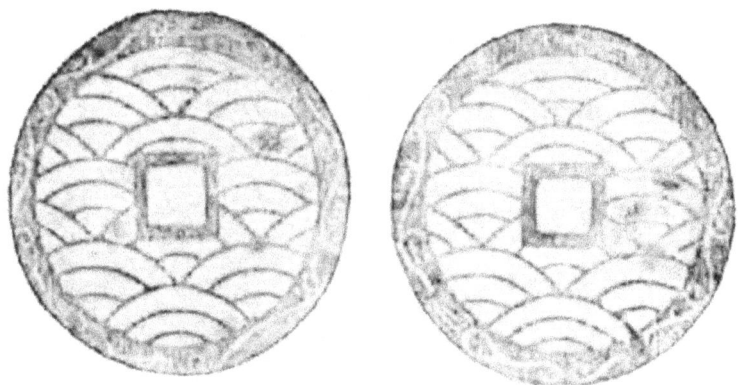

FIG. 25

Daimyo of Akita, figs. 26 and 27. In artistic merit it would entirely eclipse the other. Its association with the military prowess, real or imaginary, of their Lord, no doubt conveyed just that suggestion of the *fortiter in re* which was needed to still discontent. To the superstitious too, that is to say, to nearly every one before the Meiji era, the eight diagrams on the face, the weird Pa-

FIG. 26—Obverse.

182 PROVINCIAL COINS.

FIG. 26 — Reverse.

Kua, as they are known in Chinese, invented in bygone ages by the sage ruler Fou-Si; called in Japanese the "Hakke," this mystical device to read the future out of the Unconscious, must have appealed, as the emblem of knowledge that was more than human. On the reverse there is the Phoenix, or Howo, the sacred

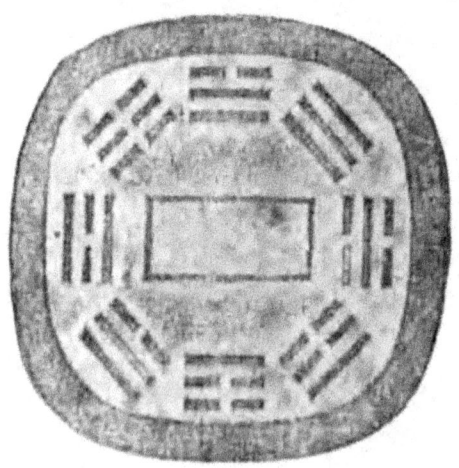

FIG. 27 — Obverse

FIG. 27—Reverse T.

token of mortality which unites the East and West. It is indeed a strange coin, perhaps the most original and bizarre that the world has seen. On the edge of the "Tsuyo" sen or current money, there is stamped on

FIG. 28

either side, the Chinese character "kyu" (久) in allusion to the period Bunkyu. There are several varieties of this coin in my collection, due mainly to differences in the arrangement of the flowery flames that surround the Phoenix.

Another peculiar coin hails from Akita. It is made of lead, is of rectangular form, with a round hole, and was probably cast in the second year of Bunkyu. It exists in two sizes. The first, fig. 28, has the inscription "Do-Zan Shi-Ho" on the obverse, meaning the "Precious Treasure of the Copper Mine," while on the reverse there is "To Hayaku Kyu Ni," "Value One Hundred, (Bun) Kyu second." The lesser, fig. 29, has bevelled corners,

FIG 29.

and bears the same motto as the other, the character "Ho" being written in the abbreviated style. On the reverse there is written "Kyu ni Go Jiu," (Bun) "Kyu second Fifty," indicating its nominal value as fifty mon.

PROVINCIAL COINS.

HAKODATE. The currency of Hakodate, Oshima province, was in effect, that of the great Northern island of Japan, the Hokkaido. It was an iron coin, and the figures here illustrating it, are Tane sen, fig. 30. This coin

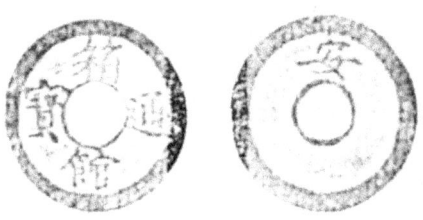

FIG. 30 T

is round, and in the common variety, the hole also is round. - It has the characters "Hakodate Tsu-Ho" on the face, and on the back the character "An" is cast as the first part of Ansei, in the 3rd year of which it was made. It was not issued however, till the 4th year of that period. The characters are said to have been written by one Ota Tamesaburo. A Shiken sen exists in which the hole is not round but octagonal and the writing of the character "An" is different from that of the first coin.

VI.

GOLD AND SILVER CURRENCY.

For the last seven or eight hundred years, perhaps even a longer period, gold, in the form of dust or grains, has been in use as a means of reward or for presentation, and sometimes payment. This gold was handled in bags of paper; and the custom of presenting money in paper bags of special design, fig 1, coated with

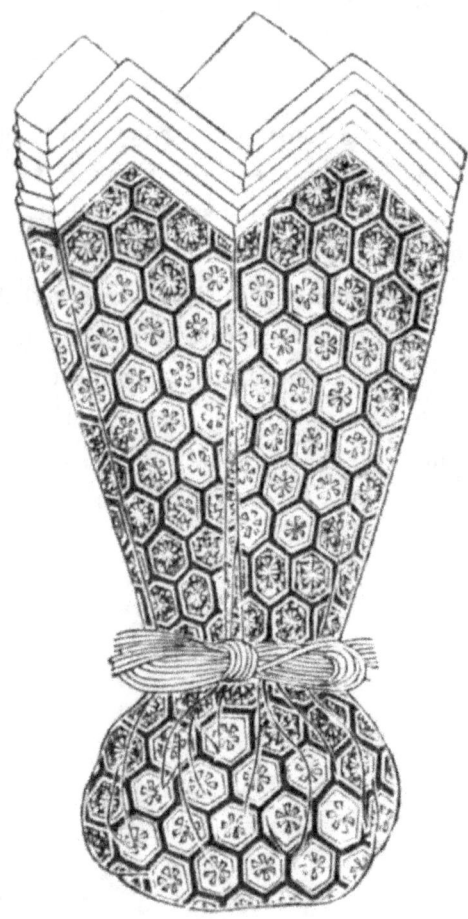

FIG. 1

PLATE 7—GENROKU OBAN
(Obverse)

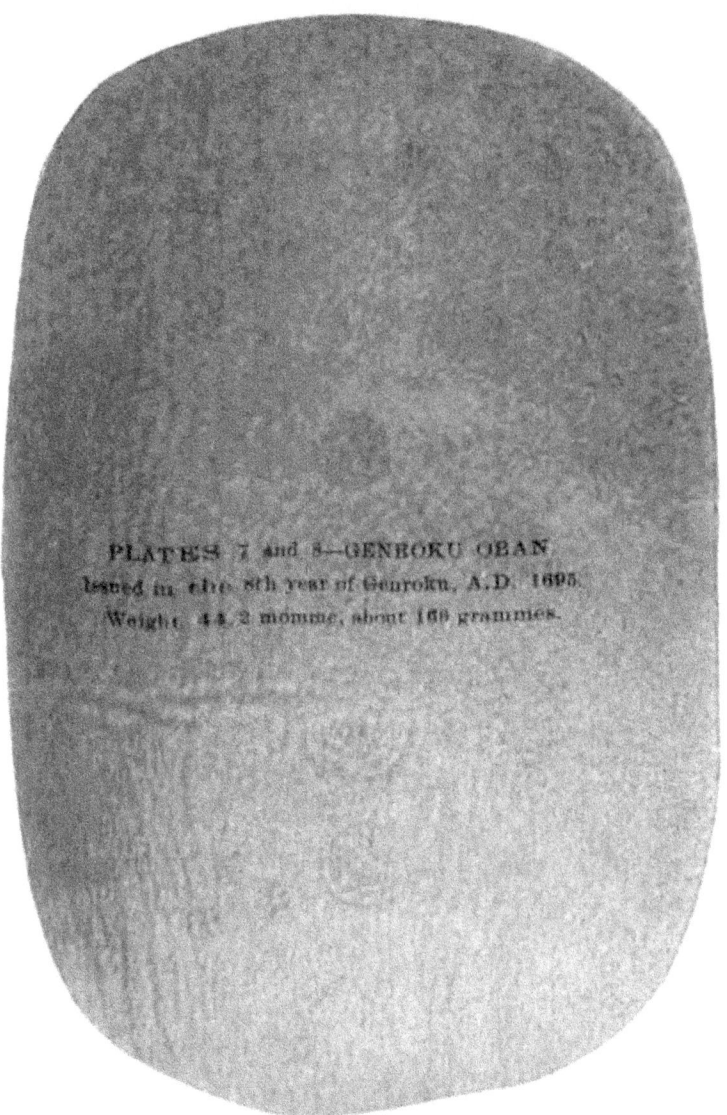

PLATES 7 and 8—GENROKU OBAN
Issued in the 8th year of Genroku, A.D. 1695.
Weight 44.2 momme, about 160 grammes.

PLATE 8—GENROKU OBAN
(Reverse)

PLATE 8—GENROKU OBAN
(Reverse)

1734. Its weight was 44.2 Momme, about 166 grammes. On the obverse are four crests of the Kiri, with the value, ten ryo, and the signature Goto. On the reverse are the character "Gen", two crests of the Kiri, a signature mark and sometimes some small independent characters. The Tokyo Koban of this issue, plate 17, No. 1, has two Kiri crests, the value (one ryo) and the name Mitsutsugu on the face, while the back has a signature mark and the character "Gen", in reference to the period of Genroku, with one or two independent characters. Its weight was 4.8 momme, about 18 grammes. There are two or three varieties of the Genroku Oban and Koban. The Ichi Bu coin, plate 17, No. 3, has two Kiri crests with "Ichi Bu" on one side and "Gen" with Mitsutsugu on the other. It was issued at the same time as the Oban and was stopped in the 3rd year of Kyoho, 1718. A smaller coin called the "Ni Shu Ban Kin," or Two Shu (there were four Shu in one Bu) is made of inferior gold, plate 17, No. 4. It has the Kiri crest and "Ni Shu", (two Shu) on one side, with "Gen" and Mitsutsugu on the other. It was issued in the sixth month of the 10th year of Genroku, 1697, and stopped in the 7th year of Ho-ei 1710. Between the 8th and 11th years of Genroku, 31,795 Oban were issued, while the Koban, Ichibu and Nishu totalled 13,936,220 ryo.

In the fourth month of the 7th year of Ho-ei, 1700, a Koban was issued, slightly smaller than the Genroku coin, from which it is said to have been reminted. There were complaints about the poor quality of the Genroku Koban; and it was decreed that as it was not of sufficiently good quality for the currency of the country (it contained only 56.4% of gold), it had to be changed. The new coin contained 83.4% of gold, but its diminished size shews that the mint did not lose much by the exchange. The obverse resembles that of the Genroku Koban; the reverse has the character "Ken,"[*] which in the Chinese classic on divination means "Gold." It has also a signature mark and occasional characters at the lower end.

Another Koban, plate 18, No. 1, appeared in the fourth month of the 4th year of Shotoku, 1714, having about the same size as the Genroku coin, which it resembles in the obverse. The reverse has a signature mark and two lesser characters, which need not be specified. It weighed 4.8 Momme, about 18 grammes.

An Oban was made in the 10th year of Kyoho, 1725, weighing 44 Momme, about 166 grammes, plates 9 and 10. It was recoined from the Genroku Oban on the standard of the Keicho Oban, which contained 73.46% of gold, the best quality of all. It is sometimes called the "Shin Kin Oban", or new gold Oban. On the face it bears four impressions of the Kiri, with "Jiu Ryo", ten Ryo, and the name Goto. On the reverse it has two crests of the Kiri, a signature sign, and occasional characters. There are several varieties.

In the fifth month of the 1st year of Gembun, 1736, a Koban was issued, weighing 3.5 Momme, about 13 grammes, plate 20, No. 1. It is but slightly larger than the Ho-ei Koban, which it resem-

---

[*] "Heaven" in its ordinary signification. Probably used in its derivative sense "Highest."

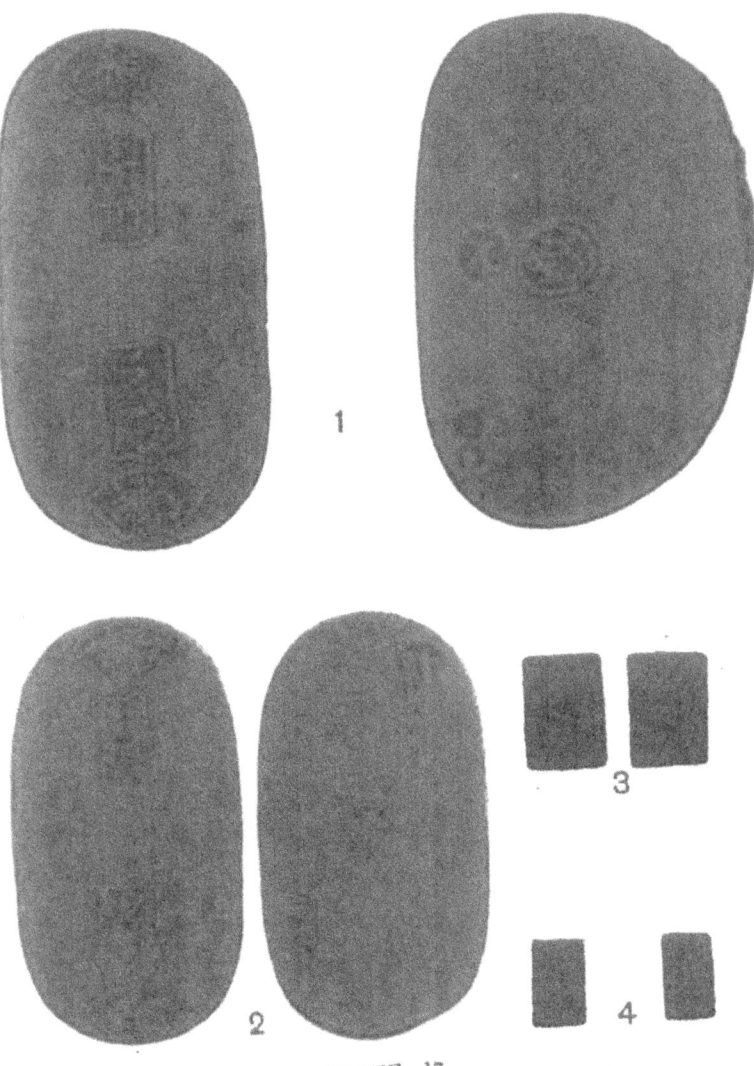

PLATE 17

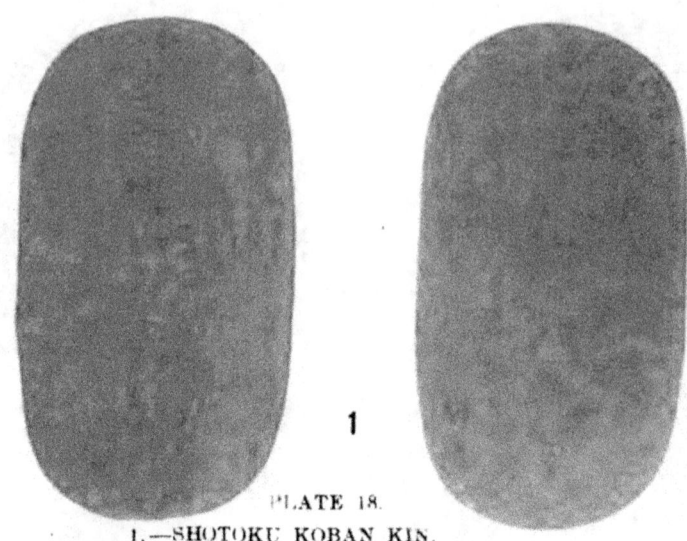

PLATE 18.
1.—SHOTOKU KOBAN KIN.
2.—ANSEI "SHO JI" KOBAN KIN.
3.—ANSEI NI BU KIN.

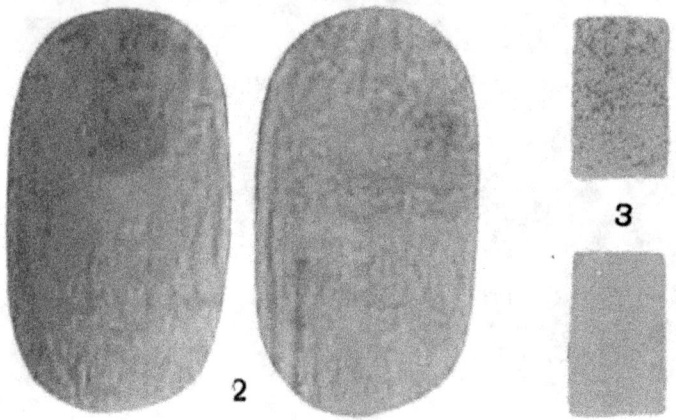

PLATE 18.

PLATE 18.
1.—SHOTOKU KOBAN KIN.
2.—ANSEI "SHO JI" KOBAN KIN.
3.—ANSEI NI BU KIN.

PLATE 19.
1.—KYOHO KOBAN KIN.
2.—TEMPO KOBAN KIN.
3.—KYOHO ICHI BU KIN.
4.—TEMPO NI SHU KIN.

PLATE 20.

1.—GEMBUK KORAN KIN.
2.—BUNSEI KORAN KIN.
3.—BUNSEI NI BU KIN.
4.—BUNSEI ISSHU KIN (One shu Gold.)

In the same year a Koban of small size, called the "Sho Ji" Koban, from the presence of the character Sho on the reverse, was issued, plate 18, No. 2, its percentage

FIG. 12

of Gold was 56.97 and it weighed 2.4 momme, about 9 grammes. It has the Kiri crest above and below on the obverse, and its value "One Ryo," with the name and signature of Mitsutsugu. On the reverse it is stamped with the character Sei, or Sho, hence the name. This has also the usual signature mark and incidental characters.

In the first year of Manen, 1860, a diminutive Koban, Plate 21, No. 2, known as the "Shin", or new Koban, with the two Kiri crests and the official value "One Ryo", and usual name, on the face. The reverse has the signature mark and occasional characters. Its weight was .88 momme, about 3.3 grammes, but it contains a trifle more gold than the former viz. 57.36 %. As, however, it weighed less than one half of the "Sho" Koban, it will be seen that gold must have risen to about 100% premium in one year.

The rise in the price of gold may also be seen by comparing the following attenuated Manen gold coin of two Shu value, Plate 21, No. 3 with that of the Tempo period. The weight of the Tempo coin of this denomination was 4.3 momme, 16 grammes, while this was only 2 momme, about 7.5 grammes, less than half. The Tempo coin, moreover, contained 29.8%, while this had only 22.9% of gold.

Next to the "Hatome sen" of the Loochus the smallest coin made in Japan is the gold one, made at Kofu in the period of Shotoku, plate 21, No. 4.

Oblong lumps of silver, more or less diluted with copper, are seen in plate 22, and figs. 13, 14 and 15. They have no right to be called circulating coin. They were however, made by the government, and are the survival of a custom supposed to date back some seven or eight hundred years, of giving official recognition of meritorious services by presenting a token of this kind. The earliest known piece, plate 22, is said to date back to the time of Hideyoshi, but this is open to doubt. There is evidence however that one was made in the period of Keicho, 6th year, 1601. The weight was supposed to be 43 momme, but owing to uncouth form and rough casting, these "Cho Gin" or "Long Silver" pieces frequently fell short of this amount. To correct the deficiency, pieces of silver of various weights, figs. 16 (Keicho), 17 (Genroku), 18 (Ho-Ei), 19 (Gembun), 20 (Tempo), 21, 22, 23, (Ansei) were added to the gift. These have been described in some works as "Bean" *money*, but this is quite incorrect, the

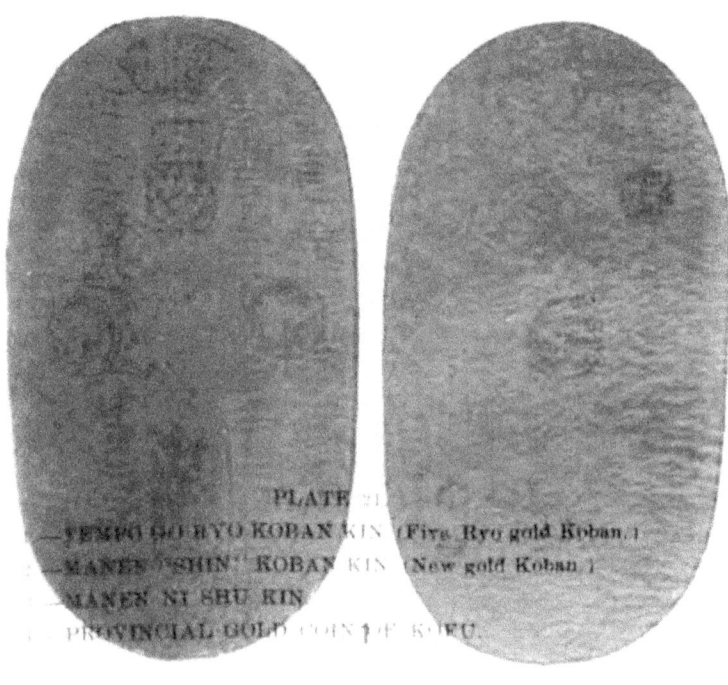

PLATE 21
1.—YEMPO GO RYO KOBAN KIN (Five Ryo gold Koban.)
2.—MANEN "SHIN" KOBAN KIN (New gold Koban.)
3.—MANEN NI SHU KIN.
4.—PROVINCIAL GOLD COIN OF KOFU.

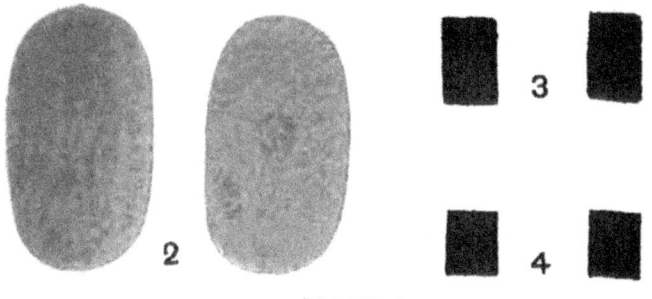

PLATE 21

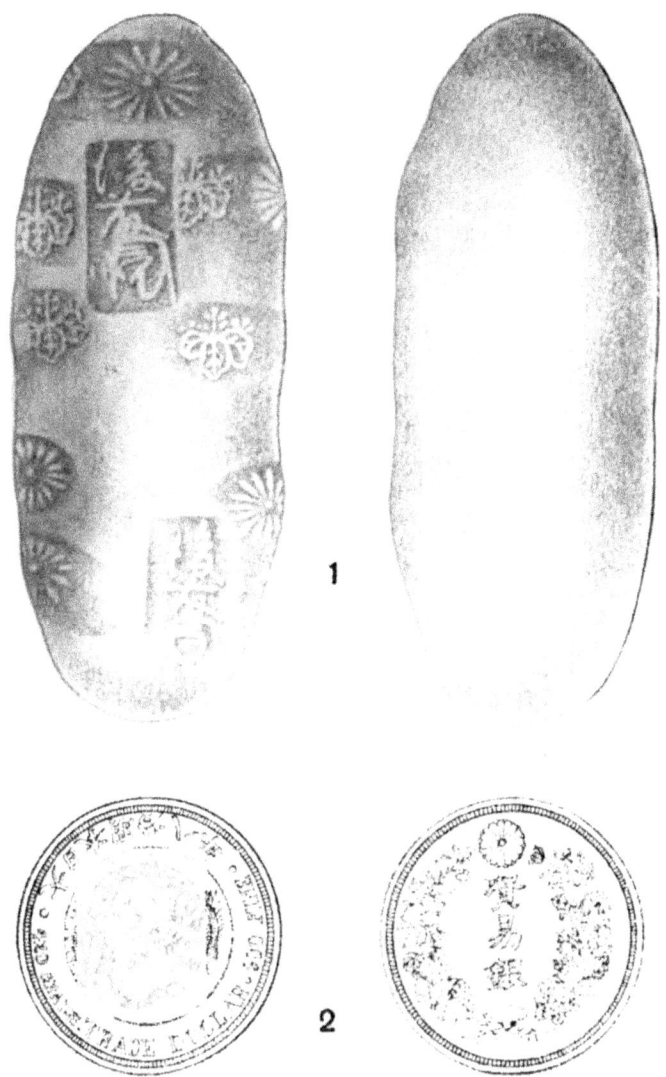

PLATE 22

GOLD AND SILVER CURRENCY. 203

expression "Mame Gin" or "Bean Silver," having reference to their usually round or bean like form. They all represent Daikoku Ten,* the god of wealth, and have the year period cast in the centre of each figure. These oblong pieces, "Cho," or slab silver, as they were called and their accompanying "Mame" or bean silver,

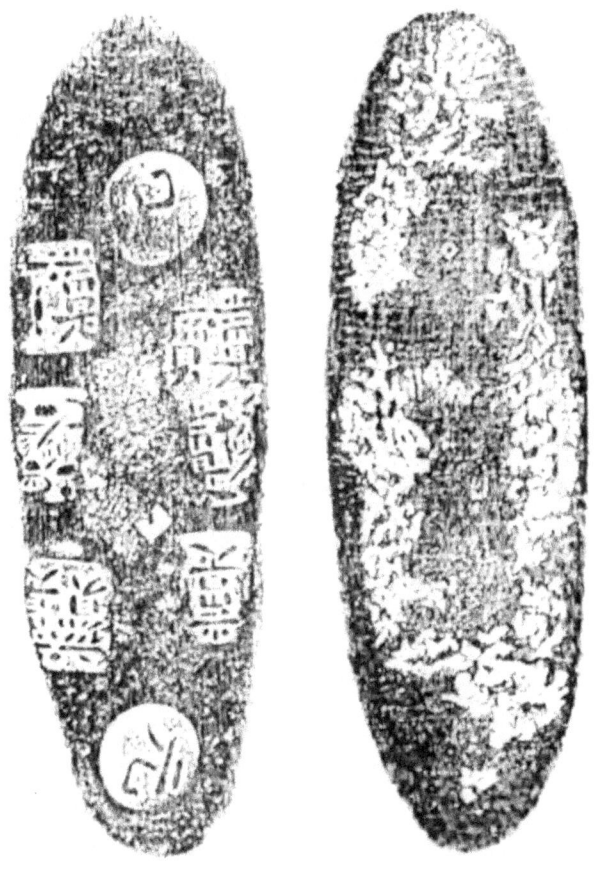

FIG. 13

* See Chapter 7.
No. 1, Plate 22, is an exception.

varied in the percentage of silver according to the period in which they were made. Fig. 13 shews a "Cho Gin" of the Genroku period, while figs. 14 and 15 illustrate

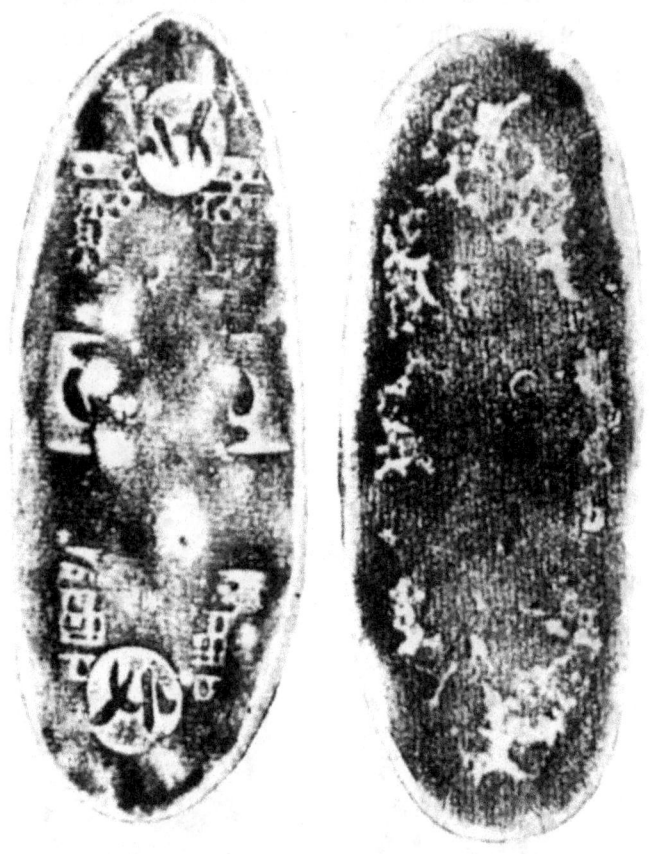

FIG 14

those of Bunsei and Tempo. In the case of the Tempo piece the percentage of silver was only 26. Of this, with the "Beans," 182,108 kwamme were cast. Although not intended for circulation they could be guaranteed for circulation at the exchange bureaus of the government

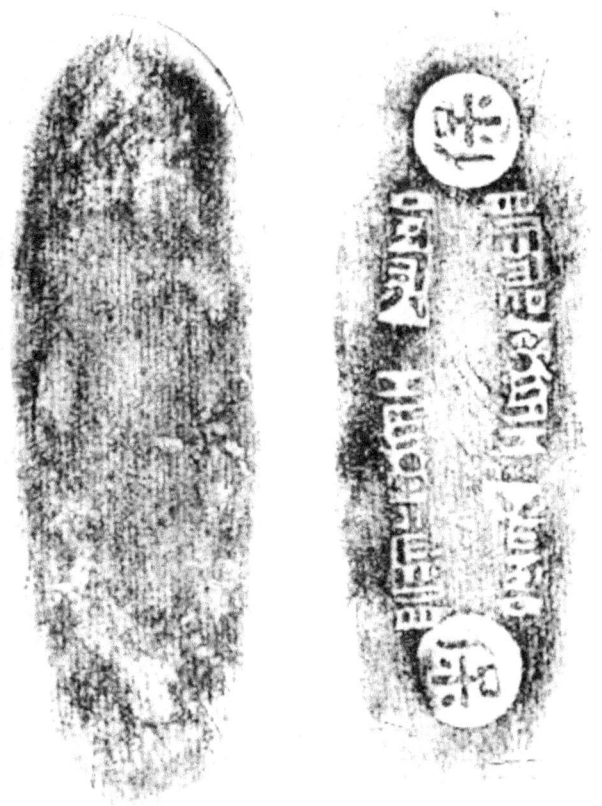

FIG. 15

for the purpose, and sold at the "Ryogai-Ya", or money exchanges. In the former case, they were weighed and corrected to one ryo of silver, then wrapped up and stamped as a guarantee of weight. In this form they could be used as money. Some of the forms of the "Mame Gin" are quite grotesque, as in fig. 21. It is probable that the oblong pieces, and also the "Mame

FIG. 16

FIG. 17

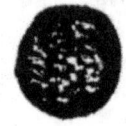

FIG. 18

FIG. 19

FIG. 20

FIG. 21

FIG. 22

FIG. 23

MAME GIN.

GOLD AND SILVER CURRENCY.

Gin", were given as presents amongst private persons and in this manner may have been used for small purchases, without always being referred to the exchange offices.

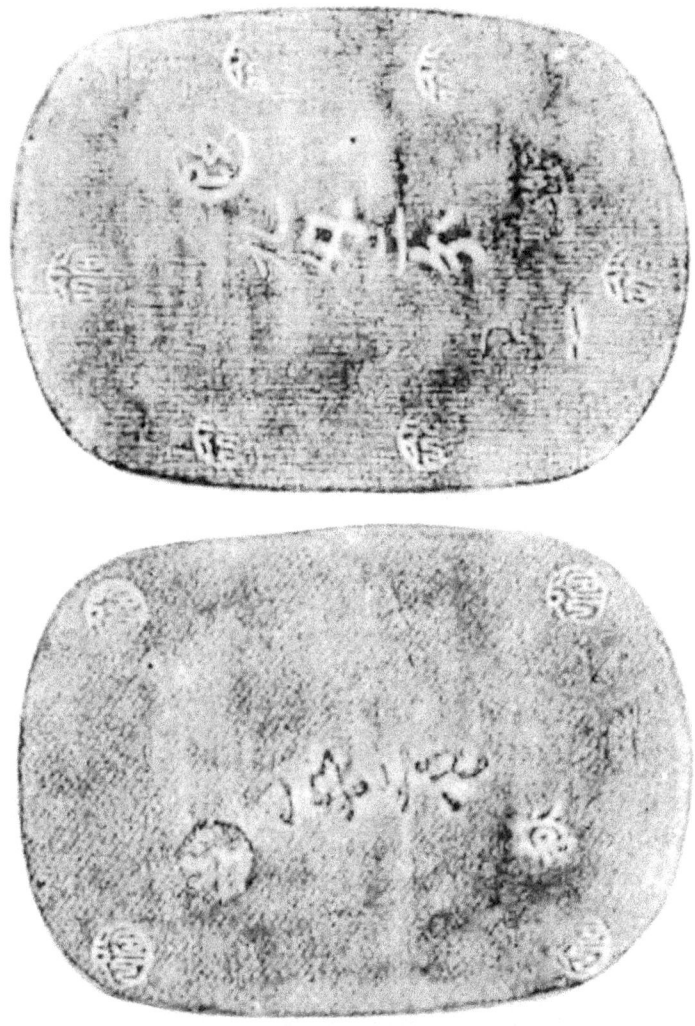

FIG. 24

208   GOLD AND SILVER CURRENCY.

The silver Koban of Akita, in the province of Dewa, and one of the Yamagata province, are seen in figs. 24 and 25. Though not government currency, they circulated in and even out of their provinces, and

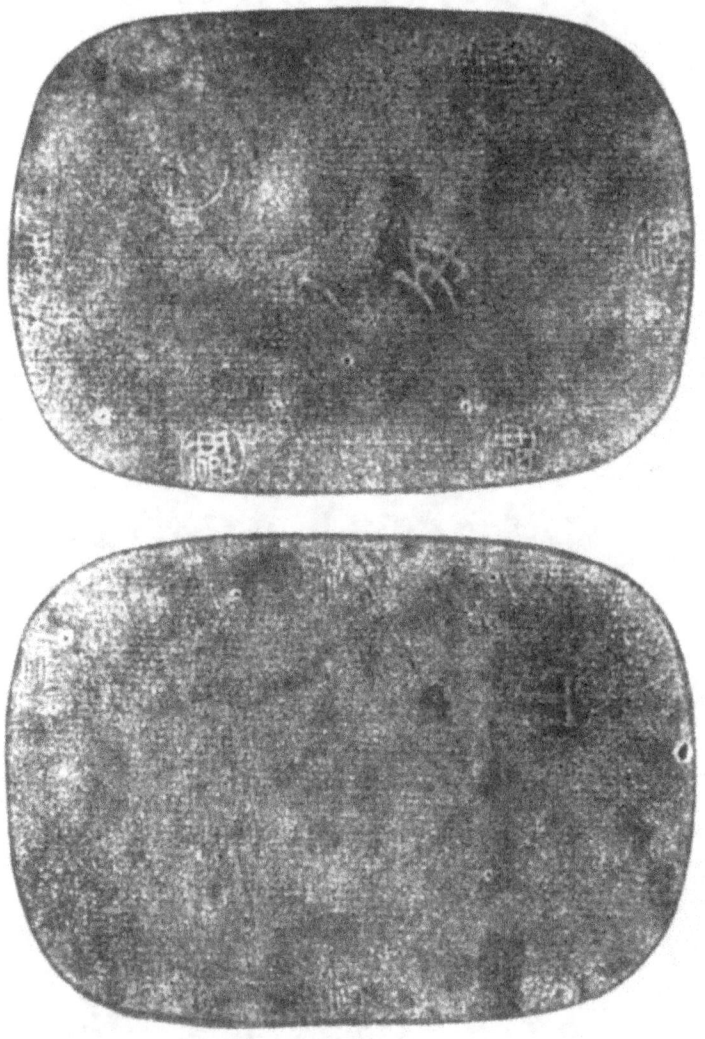

FIG. 25

are samples of the coinages which were made by several Daimyos in their own territories. The Akita silver Koban were made in the 2nd year of Bunkyu, 1862, and are simply sheets of silver, trimmed to their weight and stamped with the archaic form of "Yu" "abundant," round the margin, "Kai" (Aratame), Inspected, and "Aki", for Akita. This one is also stamped with "9 momme, 2 fun." The Yamagata silver Koban is stamped on the margin with "Yu" (different character), meaning to circulate. It is also stamped with "Kai" (Aratame), "Inspected," and it weighed "8 Momme." On the reverse is the character "San", (Japanese, Yama), a mountain, the first syllable of Yamagata.

In the province of Akita, there was also made a silver coin of the value of one Bu, the fourth of a ryo, fig. 26. On the face it has the crest of the Satake

FIG. 26

family, the Daimyos of Akita at that time, in the form of the leaves and flowers of the Sasarindo, the badge of the Minamoto family. Below is written "One Bu Silver". On the back is "Aki", as seen on the Koban and the "Nami" sen, and "Dozan Tsuho" or "Current" "Treasure of the Copper Mine."

A small silver coin of the Tajima province may be added as a sample of these provincial silver coins, fig. 27.

FIG. 27

On the face it has the characters "'Tajima" and on the reverse "Nan Ryo,"* which was equivalent to two Shu. The silver mine from which it was minted is said to have been discovered in the period of Engi, A.D. 901-22 though the records do not date further back than the 11th period of Tembun, 1542.

THE MEIJI CURRENCY.

The period of Wado first witnessed the issue of Government coin in Japan and it was then also that the story of her earlier civilisation first sought the light. The period of Meiji is distinguished by the change in form of her bronze coinage from the ancient and useful "cash" model, with its central hole for stringing the coin, to the more solid "copper" of Europe, while the experiment, first initiated in A.D. 760, of a three metal currency, was now established as a practical fact. More important than this, (though it does not lie within our present province), the present period of Meiji has seen the first earnest revelation of the Japanese later

---

* See page. 196

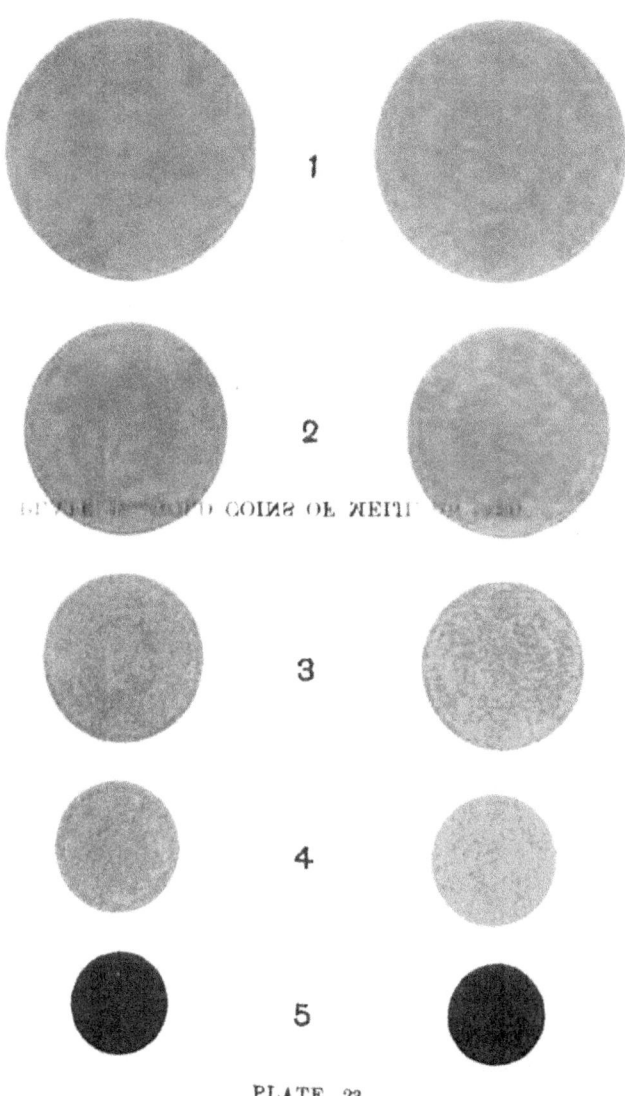

PLATE 23

civilisation to the outer world, and her affiliation with the factors of progress and enlightenment. The word "Meiji," implying "Enlightened Government," which was used to name this period, has crystallised the idea which must have been predominant in the minds of Japanese leaders and thinkers long before 1868, when the era of truly enlightened government began.

There does not exist in the history of any nation a hundred years of such progress as that which marks the 19th century in Japan. There is no century in which the difference between the opening and the close has been so marked, with respect to general culture, form of government, or material prosperity. Suffice it to say here that this adoption of western methods and ideals, which is spoken of by thoughtless persons as the civilising of Japan, is the blossom only of that tree whose roots were planted before the Wado period and whose sturdy stem and vigorous foliage were only awaiting the stimulus which would change the leaf bud to the flower. To any one who has read this book, it must be apparent that there has been no lack of "civilisation" during the thousand years preceeding the period of Meiji; indeed some of the edicts would seem to indicate rather a plethera of this. Let us hope that in its present form it will bear good fruit.

The death of the Shogun Iemochi in 1866, twelve years after the signing of the treaty with the United States, left the way open for the return of the temporal power to its rightful source. As there was no direct heir to the Tokugawa dynasty, Hitotsubashi was, after considerable pressure, induced to accept the office, but he felt that the trend of events was out of harmony with a dual authority and in November 1867 he resigned. While proposing this step to the Daimyos he remarked, "It appears to me that laws cannot be maintained in face of the daily extension of our foreign relations unless the government be conducted by one head and I propose therefore to surrender the whole governing power into the hands of the imperial court. This is the best that I can do for the interests of the empire." The resignation was accepted, but Hitotsubashi was asked by the Emperor to continue office until things were properly arranged, and in the meantime the ex-shogun was made an unwilling participator in the rebellion of 1868 out of a mistaken feeling of loyalty to his vassals, whose swords were stirred by their own selfish grievances. Although he finally resigned in the same year, his daimyos continued the struggle till 1869.

The Emperor Komei having died in 1867, he was succeeded by H. I. M. Mutsuhito who thus unites in his person the supreme authority in the affairs of the realm and the sacred office of spiritual Chief, the representative of that unbroken line of ancestor Kings whose remote origin in the archaic past of the Yamato Minzoku* reaches beyond the confines of tradition.

In the 2nd year of Meiji, an order was issued to the effect that the "Kwammon" or kwan of coin, would be equivalent to one ryo of gold. In the following year, Mr.

---

* The so called "Yamato" race who arrived in Japan probably about 1000 B.C.

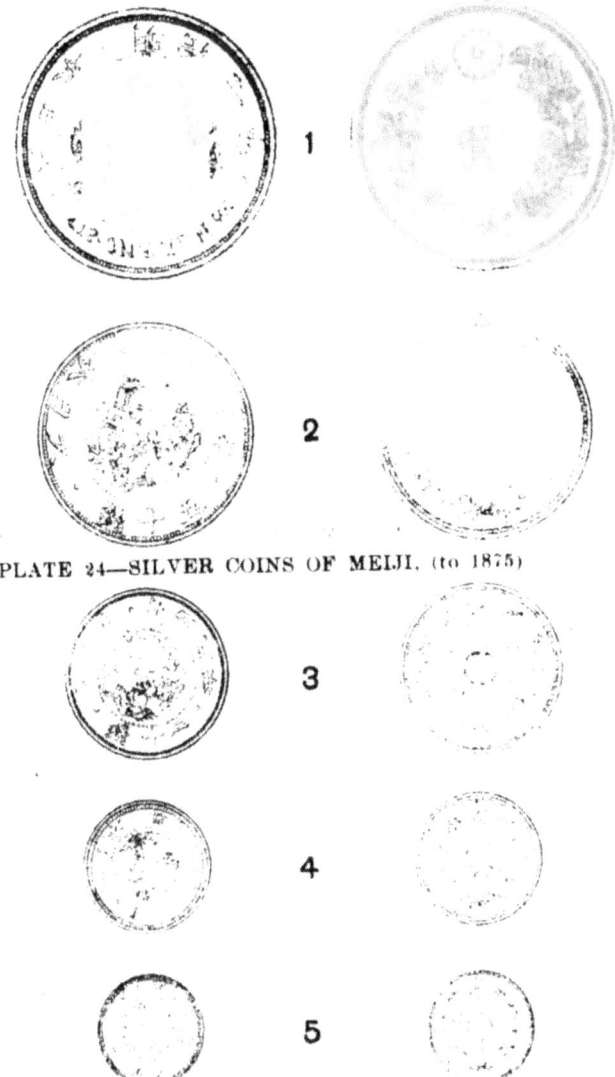

PLATE 24—SILVER COINS OF MEIJI. (to 1875)

PLATE 24

THE MEIJI CURRENCY. 213

Kinder and staff arrived from England to organise the mint at Osaka. Near the end of this year the coinage of money by stamping with engraved steel dies instead of by casting was commenced. For a fuller description of the regulations and other details regarding the institution of the Meiji currency, I would refer the reader to the excellent resumé by Mr. Van de Polder in the Transactions of the Asiatic Society of Japan for the year 1891. It will suffice here to give a list of the coins issued and circulated during this period, eliminating a few unimportant varieties.

Plate 23, No. 1,   20 yen gold piece.
"   "   " 2,   10 "   "   "
"   "   " 3,   5 "   "   "
"   "   " 4,   2 "   "   "
"   "   " 5,   1 "   "   "
Plate 24, No. 1,   1 yen silver.
"   "   " 2,   50 sen "
"   "   " 3,   20 "   "
"   "   " 4,   10 "   "
"   "   " 5,   5 "   "

The 5 sen nickel coin is illustrated in fig. 28, and a

FIG. 28

curious silver piece is seen in plate 22, No. 2, called the "Boeki" coin, from the characters which are stamped on one side, with the translation on the other, in English, "Trade Dollar," together with the weight and degree "420 Grains, 900 Fine".

  Plate 25, No. 1, 2 sen copper
  " " " 2, 1 " "
  " " " 3, ½ " "
  " " " 4 1/10 " " called the "Rin."

A specimen of the "Shiken" or Trial sen of the Meiji era is illustrated in the following chapter.

Space does not allow us to follow the extraordinary fluctuations of the gold currency in its relation to silver during the earlier years of the Meiji period. Suffice it to say that gold is now firmly established as the standard of currency in this country and that copper, which for so long acted as the current medium of Japan, now runs its course as a useful but subsidiary stream to that of the nobler metal. The glory of the "Do Sen" hath departed, but its romantic history will not soon be forgotten.

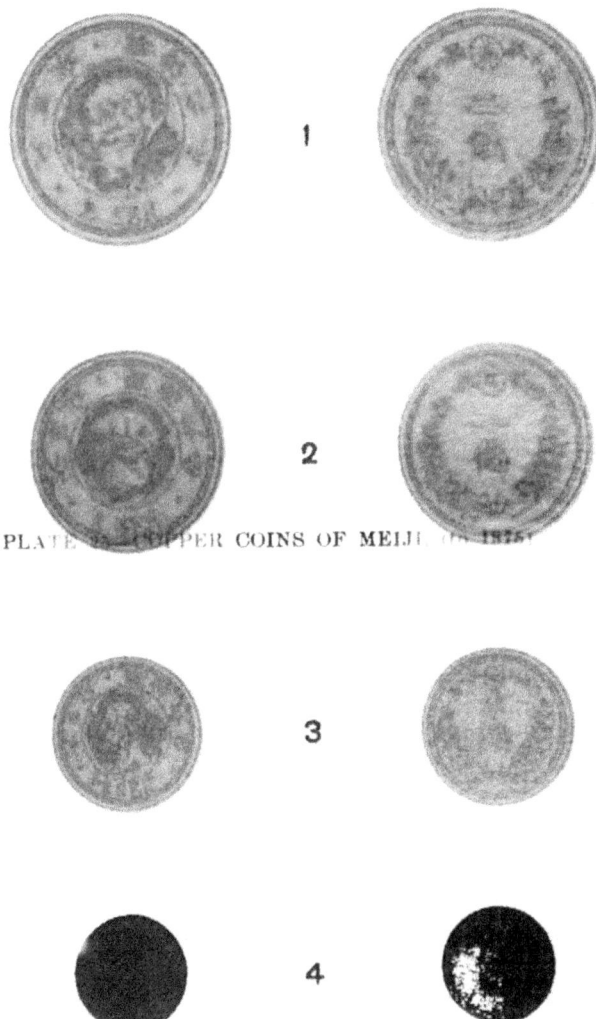

PLATE 24.—COPPER COINS OF MEIJI 8 (1875)

PLATE 25

VII.

EXPERIMENTAL AND ORNAMENTAL COINS.

It has been stated in a former chapter that specimens of coin have been made and submitted for government approval, either by the officials of the central mints or those of the provinces. These are known as "shiken", or experimental sen. This term is particularly applied to those coins that have been refused the sanction of the authorities and it will be here used in this sense. The "Niji" Hoei, page 148, and some of the Kwan-Ei sen may be cited as examples. In the case of some of the Provincial coins, and those government sen of a denomination corresponding to certain of these "shiken" sen, I have, for the sake of continuity, placed the latter with their more favoured brethern. There still remain however some experimental coins which could not be so classed, and they may be fitly illustrated along with the ornamental and fancy coins, from which in some cases it is not easy to distinguish them. In historical order, the first of these trial sen was the "Kenkon Tsuho" mentioned in chapter 3, page 80, as having been sanctioned for issue in the period of Kemmu, 1334, during the reign of the ill-fated Emperor Go Daigo, but of which no authentic specimen exists. Another coin about which some doubt exists, but which probably represents a "shiken" sen of the period, is called the "Cho-Roku Tsu-Ho", or Current Treasure of Choroku, page 87. It is said to have been cast during the period of Choroku, 1457-1460, in the reign of the Emperor Go Hana-

216   *EXPERIMENTAL AND ORNAMENTAL COINS.*

zono, while Ashikaga Yoshimasa was Shogun. Three specimens have been known, but so far as I am aware there is no record as to the origin of this coin.

The next in order is the "Kei-An Tsuho," fig. 1, or

FIG. 1

Current Treasure of Keian, "Peaceful Gladness," a coin, supposed to have been made during the period of Keian, 1648-52, but not circulated. A lead and copper sen of this size are known and also a smaller one of silver. The reverse has the moon and star and the characters "Cho No" or "Lasting Capability." The Emperor Go Komyo was then on the throne and the Shogun was either Iemitsu, 1623-50, or Ietsuna, 1651-80.

The following coin, fig. 2, is rather a desideratum to

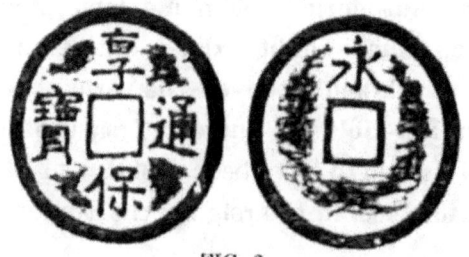

FIG. 2

the Japanese coin collector and is getting scarce. It is called the "Kyo-Ho Tsuho," or Current Treasure of

EXPERIMENTAL AND ORNAMENTAL COINS. 217

Kyoho, "Receiving, Holding"* and was cast in the first year of Kyoho, 1716, during the reign of the Emperor Nakamikado. The obverse bears the characters as above, while the reverse has the character "Ei", "Lasting," possibly to indicate its intention to replace the popular Kwan-Ei sen, which neither it nor the Ho-Ei coin succeeded in doing. It will be remembered that this character "Ei" was also used on the sen which succeeded the Kwan-Ei, namely the Bunkyu Ei-Ho. The "Teikyo Tsuho," or "Current Treasure of Teikyo" (or Jokyo), "Chastity Receiving",* fig. 3, is a silver coin, the copper

FIG. 3

one which is sometimes seen being always engraved, not cast. Indeed the genuine silver shiken sen is almost never seen. It was made during the period of Teikyo 1684-88.

FIG. 4

---

* If it is remembered that only a limited number of auspicious characters were used for the Nengo, or year names, and that these were frequently placed together to be read as separate announcements, it will be understood that it is often impossible to give connected meanings to the translation.

218 EXPERIMENTAL AND ORNAMENTAL COINS.

The Gen-roku Kai-Chin, or "Commencing Precious Article (Treasure) of Genroku," fig. 4, "Commencing Official Emolument", was cast in the 6th year of Genroku, commencing 1693, the year of the Bird. This is expressed by the picture of the hen on the reverse. Here also is inscribed its value, 1 fun, that is to say, the 10th part of a momme. The next coin, fig. 5, was also coined in the 6th

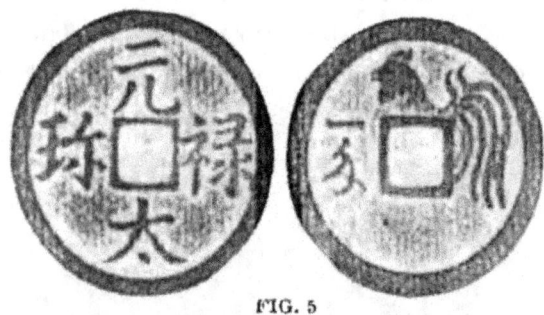

FIG. 5

year of Genroku. It bears the legend "Gen-Roku Tai-Chin," or "Great Precious Article of Genroku" which, like the Genroku Kaichin, reads round the coin as in the antique sen. The year of the bird is indicated by the picture of a cock on the reverse, on which also is stated the value, "1 momme". The discrepancy between the values and sizes of these two coins, the first being one tenth the value of the second, is sufficiently absurd to have prohibited their use. The following coin, fig. 6, was pro-

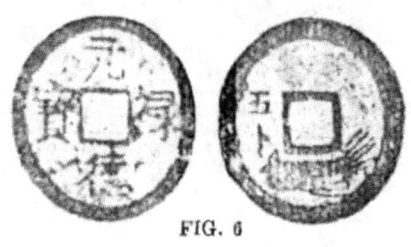

FIG. 6

EXPERIMENTAL AND ORNAMENTAL COINS.

bably cast in the same year, as the reverse bears also the sign of the Bird, together with the value, 2 fun. The obverse has the characters "Gen-Roku Toku-Ho" or "Good Treasure of Genroku".

Another Shiken sen which was probably made about the Genroku period, though the date is not accurately known, is inscribed on the face with "Gin-Ei Tsu-Ho" or

FIG. 7

"Current Treasure of Silver Glory" (or Prosperity). The reverse is plain.

There are several varieties of the following coin, which bear the inscription "Gin-Dai Tsu-Ho". "Gindai" means "Substitute for Silver", the metal of the coin in question containing a large proportion of tin and zinc, so that it has a white appearance, like that of the "Haku-Do" Sen, page. 174.

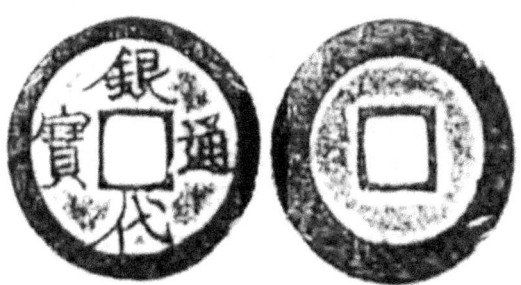

FIG. 8

220   EXPERIMENTAL AND ORNAMENTAL COINS.

In fig. 8 the reverse is plain. This is the typical shiken sen of this denomination, though a smaller one is also probably genuine, and forgeries are to be easily found. Fig. 9 is more rare. The handwriting is

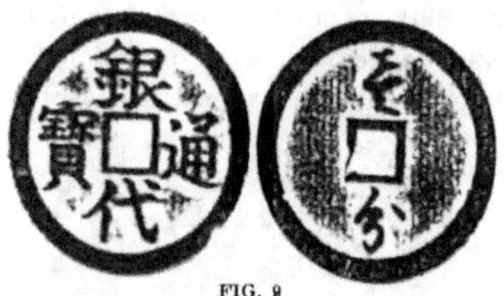

FIG. 9

different and the coin beautifully finished. On the reverse, in the running style of writing, is "Ichi Bu", or "One Bu" which, if it refers to the silver standard, is surely an extravagant valuation.

Fig. 10 also represents a light coloured shiken sen, of what date or place, is unknown. Perhaps it ought to be placed with the pleasure or fancy coins. On the obverse it bears the "Fundo Jirushi" (or shirushi), the emblem

FIG. 10

of weight, and the characters "Tai-Sei-Kai", "Great Commencing Life" (Birth). On the reverse is "Ichi Hyaku Ei Sen," "One Hundred Enduring Sen."

EXPERIMENTAL AND ORNAMENTAL COINS. 221

A coin was made in Nagasaki, probably for the inspection of the local Government, (see pages 156 and 168) bearing the character "To-Sen Tsu-Ho" or "Foreign sen Current Treasure", fig. 11.

 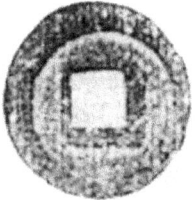

FIG. 11

During the period of Bunkyu, 1861-63, a large and handsome sen was made, under the order of the Tokugawa Government, fig. 12. It is slightly larger than the "Hoei Tsuho" (page 146), and the experience with that coin probably deterred the authorities from putting this one into circulation. On the face is written "Bun-Kyu Tsu-Ho", or Current Treasure of Bunkyu; the reverse

FIG 12

has "To-Hyaku-Mon," "Value One Hundred Mon," with a signature beneath.

At Mito, two interesting coins were made, one of which at least may claim to have had a limited circulation: as however I have not been able to secure absolute evidence on this point, I place them on the list of the Shiken sen. The first, fig. 13 T, was cast in the 3rd year

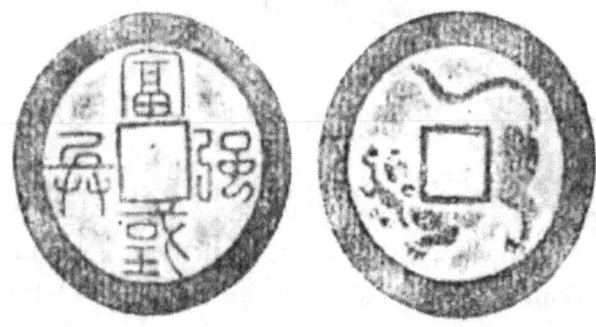

FIG. 13 T

of Keio, 1867, from the bronze cannon which the Daimyo Mito had made out of the temple bells, in order to repel the western barbarian. The idea originated with one Kawasaki, a smith, if I remember rightly, but as a speculation it was failure. From the artistic point of view, this and the following coin are *facile princeps*. One one side it has the inscription in the Tensho style "Fu-Koku Kyo-Hei" which means "Make rich the country, strengthen the army", both eminently patriotic sentiments which express the ardent aspiration of all modern Japanese. On the other side is a beautifully executed relief casting of a tiger.

This large coin was sold for 100 mon, but did not find a market. Sometime in the beginning of Meiji, a slightly

EXPERIMENTAL AND ORNAMENTAL COINS. 223

FIG. 14 T

smaller coin, fig. 14 T, was made by Kawasaki and had a limited sale at about twelve times the price of the other. It is also a work of art. On one side, if we read them in the order of the earlier coins, are the characters "Jiu-Hi-Nan-San" which mean "Long Life compared to a Southern Mountain," the ideal of strength and permanence. On the other side is an excellent representation of Daikoku Sama, whose portraits may also be found in plates 8 and 9.

It will be understood that figs. 13 and 14, which are Tane sen, are slightly larger than those of the ordinary sen. These tracings of coins, though faithful with respect to the characters, cannot shew such pictures in full detail. Several other coins were made in this centre of culture, which partake more of the nature of

FIG. 15

FIG. 16

ornamental than experimental coins. Figs. 15 and 16, are examples. The central hole in both is round, and the inscription the same, viz, "Kwa-Kai Sei-Ko", "Open Flower, Delightful Fragrance". The reverse of fig. 16 has three stars. The metal of fig. 16 also is much whiter than that of fig. 15. Yet another specimen, fig. 17, is without writing. Both sides shew some

FIG. 17

ornamentation, one may be a conventionalised form of the dragon.

Fig. 18 is a sample of casting made for the inspection of the mint or government officials. It looks like a preliminary casting for the "Hoei Tsuho."

In the second year of Meiji, samples were made of coin based on the model of the old sen, which however

EXPERIMENTAL AND ORNAMENTAL COINS.

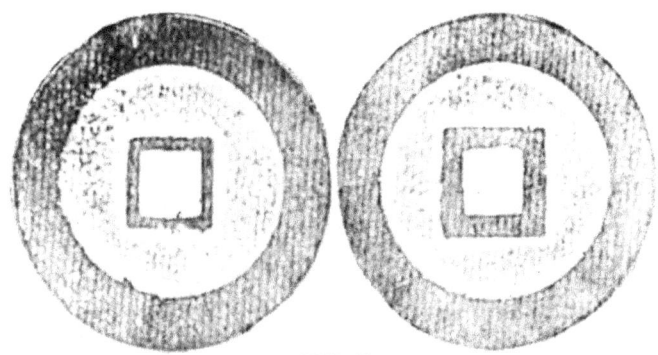

FIG. 18

were discarded in favour of the presnt Meiji coin. Fig. 19 shews one of these. They were cast with various values upon them.

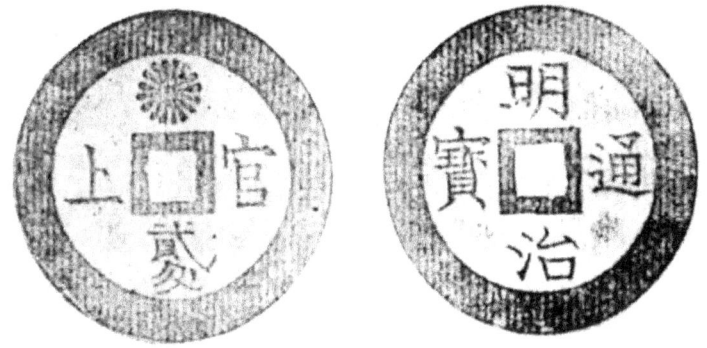

FIG. 19

This one bears the motto "Melji Tsu-Ho", or "Current Treasure of Meiji" on the obverse, with the Chrysanthemum crest on the reverse, its value "'Two Momme" and "Kwan Jo," "Imperial Government". These are very rare.

What the farce is to the drama, so are the "E" sen to the legitimate currency of Japan. In reality they are not sen, but tokens, often very curious and whimsical, designed for quite other purposes than that of a circulating medium. They are called "E" or picture sen, because they usually, though by no means invariably, bear some pictorial design or ornamentation, and moreover they resemble in shape and material, the current coin, called sen. Some of these picture sen have been cast in the government mints and have thereby, it may be presumed, received official sanction for their production. There are over a thousand varieties known. Dr. Majima, who is an authority on these fancy coins, has illustrated nearly that number in his work called the Ga Sempu.

For the purpose of giving a general idea of these however, a tenth of this number will be sufficiently illustrative. There seems to be little doubt that the picture sen of Japan did not originate in this country, but came from China, the source of many things both wise and foolish. In that country they were, and are still, used as amulets. No doubt they came over with the great influx of Chinese coin during the later mediaeval period, and were known at the court of Ashikaga Yoshimasa. It is said that the first picture sen, known as "Rokujo sen", were made during this time, but according to Dr. Majima and others, the sen which are now known by that name cannot claim this antiquity. It would appear that the oldest specimen of these sen is not earlier than the Tokugawa dynasty, but it may be that earlier specimens have disappeared, as might easily happen to fancy coins or gems, which were produced in limited amount, and that the original "E" sen was made during the time first noted, at Rokujo in the ancient capital of Kyoto. It will be noticed that the specimen illustrated in No. 1, plate 1, bears on the face the name "Wado Kaiho" (or "Kaichin"), the first coin of Japan. This is the motto of all the Rokujo sen, but the inscription on the back varies in different cases and sometimes there is no inscription at all on the reverse. Occasionally the characters "Wado Kaichin" are written in the old order, namely round the coin, or they may be arranged in the order of the later coins, while in a few cases they read from above downwards and from left to right instead of from right to left. In No. 1, plate 1, the inscription on the reverse reads "San Jiu Ban Jin," "The Thirtieth Deity," in one direction, and "Jiu Rasetsu Jo," Awful Female Demon"* in another. Most of the inscriptions on these Rokujo sen indicate their superstitious origin and bear out the assumption that they were originally designed for use as amulets. It says much however for the practical common sense of the Japanese people that this use of such medals was not very widespread, and that few of the E sen appear to have been been countenanced from a belief in their efficacy as a means of enchantment, or magic. The reasons which have led to the production of these sen. are various and may be grouped under the following heads.

1.—Those which have been made in a government

The word "Rasetsu," according to Brinkley's dictionary refers to the demons "who are said to devour human beings."

mint to celebrate the commencement of a new coinage, or even the opening of the seasons' work.

2.—Those that have been made in a government or private mint either for its special Lares or the festival of some deity.

3.—Those that have been made in a government or private mint for the celebration of the "Muneage" (completed framework rejoicing) of a temple or house.

Fig. 20 though quite modern, is of some interest as

FIG. 20

its *raison d'etre* is stated on the reverse, "Mune Age"; the obverse bearing the words "Matsuzaka Kwaisha."

4.—Those that have been made in a private mint as congratulatory coins or medals.

5.—Those made in the latter places to sell for gambling purposes, or as curiosities.

I shall now describe the E sen illustrated in the following plates:

Plate 1, No. 2. "✿ Gyoku Kwasen", bearing the characters "Kwa Sen" after one of the most ancient coins of China, and having a tree (So) and two jewels (Gyoku) above.

No. 3. "Sanko Kaichin." This coin is of silver,

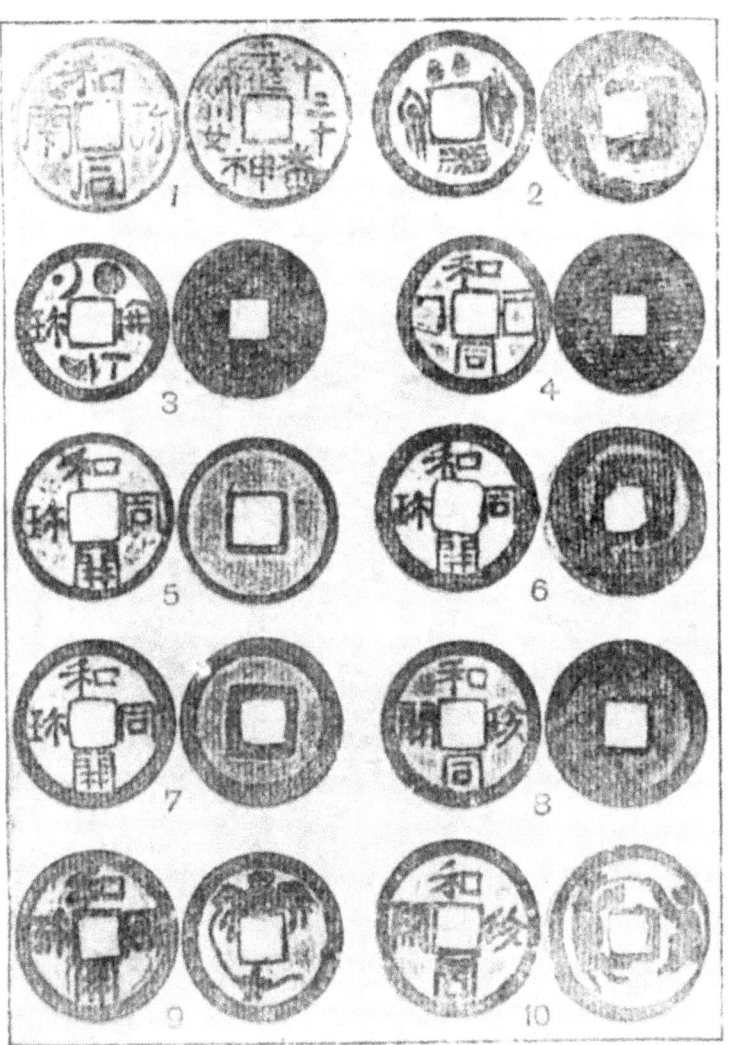

PLATE I.—E SEN.

though also made of bronze. "Sanko" means the three luminaries, sun, moon and star, which are shewn above. The "Kaichin" or "Kaiho" are taken from the Wado coin. Below is a "Mino" or straw rain cape, and a "Tsuchi" or hammer.

No. 4. This is also in silver and is called "Wado Masukage," after the Wado characters. There is also a hieroglyphic illustration of the "Masu," or measuring box for grain, and a "Kagi" or key.

No. 5. A silver "Wado Kaiho" made as a pleasure sen, probably within the last two hundred years.

Nos. 6 and 7. The same in copper, probably made in a mint for the Kwanei sen.

No. 8. A similar coin in copper, with the "Kaichin" reading from left to right.

No. 9. "Wado Kaichin Hikidashi" sen. The latter expression means pulling out, (a colt, in this case) in reference to the picture on the reverse, where the young horse is seen with his back bending under some burden.

No. 10. "Wado Kaichin Saruhiki Goma." The characters are displaced as in fig. 8 and the monkey, (Saru) is pulling (Hiki), what is supposed to be a colt, though it looks more like a tortoise. These horse coins are amongst the earliest of the E sen and there is little doubt that the idea of using this design came from China, where equestrian pictures are found on the amulets. I have several of these Chinese sen which appear to be of much earlier date that those of Japan. The "Koma" or young horse sen were frequently used for gambling purposes.

230 EXPERIMENTAL AND ORNAMENTAL COINS.

Plate 2, No. 1. "Yoshida Koma" sen. Made at Yoshida in the province of Mikawa and bearing the characters "Yoshida". This place was quite celebrated for its manufacture of E sen and is one of the mints for the Kwanei Sen.

No. 2. "Nogoma" or "Colt (possibly pony) in the field." It does not seem to be happy. Perhaps it has an antipathy to the pack, or swelling, on its back.

No. 3. "Ikwangoma" so-called because the man with the horse is suppose to be in court dress (Ikwan). In the original coin the figure above is a bag of gold dust, with the string hanging down at each side. The figure on the right consists of three "Hoshu", see page 231, on a chalice.

No. 4. "Eiraku Goma". This E sen is made from a stamp consisting of a Chinese Eiraku coin, from which all the characters have been erased, excepting the "Ei" (永). It is by no means common. The horse too, is shewing his metal.

No. 5, bears on the obverse the characters, "Kai-Un Jin-Ho" which may be rendered "Commencing of Success Sacred Treasure." On the reverse is a horse with a "Gohei"* above.

No. 6. "Eiji Koma." The character "Ei" (永) is *below* and is copied from one of the Kwanei sen. The "horse" reminds one of Mahomet's coffin, "suspended between heaven and earth.".

No. 7. "Hyotan Goma." The first word means a gourd, and the picture of the horse coming out

---
* "The emblems in a shinto temple, of the ancient offerings of cloth. They are now usually strips of white paper" Chamberlain and Mason. These offerings undoubtedly antedate the use of money in Japan.

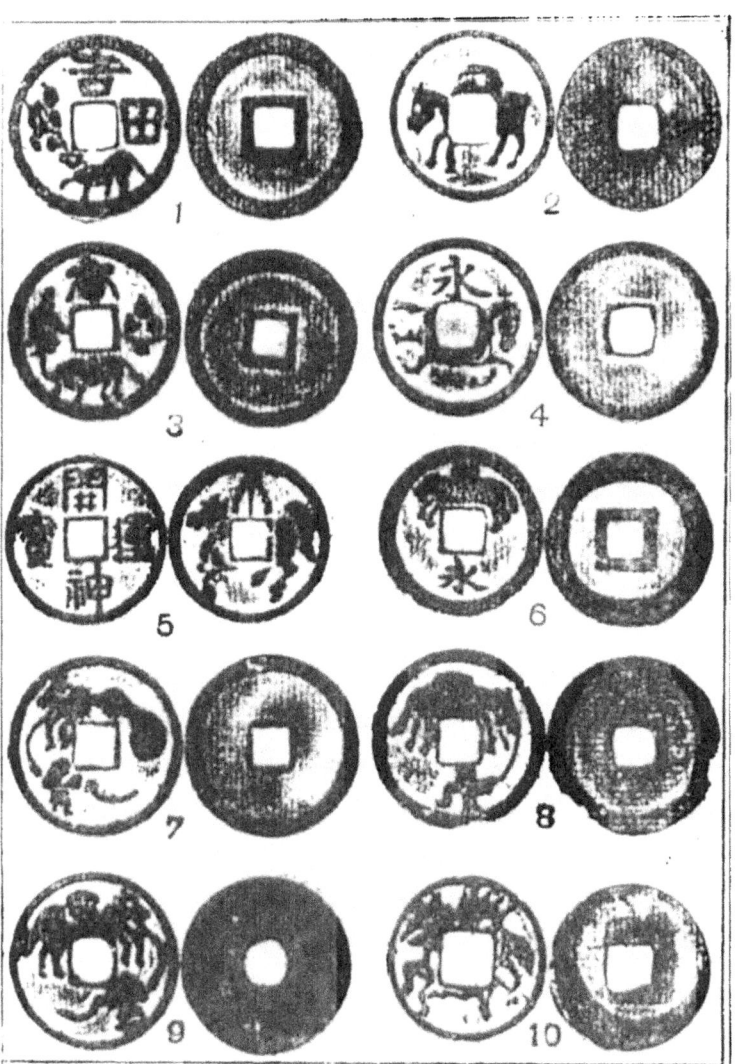

PLATE 2.—E SEN.

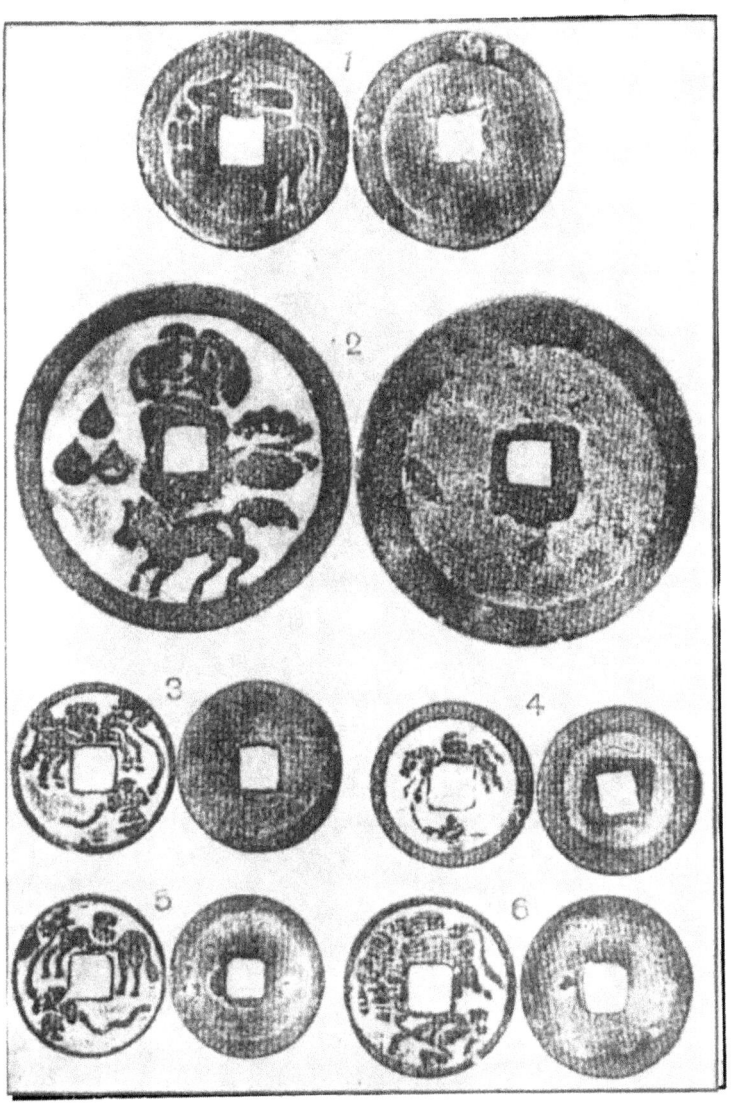

PLATE 3.—E SEN.

of the gourd refers to the popular saying "Hyotan kara koma," a horse coming out of a gourd; lit. to produce an unexpected result. (Brinkley).

No. 8. "Katate Goma." Pulling the horse in with one hand.

No. 9. Koma sen with round hole.

No. 10. This frisky something is also supposed to be a horse. The coin is somewhat worn, but the reverse is interesting.

Plate 3, No. 1. "Hikidashi Goma;" drawing forth the horse. It is a large medal, of pure copper, struck instead of cast.

No. 2. "Sanpuku (fuku) Koma sen exhibits what is said to be a horse and three essentials of fortune, namely the god Daikoku, of whom more presently, a bag of gold and three "Hoshu,"* transcendent gems. What the Hoshu-no-tama is I have not been able to discover. It is an emblem in some way connected with the Buddhist ritual in Japan, but its origin is lost in the remote past. In the "Handbook of Japan" by Professor Chamberlain and Mr. Mason, it is suggested that it may be identical with the "Nyo-i-rin, properly the name of a gem which is supposed to enable its possessor to gratify all his desires."

No. 3. "Hiki-ire Goma," "Pulling the colt in. Why "in," is not clear.

---

* This word might be "Hoju" from "Ho" treasure, and "Ju" a ball. The latter character is composed of "Gyoku" a precious stone, and "Shu," red colour. It would therefore refer to a red ball. It is represented in two forms, one with and one without flames. Possibly it is a survival of ancient Fire Worship.—N. G. M.

232 EXPERIMENTAL AND ORNAMENTAL COINS.

No. 4. "Hikidashi Goma;" drawing the colt out.

No. 5. The name of this I do not know. It might be called "The last straw."

No. 6. This is not a lion, nor an infuriated bull, but a horse drawn by a monkey and is therefore called "Saru (monkey) Hiki Goma."

Plate 4, No. 1. A large medal with a rope-like margin and somewhat similar decoration around the central hole, which is relatively small. On the face are a pine tree, a flying stork, a peasant with straw rain cape and an active horse.

No. 2. "Wado Kaichin Saru Hiki Goma." This is a another example of the left hand writing of "Kaichin." On the reverse is a monkey, apparently exhausted by his attempt to pull a refractory colt.

No. 3. The characters "Wado Kaichin" are here written in the ancient order and the monkey, though on his back, still pulls with both hands.

No. 4. Possibly a theatre ticket.

No. 5. This is a large presentation of the famous "Kwanei Tsuho" and bears on the reverse the characters "Namu Amida Butsu," "I adore the Eternal Buddha". It may be thought that this and the following medals with Buddist inscriptions, were intended as amulets, and in some cases they may have been so regarded by the superstitious, but in the majority of cases, they were issued on the occasion of certain religious festivals, or to commemorate the opening of temples. On these occasions they were bestowed upon the subscribers and perhaps visitors generally.

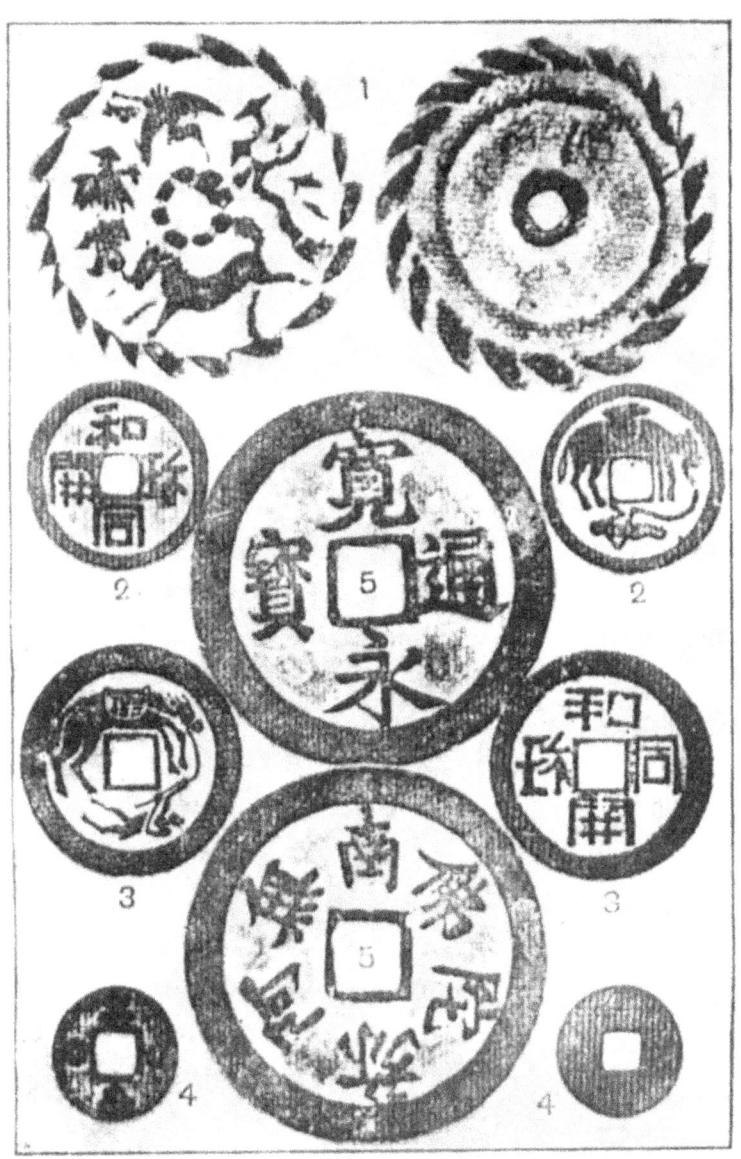

PLATE 4.—E SEN.

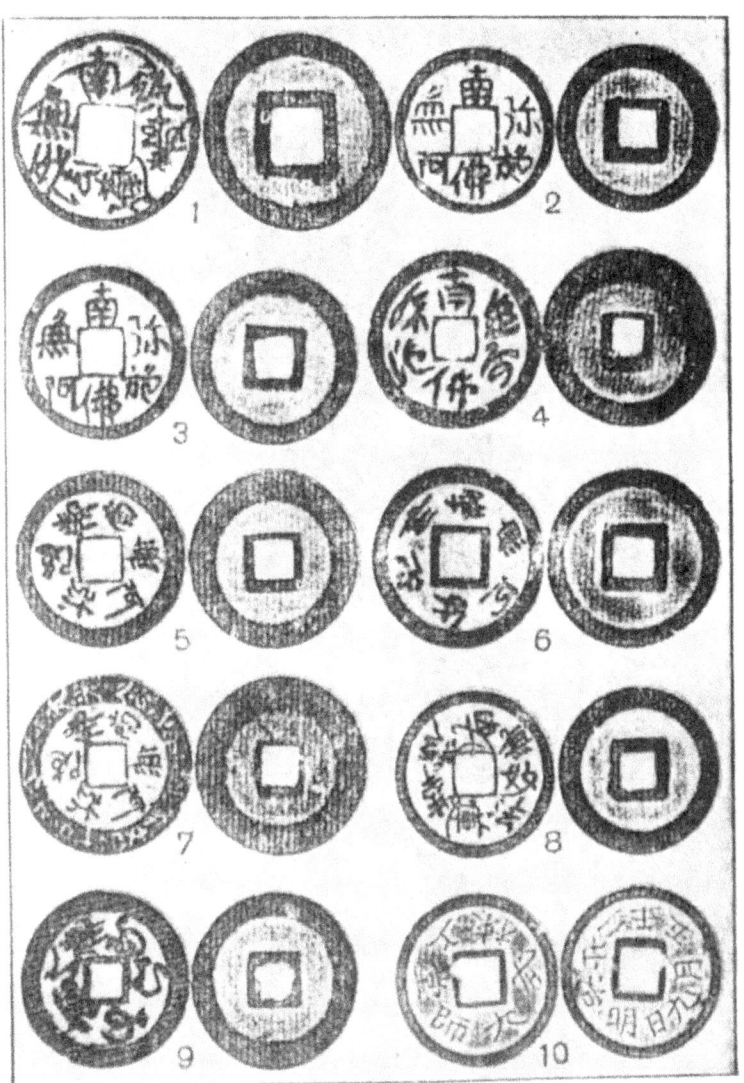

PLATE 5.—E SEN.

The texts inscribed thereon have the same intention as the texts of other religious systems, namely to hold the attention of the laity and thus to keep in mind their precepts or admonitions. These text bearing sen are quite numerous, but I shall only describe a few of the better known ones.

Plate 5, No. 1, called "Nembutsu" or praying to Budda, "from the inscription on it, and "Kuruma Nembutsu" from the fact that it reads round (in this case from left to right) like a wheel, possibly in allusion to the praying wheel. The inscription reads "Namu Myo Ho Renge Kyo," "Adore the Wonderful Doctrine of the Lotus' Scripture." Those who have heard this text recited in the Buddhist ritual, will not fail to recall the solemnity of its sonorous accents.

No. 8. This is a smaller specimen and the inscription, in a different handwriting, reads from right to left.

No. 2. "Namu Amida Butsu", "I adore the Eternal Buddha." The characters here read, one above, two to the left, two to the right and one below.

No. 3. The same. Size and handwriting different.

No. 4. The same. Reads first above, then two to the right, two to the left and one below.

No. 5. The same. Reads round the coin like the figures on a clock.

No. 6. The same, and read in the same order. The handwriting is different.

No. 7. The same. The rim is wide and carries an inscription which is not quite legible.

No. 9. The same written in Hiragana (Syllabic writing), except the last word (Buddha) "Butsu," which is in character.

No. 10. This is made of pewter and bears on the face "Dai Shi Do Jo To Shiki," "Temple of Daishi Ceremony of Erection" (Muneage). On the reverse it has the date, namely the 9th day of the fifth month of the 22nd year of Meiji,

Plate 6. I shall first invite attention to No. 6 on this plate, which represents the deified personage who is worshiped as Tenjin, his name while in the flesh having been Sugawara-no-Michizane. (See chapter 2, page 71, footnote.) This sen ought to be the pioneer of the E sen for, according to tradition, in the first year of Bummei, 1469, several thousand Engi Tsuho coins (antique group) were found at the village of Nagasu in the province of Settsu: these were recast into the form of the Tenjin coin in order to commemorate the sojourn of Sugawara-no-Michizane at this place, over five hundred years previously, on his way to his exile in Kyushu. It is said that in the first year of Temmei, 1781, several thousand of the same coin were again found at the same place and half of them were sent to Kitani to be recoined as mementoes of the great Tenjin. Dr. Majima says that none of these Tenjin sen appear to be so old as the period of Bummei, but that it is possible that they were then so made. It will be readily understood that the liability of E sen to disappear, must be greater than that of circulating coin, if only for the reason that they are produced in less numbers, but it

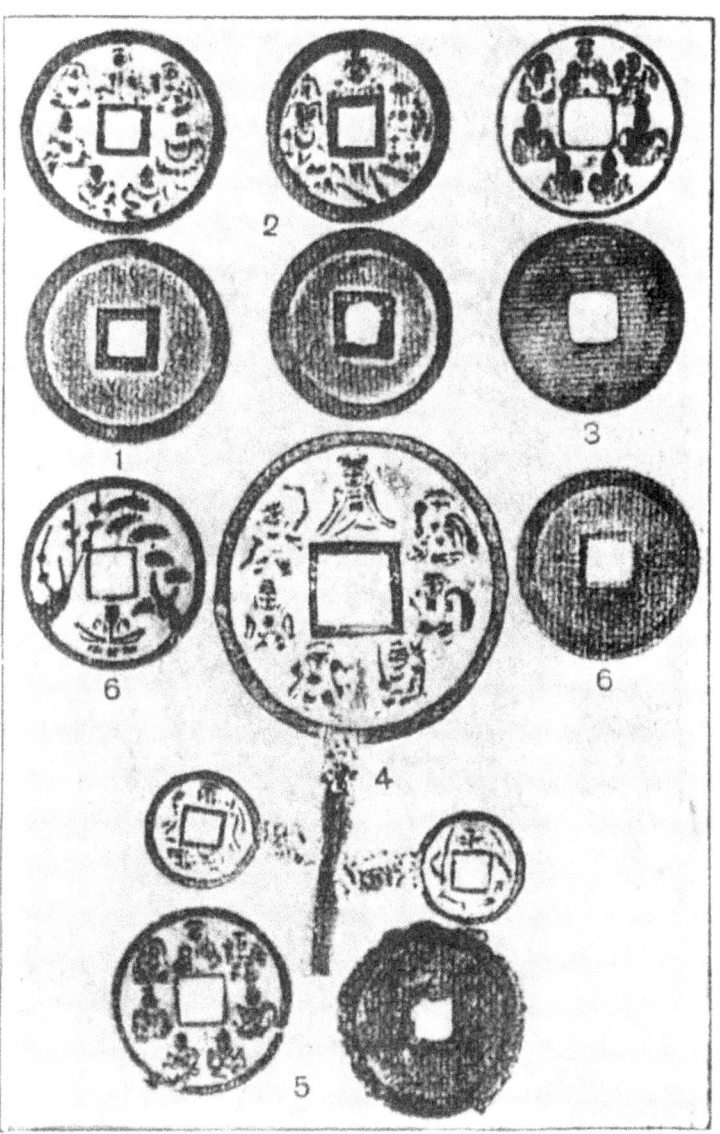

PLATE 6.—E SEN.

EXPERIMENTAL AND ORNAMENTAL COINS. 235

is improbable that several thousands of such coin could entirely pass out of existence. It seems to me more likely that only a few, if any, were made at the earlier period referred to. There are three kinds of this sen. No. 6 represents Tenjin sitting under the plum and pine trees, two of the emblems of luck, and the former his favourite flower.

The Shichifukujin, or seven Gods of Luck. In Japanese, the expression Kami, which is usually translated as "God" does not necessarily refer to a Supreme Being, but rather to a superhuman being, the word Kami being used in the sense of superior, or above humanity in general. An interesting paper by Signor Carlo Puini in the Transactions of the Asiatic Society of Japan, 1880, gives much information on the question of the Shichi Fukujin, or the Seven Gods of Happiness. He states that three degrees of Kami are known, viz., the celestial, the terrestial and the human Kami.

There can be no question that the Kami, Gods, or superior beings of the Japanese pantheon, have various degrees of power and special functions, or perhaps rather limitations of purpose, ascribed to them, though the sphere of activity, or utility in one, may overlap with that of another. The word Kami is of very ancient origin and is properly applied to initial intelligences, or to those ancestors whose distant origin in the mythological period, or whose deeds of surpassing excellence, entitle them to rank above ordinary humanity. The former are the recipients of conventional reverence, but the latter, with their direct human connection, have more influence over the affairs of men, either through the use of the special potency with which they are endowed, or as mediators with the "Powers that be".

The Shichifukujin are named respectively: 1 Ebisu, 2 Daikoku, 3 Benten, 4 Fukurokujin, 5 Bishamon, 6 Jurojin and 7 Hotei.

Strange to say, only one of these belongs wholly to the ancient Shinto religion, whose simple and primitive, but coherent and effective, ancestor worship has been complicated by additions from Buddhist and even Taoist sources. Signor Puini points out that of the seven Kami, Yebisu only is of entirely Japanese origin, and that three, viz., Daikoku, Bishamon and Ben-zai-ten are of Buddhist creation, while three are of Chinese origin, "of whom the last two are somewhat Taoist". These seven are shewn in Nos. 1, 3, 4, and 5, and three, namely Ebisu, Daikoku and Benzaiten, (commonly called Benten) in No. 2, but it is not easy to discern their special characteristics. It will be sufficient to illustrate the first two, namely Ebisu and Daikoku, which are the most frequently found.

No. 4, representing the seven gods of Luck, is one of those extraordinary medals produced on occasions of rejoicing by the festive employees in one of the government or private mints. The connecting strip of metal is purposely left uncut and the smaller medals thus remaining attached, shew the images of Ebisu on the right and Daikoku on the left.

No. 5 resembles No. 3 except that it is made of iron.

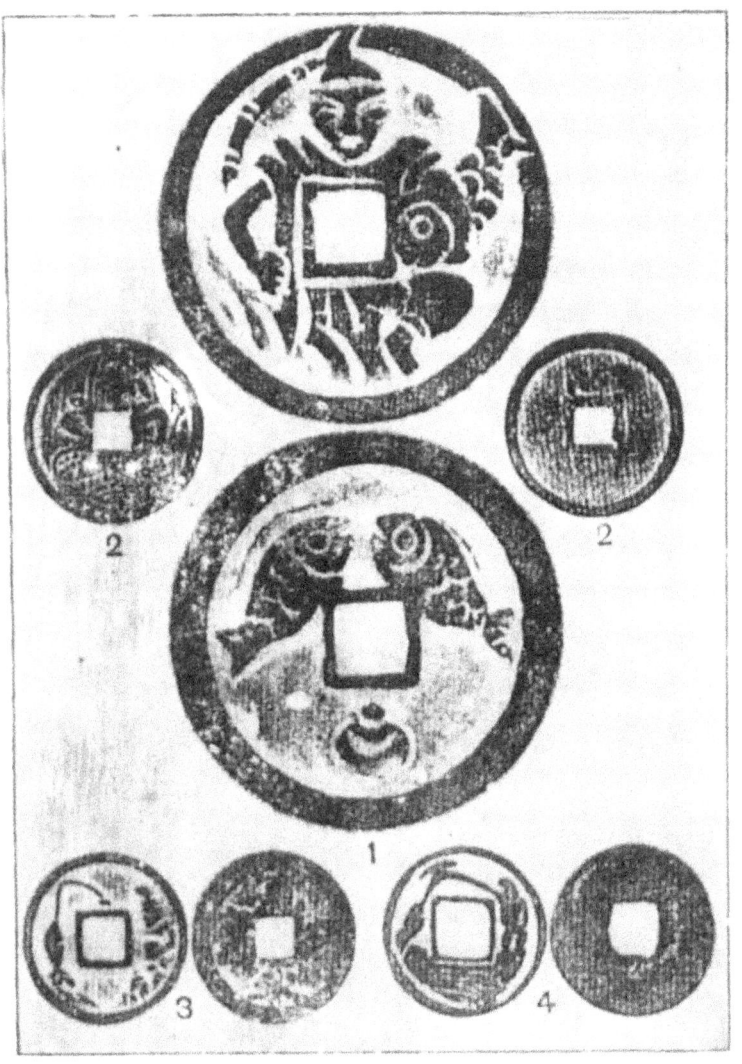

PLATE 7 — E SEN

Plate 7, fig. 1. This is a large likeness of the God Ebisu, the only one of the Shichifukujin who can claim an undisputed native origin. In his left arm he grasps a goodly fish of the kind called "Tai", a variety of sea bream and much esteemed. On the left is the bamboo rod shewing its elastic curve to a degree that would have astonished the author of "The Compleat Angler" and may furnish a theme for a future edition of "Fisherman's Luck". The God himself looks a trifle uncertain about the lower extremities (he had weak legs as a lad), but he grasps the big fish round the gills with a determination as great as its own (which is also traditional). On the reverse we behold two other noble specimens of the mighty angler's skill and below, the mystic "Hoshu", the wishing ball, which satisfies all desires, even that of the amateur angler.

No. 2, shews the same god sitting on the waves with fish and rod. It is struck in pure copper and is probably more than two hundred years old.

No. 3. Ebisu at work. The reverse has the "Kwanei Tsuho".

No. 4. Ebisu catching fish, or being caught, which is it?

Nos. 7, 8 and 11 also shew him in his classical attitude. These are cast in iron.

Ebisu is the "Patron of Honest labour". His original name is said to have been Hiruko. He was the offspring of Izanagi and Izanami, the male and female Deities who created the world and the terrestrial Kami. He was weak in his legs (perhaps from infantile paralysis) so that at the age of three years he could not stand. This was a source of grief to his tender hearted parents, so they stuck him in a boat and abandoned him to the elements. He drifted to the province of Settsu and was, probably on account of his legs, worshipped as a god. The people were savages, "Ebisu", hence his name. Whatever his real origin may be, Ebis' Sama enjoys constant popularity: if not so full of resource as Daikoku Sama, he is scarcely less esteemed.

Daikoku is usually represented sitting or standing, on bags of rice with a wallet slung on his back. He is also depicted holding a mallet called the Hammer of Happiness. "Each time he gives a blow with it, the wallet he has by him becomes filled with money, rice and, other things, according to what may be desired." Pulni, goes on to tell us, "Daikoku, the name of the second of the Gods of Happiness, is the translation, through the Chinese, of Mahâkâla, which is one of the names of Siva and other Sivan deities. This god was added to the Buddist pantheon with other Brahmanic deities."* He has got thoroughly acclimatised and seems to be happy in giving happiness to others, though in his land of birth he is supposed to be either a great heretic or a perverse destroyer.

Plate 8, No. 1. This is a "Hori" or engraved sen called "Ippyo Daikoku" or Daikoku on one rice bag.

---

* Mr. Yuzawa tells me that the Genkai also gives Daikoku the cognomen of Okuninushino-Mikoto, the ruling god (or Prince) of Izumo. This is the popular belief, through which he may claim native origin.

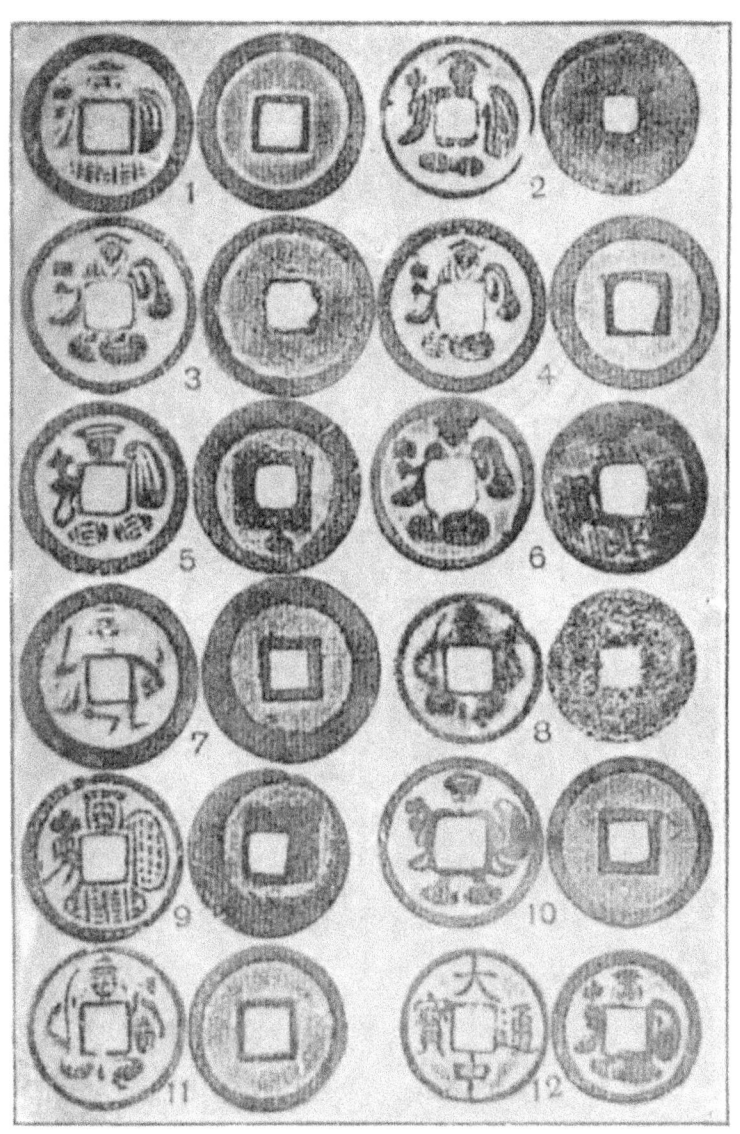

PLATE 8.—E SEN.

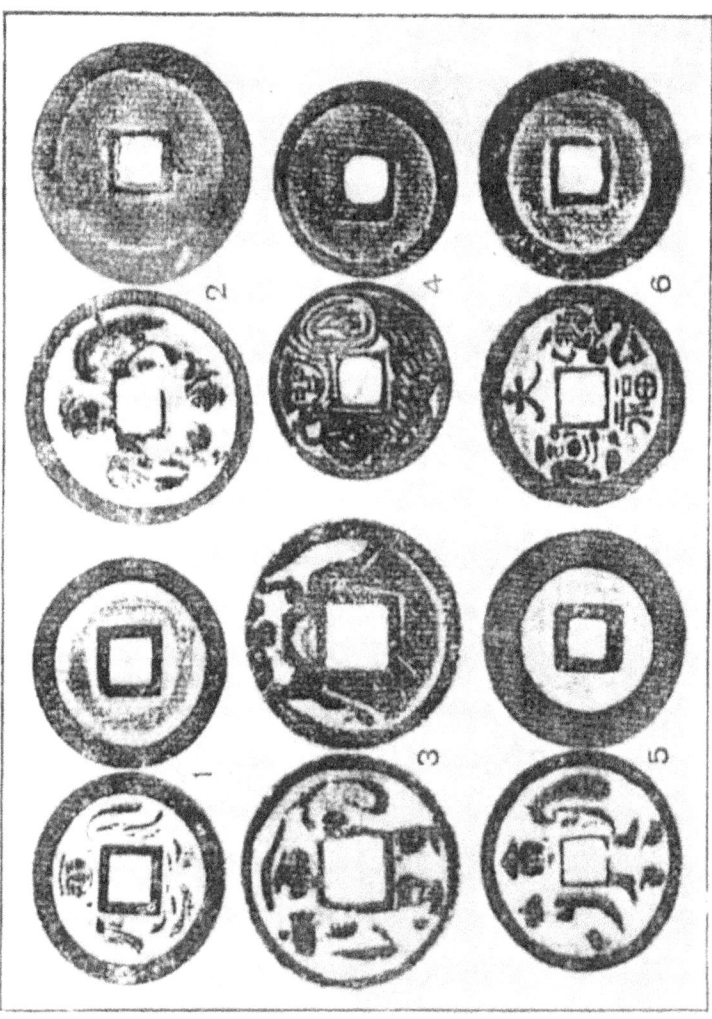

PLATE 9.—E SEN.

EXPERIMENTAL AND ORNAMENTAL COINS.

No. 2. "Kobo Daikoku", supposed to have been modelled from a picture by Kobo Daishi, who is mentioned in chapter 2. He is referred to in the "Handbook of Japan" as "The most famous of all the Japanese Buddhist saints, was noted equally as preacher, painter, sculptor, calligraphist and traveller."

No. 3 and 4. He is here distinguished by the wearing of a collar, but it is not much in evidence.

No. 5. "Kasagi Daikoku". Wearing a hat: the back has a star (Hai Hoshi).

No. 6. Here he also has a hat. The reverse bears the Kwanei Tsuho characters, rather blurred.

No. 9. " Tagane Daikoku ". So called because it looks as if it had been chiselled out. (Tagane, chisel).

No. 10. "Kumano Daikoku" made for the Kumano temple. The feet are either too large or the rice bags too small.

No. 11. Ebisu. (See page 237.)

No. 12. This bears the characters "Tai-Chu Tsu-Ho" after the well known Chinese coin of that name.

Plate 9, No. 1. This is an engraved tane sen, or probably a "Haha", or mother sen and is quite rare.

No. 2. Large Daikoku. "Yoko Muki," "Looking to the side."

No. 3. "Tachi Daikoku". Standing Daikoku. The reverse is supposed to depict the famous active volcano called mount Asama.

No. 4. "Shima Daikoku." Resembles a Shima sen. See chapter 3.

No. 5. "Tama Nori Daikoku". Rides on balls (Tama). These are doubtless the "Hoshu" or wishing balls.

No. 6. "Dai Fuku," which characters mean "Great Luck, or Happiness" and "Ni Jin, or Two Gods". These are the two favourities, Daikoku and Ebisu.

Plate 10. This is a set of "Matsuri" or festival sen. In the centre is Ebisu, above is Daikoku; to his left (our right) is the "Kwanei Tsuho" bearing the handwriting of the Kutsutani mint in the province of Suruga (where it was made, probably between the 13th, and 16th years of Kwanei). Below this sen and also to the right of Daikoku are sen with the writing "Namu Amida Butsu", while below and to the right of Ebisu is a sen with the inscription "Namu Myo Ho Renge Kyo". The reverse is that of the Kutsutani mint.

Plates 11 and 12. Ebisu and five Kwanei sen in iron, arranged in "Matsui" form.

Plate 13, No. 1. These seven "Matsuri" sen bear the inscription "Namu Amida Butsu". Where they have been made is doubtful.

No. 2. Is also a festival medal. Above is Ebisu; to his right is another picture of his honourable self, combining business and pleasure, while below is Daikoku Sama with his mallet, and his bag of tricks. The Kwanei characters peep above the central Ebisu as they do in

No. 3 of the same plate, where the two friends of humanity appear side by side. These festival sen were often set up in front of the household shrines, to pro-

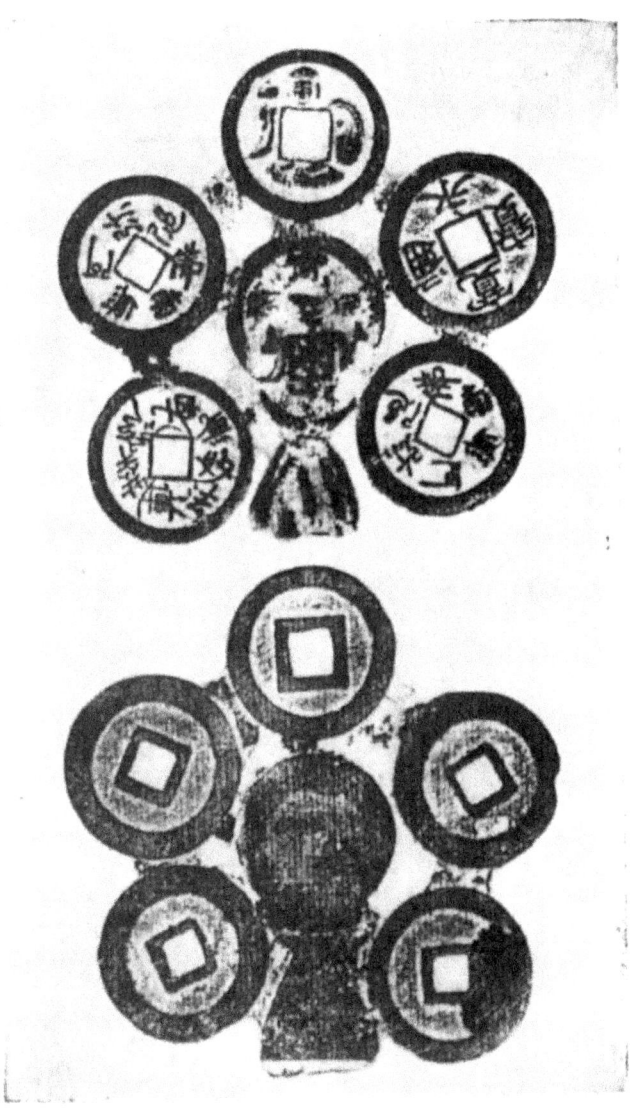

PLATE 10.—E SEN.

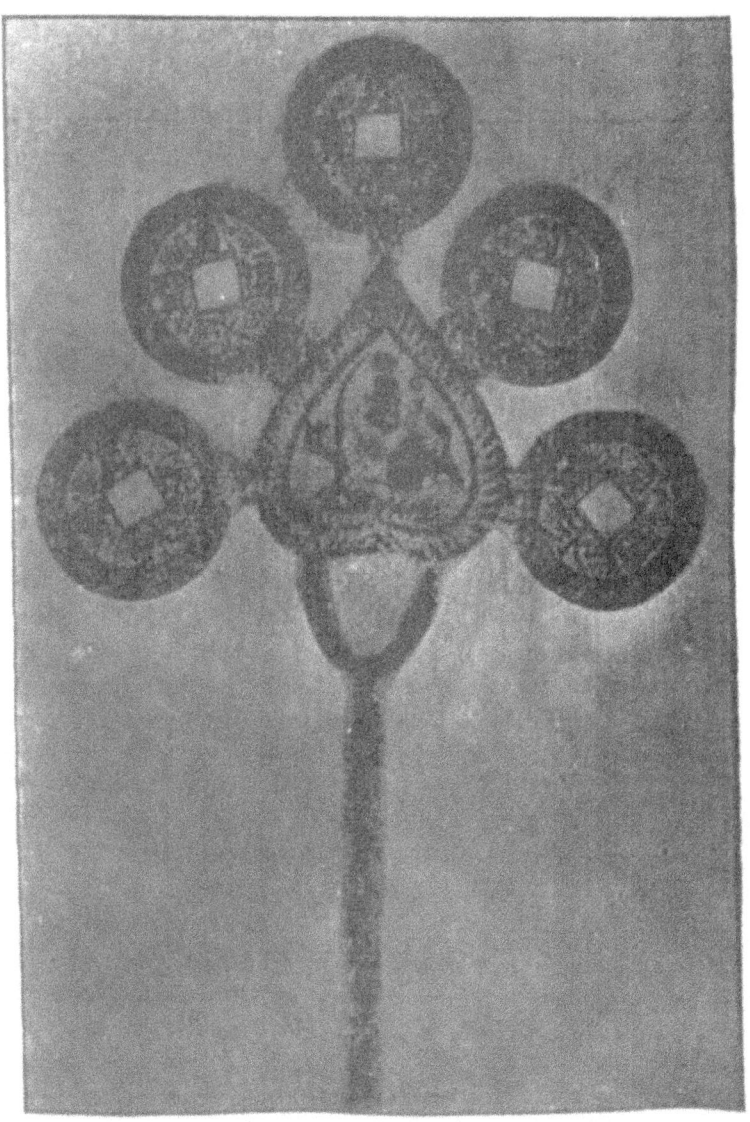

PLATE 11.—E SEN.

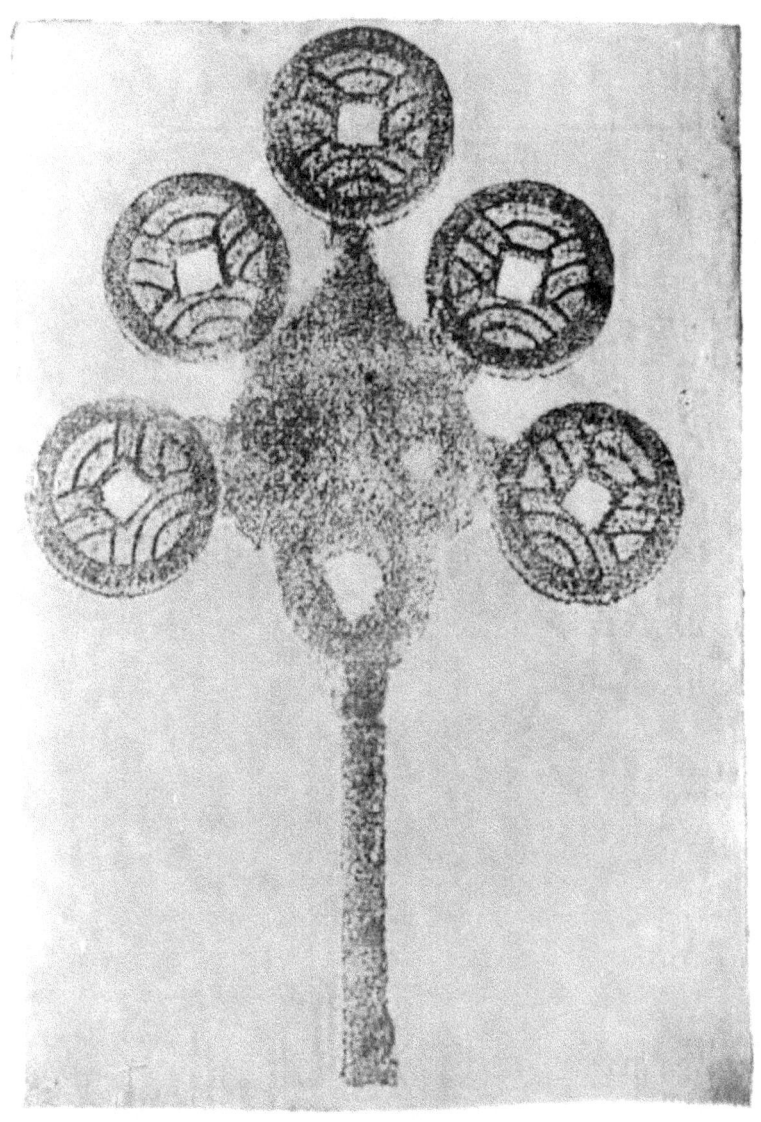

PLATE 12.—E SEN.

PLATE 13.—E SEN.

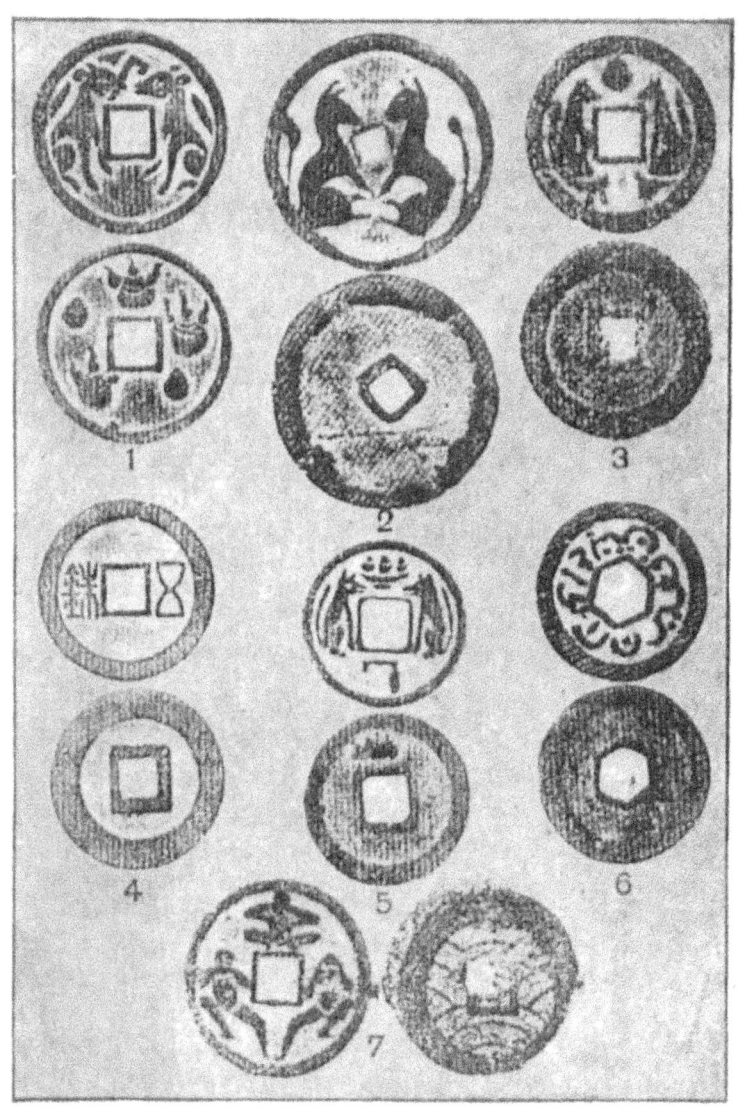

PLATE 14.—E SEN.

pitiate the Lares and Penates, doubtless with most gratifying results.

We come now to the most popular of all the deities, namely Inari Sama, whose messenger is the fox and whose deeds would fills a dozen volumes. He (she or it) has been identified with the god Uga, and if this be correct, Inari is entitled to rank with the Shichi Fukujin or seven gods of Fortune, for this Uga is a form of Benten.* Like the latter, he takes the fields and their produce, especially rice, under his protection; his shrines are the most numerous in the land and nearly every house, whether Buddhist or Shinto, has an altar wherewith to propitiate and to render him grateful thanksgiving. He is essentially an "Arigatai Kami Sama" or "Grateful Mr. Deity" and offerings of rice cakes, incense and rushlights are daily to be found tempting his appetite, and otherwise giving him immense satisfaction. It may truly be said that these little acts of devotion have lightened many a dark and fearful moment and, if not without, at least the god *within* the human breast, responds to the pious offering and bestows the blessing of hope on the anxious wife or mother.

Plate 14, No. 1. Inari sen. There are always two foxes as ministers (sometimes regarded as incarnations) of Inari. One of them has the mystic key to unlock the hidden stores of plenty. On the reverse are the five "Hoshu" or "Hoju", three with the sacred fire and two without.

No. 2. Large size Inari sen. The central hole is small and its angles are differently placed than usual.

---

* Benten is a Goddess.

No. 3. Inari sen of iron. Above is the Hoshu.

No. 5. Inari sen with three Hoshu on a chalice and the mystic key below.

No. 7. Koshin sen. I will again quote from Chamberlain and Mason. "Koshin, a deification of that day of the month which corresponds to the 57th term of the Chinese sexagesimal circle, and is called in Japanese "Ka-no-e Saru". This being the day of the Monkey, it is represented by three monkeys (sam biki-zaru) called respectively, by a play upon words, "Mizaru", "Kikazaru" and "Iwa-zaru", that is, "the blind monkey", "the deaf monkey", and the "dumb monkey." Stone slabs with these three monkeys in relief are among the most usual objects of devotion met with on the roadside in the rural districts of Japan, the idea being that this curious triad will neither see, hear, nor speak any evil."

No. 4. This is an imitation of the ancient "Go Shiu" coin of China.

No. 6. Called the "Yaban Ji" sen, or "Barbarian Writing" coin, although classed with the E Sen, it does not properly belong to this group.

Plate 15, No. 1, is rare. It is called the "Kwan Tsuki Fuji" sen, or "Ringed Wistaria" sen. It has round marks, or balls, probably Hoshu, on the back.

No. 2, of the same plate, has no ring, but has nine balls on the back. No. 4 is a large copy of the Wistaria design.

No. 3. This might have been described along with the Ebisu sen. It is a large, somewhat heart shaped ring, with a Matsuri medal of Ebisu in the interior.

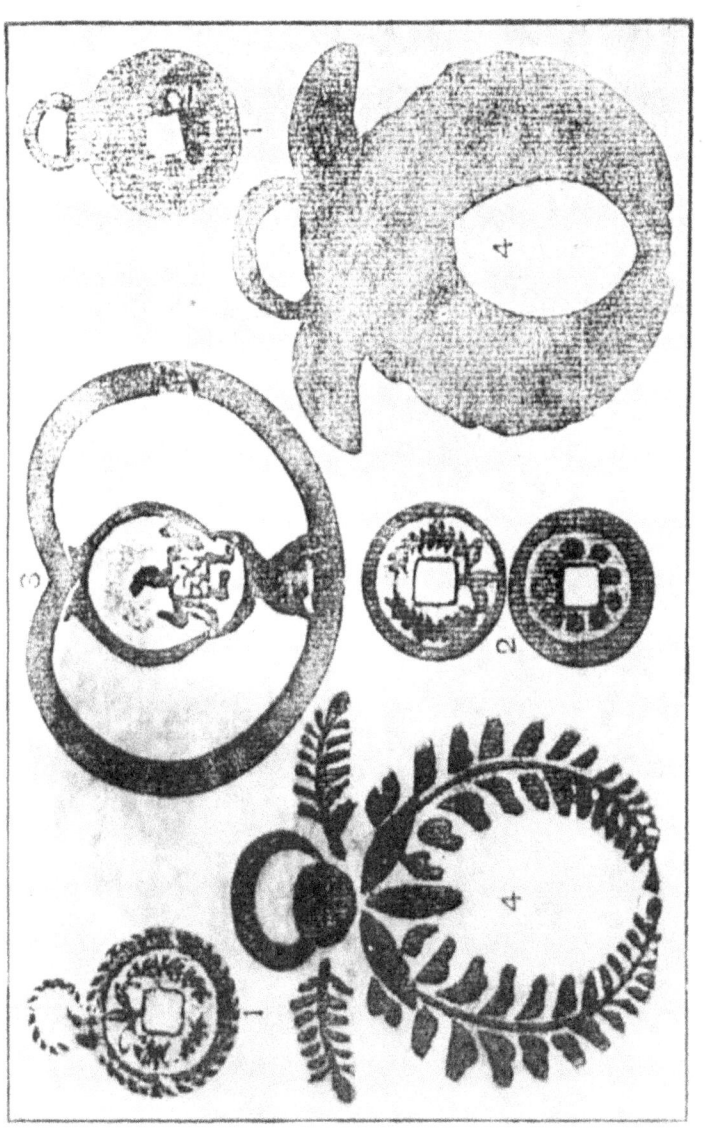

PLATE 15.— E SEN.

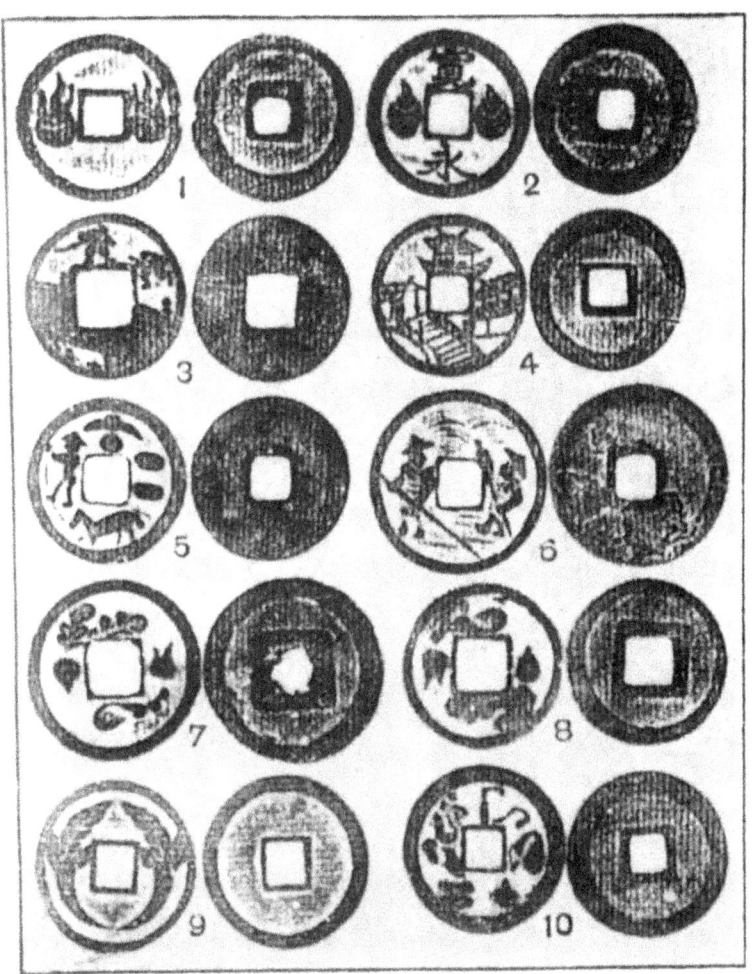

PLATE 16.—E SEN.

EXPERIMENTAL AND ORNAMENTAL COINS.

Plate 16, No. 1. We come again upon the Hoshu, or Hoju, with the sacred flame leaping high; in No. 2 of the same plate the characters "Kwanei" are seen above and beneath.

No. 3, represents an incident of medieval Japan. Benke, a famous man at arms, challenged the world (of Japan) and met with his match in the person of the youthful and noble samurai Ushiwaka, afterwards the great Yoshitsune, the most romantic figure in Japanese history. He was half brother to the Shogun Yoritomo whom he established in power, but having excited his jealousy he fled to the north of Japan where he is still held in remembrance by the Ainos. It is a popular belief, slender though the evidence is, that he escaped to China and became the famous Genghis Khan. This coin represents the meeting of Ushiwaka and Benke on the Gojo bridge at Kyoto, and the discomfiture of the latter.

No. 4. A "Yakata" or mansion.

No. 5. Shakin Goma or colt sen, with gold dust (bag). See page 861

No. 6. Two men on a raft.

Nos. 7 and 8. "Kabu" or turnip sen. The right hand figure in both coins suggests the "Hoshu."

No. 9. "Daikon" sen. This is a kind of radish with some turnip features and is much esteemed as a relish.

No. 10. "Uchidashi Daikoku". Much is here left to the imagination. Daikoku seems to be striking an attitude as he strikes (Uchi De) with his hammer, the various treasures out of his magic bag. See the key, the bag, (no longer bulging,) the Hoshu and the rice bags.

Plate 17, No. 2. This E sen depicts some of the treasures, viz., the hat, hammer, straw cape, key and oblong coin of gold. (Kasa, Tsuchi, Mino, Kage, and Koban).

No. 5. This gentleman known as Shojo, uses a ladle to fill his cup with the alcoholic beverage called saké. His capacity was phenomenal. The name Shojo means man-ape, and is supposed to be peculiarly fitting in this case, as monkeys are credited (among the ignorant) in Japan with a fondness for strong drink. Shojo is usually represented with red hair. Nothing is known about his nose.

No. 1. This is called the "Ryo Men", or double faced Kwanei sen. This particular specimen was made in the Asakusa mint for the delectation of the workmen and their friends. No. 3 was made in the village of Saruei, province of Musashi, in the 1st year of Gembun, 1736. No. 4 was probably made in the same mint as No. 6. The latter was cast at the village of Kameido in the Province of Musashi.

No. 7. "Mannen Tsuho". This specimen of the antique group I have placed amongst the E sen, as it is evidently not a government coin. On the back is the sun, crescent moon and a star, none of which are distinct.

No. 8. This is after (a long way) the ancient Chinese coin called the "Taisen Gojiu" or "Great Sen, Fifty" but the "Gojiu" reads "Jiugo", fifteen instead of fifty, if we read the characters in the usual order.

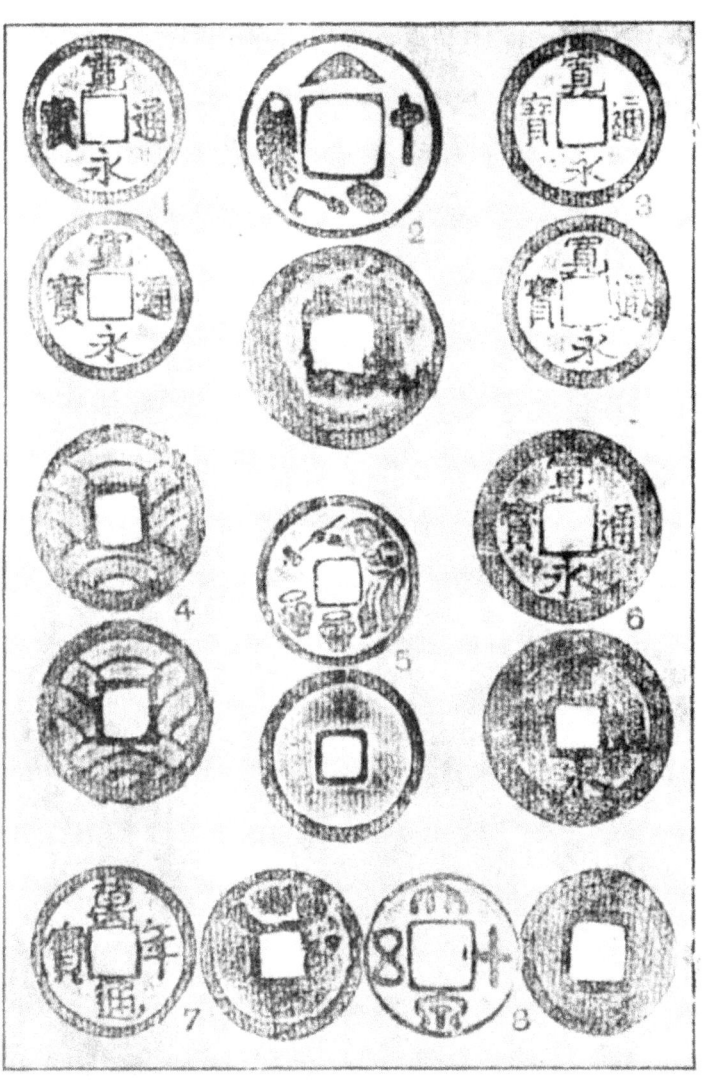

PLATE 17.—E SEN.

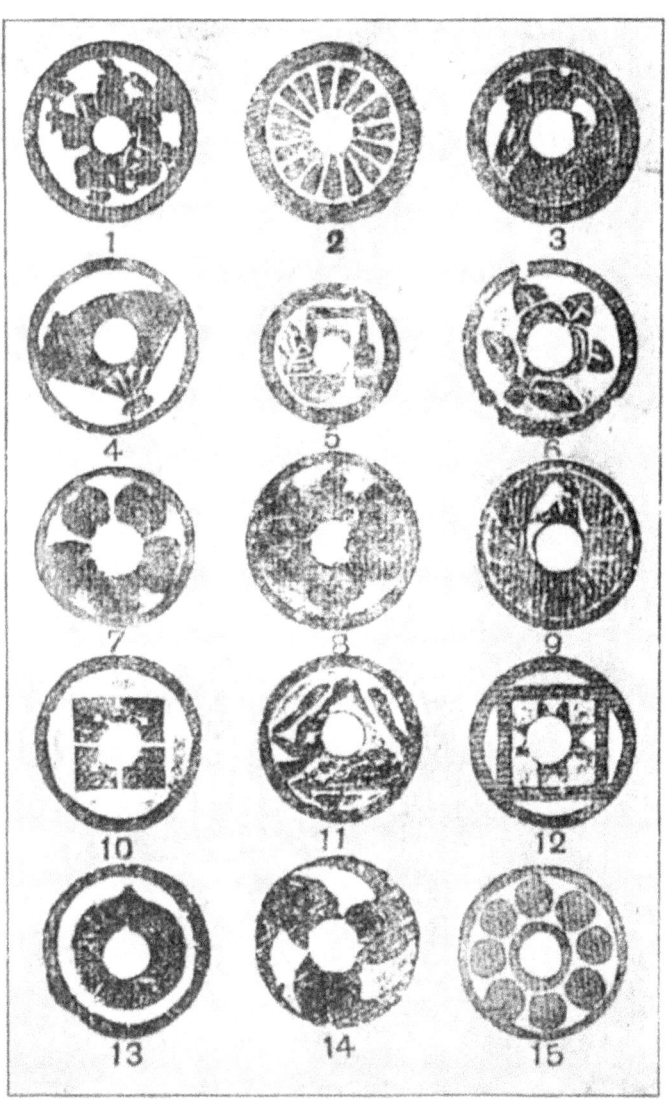

PLATE 18.—E SEN.

EXPERIMENTAL AND ORNAMENTAL COINS.

The "Kagami sen" or mirror sen, so called either because they resemble a Japanese metal mirror to the extent of being flat on one side and decorated on the other, or may be because they were made from mirror metal, are not at all entitled to the name of sen. The "E sen" are made after the manner of coins. They have a reverse and obverse and other characters of current coin. Occasionally they may have been used as coin for their intrinsic value, but this cannot be said of the "Kagami Sen". Still they are usually shewn amongst the E sen, so I bow to custom. They were playthings, childhood's toys of the nobility of other days. They are old, some of them probably as old as the time of the Ashikaga Shogunate. These illustrated in plate 18, were doubtless the pride and joy of budding Daimyo in the days when the game of pitch and toss occupied their dreams perhaps as much as the flash of the toy sword; too soon to be exchanged for the grim and relentless companion which clung to them from adolescence to the grave.* For pitch and toss, or a game betwixt this and marbles, was the function of the Kagami sen. The reverse is plain, except the honourable scars of their former vocation. I shall briefly describe the few shewn.

Plate 18, No. 1 is the god Ebisu still hugging his fish and dancing with delight; something in the right hand however, suggests the hammer of Daikoku.

---

* Sometimes as early as 6 years of age, the Young Daimyo wore real swords and were so saturated daily with etiquette, including the formal mannerisms accompanying "Hara Kiri," or *Felo de se* by disembowelling, so that even at that tender age, their behaviour was more like automata than living children.

246 EXPERIMENTAL AND ORNAMENTAL COINS.

No. 2 is the Imperial crest, with its sixteen petals, the royal chrysanthemum.

No. 3 can be no one but Daikoku Sama.

No. 4. The "Ogi" or folding fan with the sun or hole, if you like, as ornament.

No. 5. Mystic key and Hoshu.

No. 6. Tachibana or orange blossom and leaves.

No. 7. Sakura, or cherry blossom.

No. 8. The Kiri crest seen on the gold coins in chapter 6.

No. 9. Maizuru or flying crane, the badge of the Mori family.

No. 10. Another coat of arms, the Yotsume or "Four eyes."

No. 11. Fujiyama, the far-famed mountain.

No. 12. A mon or crest.

No. 13. Hoshu is it? or turnip?

No. 14. The Mitsudomoe, probably three magatama. (See plate 1, first chapter.)

No. 15. Eight jewels, or stars. *En passant* we note that the stars depicted in the pictures of China and Japan are properly represented by round bodies instead of by radiant points.

Plate 19. All the numbers of this plate with the exception of No. 20, are fancy coins in silver, imitations of Chinese sen. The names are as follows: 1, Kaigen Tsuho; No 2, Shutsu Gempo; 3, Tenho Gempo; 4, Genbo Tsuho, 5, Tins Genpo; 6, Seiso Gempo; 7, Taitei Tsuho; 8, Heian Tsuho; 9, Tenna Jimpo. The last is an ancient E sen of China, which I have introduced for the sake of

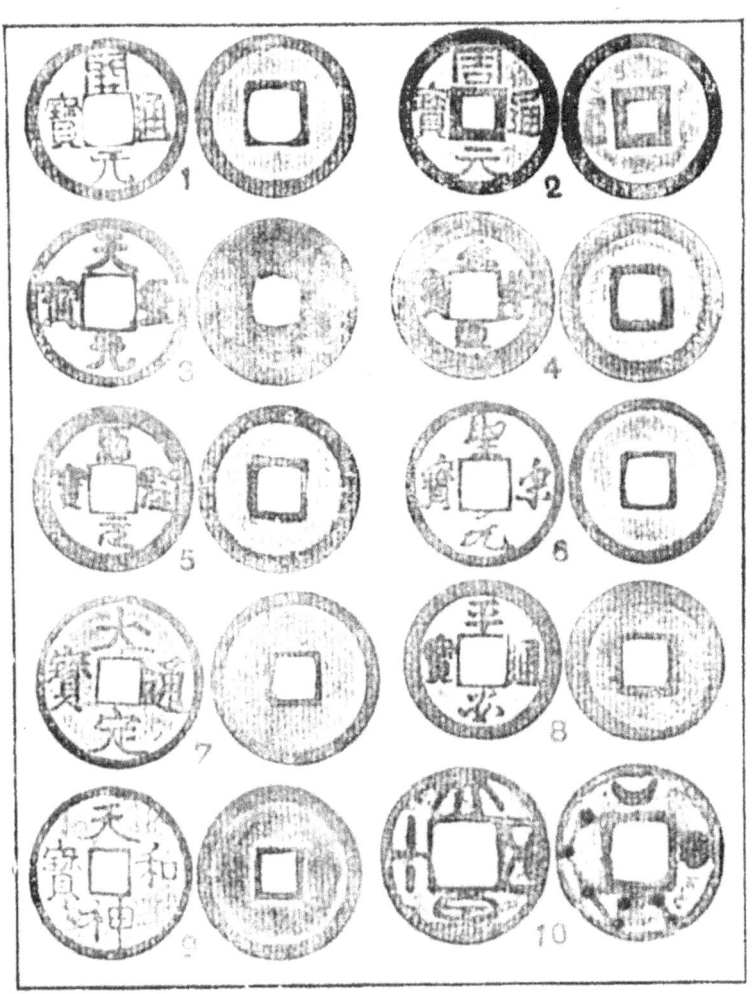

PLATE 19.—E SEN.

EXPERIMENTAL AND ORNAMENTAL COINS. 247

comparison. It is modelled after the "Taisen Gojiu" coin, but the reverse has the Sun, Moon and the constellation of Ursa Major.

Some of the Eiraku sen seen in plate 6, chapter 3, and perhaps the "Ban" sen of the same denomination,

FIG. 21

plate 7, were "Raku" sen, or fancy coins. Fig. 21 illustrates a large and finely made one of copper which probably belongs to this class.

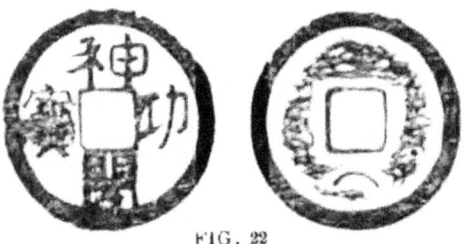

FIG. 22

Fig. 22, shews the "Tsume Jingo", copied from an old Japanese work. It is referred to at page 52.

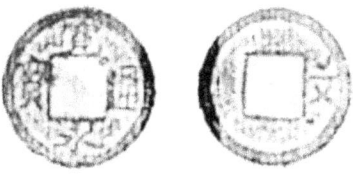

FIG. 23

EXPERIMENTAL AND ORNAMENTAL COINS.

FIG. 24

Figs. 23 and 24 represent forgeries of the famous Kwanei "Bun" sen, page 121. These were made in Annam, apparently from a verbal description only, as the likeness is far to seek.

APPENDIX A.

The following characters are to be found on the antique sen, and some others. The archaic forms have been taken from the Setsu Mon, a Chinese work of the first century A. D.

The interpretation given by this learned authority appears to be influenced by the mystical philosophy of that period and is frequently rather far-fetched. I have sometimes therefore ventured on explanations which seem to me more simple and natural.

The archaic forms too, are in the transition stage between the rude outline picture and the later ideograph, so that confusion is possible. For instance, in paragraph 9, the curve of the archaic character To, a sword, is not so clearly indicative of the rounded pommel of a sword (still surviving in the ornamental knob of the modern weapon), as it is in the same character which is inscribed on an archaic coin of my Chinese collection, where it forms the greater part of a circle. The archaic pommel was sometimes in the form of a ring of iron, cast in one piece with the blade and handle; a specimen in my collection has this form, which is also illustrated in Gowland's work on the Dolmens of Japan.

The identification of these archaic forms is the result, in great measure, of the painstaking search of Mr. Yuzawa, who has assisted me with much ardour and judgement in this interesting task.

---

1. Wa 和, Peace, Japan. Archaic Form

While most of the Chinese characters are compound forms, built up of other ideographs, or the essential parts of such, many of them consist of characters which are separate, though juxtaposed. The elementary characters, whether attached or not, are called radicals. The character Wa has two such radicals. The left hand radical (shewn on the right in the archaic form) was originally an outline picture of a plant with the ear hanging, full of grain. This portrayed all cereals known at the time. The right hand radical (left, in the archaic form) is an open mouth. The combination of an open mouth, with rice, barley etc., ready to fill it, is a most satisfactory condition amongst an agricutural people, and therefore a sign of **Peace** or **Harmony,** which is the meaning of this character. The title "Wa" was applied to the Japanese by ancient Chinese historians, though the character is not the same.

2. Do 銅 Copper. (Contracted Form 同). Archaic Forms 銅 and 同

冂 was one roof or covering: 口 in this connection is said to mean not merely a mouth, but anything under a single roof. Thus the signification *united* or made the *same*. The left hand radical in the complete character means metal, and was applied to the metal gold (probably in its native form) before other metals were familiar. It is pronounced "Kin", and consists of another character of the same sound, together with the character for earth, and streaks to represent the ore*. When copper was found, its resemblance to the precious metal was indicated by the addition of the character 同, (same) which is used in the Wado Kaiho coin without the qualifying radical for metal.

---

* Chamberlain, "Introduction to the study of Japanese writing." Page 107.

APPENDIX A.   251

3. Kai 開 Commencement.   Archaic Form

The resemblance of this to a gate is unmistakable. In the archaic form are seen the two hands pushing aside a bar; hence the meaning to **Open** or to **Commence**, as in our expression "the opening year" &c.

---

4. Tsu 通 Current.   Archaic Form

It is not easy to give a satisfactory explanation of this. The right hand radical I think, unquestionably contains the character earth (see the strata) and the middle vertical line indicating depth. The side lines are probably the sides of a channel and the figure above is doubtless bubbling water. This radical means to gush forth. The left hand radical is more difficult. The three upper lines can be traced in the Setsu Mon, to three legs and was probably intended to show that three legs were moved in the same time as two, hence the idea of running. The lower part of this radical is a plant on a fixed basis and means to stop. The difficulty of combining the ideas of stopping and moving is to some extent got over by the Setsu Mon, which declares that the upper and lower parts combined to form this radical, signify that movement takes place over a flight of steps without going down one by one. This character is found on most of the Japanese coins and I have therefore attempted this account of its origin, which at least leaves on our minds an impression of *rapid movement* of water, hence **Current**.

---

5. Ho 寶 Treasure.   Contracted in the Wado coin to 珎 (Chin).   Archaic Form 寶

APPENDIX A.

As in the character "Do," the enclosing line of the archaic form signifies a covering or roof. The portion immediately under the roof, the character "Chin," used in the Wado coin as a contraction of "Ho," means "rare," "precious." The origin of "Chin" is interesting. The left hand part is "Tama", "precious stone," derived, we may suppose, from the character "Earth", with a qualifying mark, (the upper horizontal line). The right hand part of Chin, represents a jar with its lid and horizontal line to shew that it is full to overflowing, in all likelihood, with some fermented liquor. A "precious" combination indeed!

Underneath this character "Chin" is "Kai" (in Chinese "Bai") a shell, easily recognised in the archaic form. In ancient times, shells were used in China as money, just as they are in other countries at the present day (see pages 3 and 4). A "precious shell", under a roof therefore, not only reveals the rationale of the character "Ho," Treasure, but gives us a vivid glimpse of the civilisation of those archaic times.

---

6. Man 萬 Ten Thousand.   Archaic Form

The ancient ideograph is an excellent sketch of a kind of wasp or fly that swarmed by thousands, hence the meaning, Ten thousand. The antennae, the body, attenuated in the middle, and the wings pointing backwards, are well represented.

---

7. Nen 年 Year.   Archaic Form

The upper part of this character, as will be seen on reference to the first character "Wa" (Paragraph 1.), consists of rice or some other cereal. The lower is a

APPENDIX A. 253

person, represented by legs; the horizontal line is a distinguishing mark, common in these characters, and probably signifies a farmer, perhaps a female agricultural labourer. A sheaf of rice associated with a farmer well depicts the year's crop. What better event could mark the passage of a **Year,** at a time when astronomy could only have been in embryo?

8. Jin 神 Superior Being, Deity. Archaic Form

In the archaic form, the two horizontal lines mean "above", while the three vertical ones indicate the sun, moon and stars. According to the Setsu Mon, this radical derived its meaning "to reveal" or to "shew," from the fact that Heaven reveals itself by means of these three "agents"; but this is probably a later interpretation of the Chinese school. There are reasons to think that the right hand radical by itself meant "God." It has the meaning "to extend" "to develop" and came from the figure which looks very much like a serpent, though it does not seem to be the archaic form of that creature. The combination of these two ideographs to represent the idea **God, Superior Being,** is doubtless an effort of more advanced thought.

9. Ko 功 Merit. Archaic Form

The left hand radical of this character is supposed to represent a perpendicular between two levels and indicates skill, or in combination with other characters, sometimes toil; the right hand radical is a sketch of sinews and means strength. In pages 48-9 it is stated that the character "Ko" sometimes had as its right hand radical, not the character "Riki", "Strength", but "To" a "sword", and the distinguishing features of these were pointed out. The archaic form of "To", a "sword" is 刀. The curved upper part was probably a ringed hilt, like some of those seen in the tombs of the early Japanese, or on the sword or knife money of the archaic Chinese. The lower portion was a curved blade. The resemblance of this to the character "strength" is striking and is possibly the result of frequent association in archaic times. Swordmanship, or *skill* with a *sword*, was the highest degree of Merit.

---

10. Ryu 隆 Prosperous. Archaic Form 隆

The interpretation of this character is not easy. The left hand radical seems to represent a cliff or high place with steps to shew that it can be climbed, hence the idea "Prominent", "Great." The upper part of the right hand radical depicts a person, and the line behind has been variously described as a torch, applied posteriorly (which would certainly make the time seem rather long), or simply and preferably, an indication of distance or length. At least it seems that this part of the radical means "Long". The lower portion signifies "Life" shewing as it does, a plant springing from the soil.

The character "Ryu," taken as a whole, would seem to express a long life which has attained *prominence* hence **"Prosperity."**

---

11. Hei 平 Peace. Archaic Form 平

The explanation of this character is also rather a roundabout one. One part of the archaic form consists of two horizontal lines with a curved one passing downwards. This signifies the voice of a crow, the short sound of "O". The two short curved lines between the horizontal ones signify *Parting* and the whole radical may be taken to imply that parting voices delivered in a monotone (voice of a crow), indicate absence of anger and therefore **Peace.** If this explanation seems rather far-fetched, I would remark that the Setsu Mon does not state its views at all clearly and that this interpretation seems to be the most feasible.

---

12. Ei 永 Everlasting.   Archaic Form

Here, the course of a stream with its streaks of ripples, is quite apparent. It will be noticed that this is a slight modification of the character for a river, seen in the word "Kawa", page 130. The idea of length, and hence of **Lasting** and even **Everlasting**, is thus derived from this concrete example. The archaic form of water is

---

13. Fu 富 Wealth.   Archaic Form

In order from above downwards, we can trace in the archaic form, the elements needed to portray the conception of primitive **Wealth**. A roof, the numeral one, a mouth, and four rice patches,* that is to say, plenty of rice for one mouth gathered under a roof!

---

14. Ju 寿 Longevity.   Archaic Form

This is not very clear. The top knot and long line indicate hair, in the archaic character; the curved

---

* At page 61, I assumed this to be a bale of rice, though it also occurred to me (page 18) that rice fields might be equally acceptable.

lines beneath the top knot almost certainly signify *bent* or *bowed*, while the lower radical again is a mouth, probably in this case, an individual. An individual with bent back and much hair (on the body) would be an apt illustration of **Longevity**.

15. Sho 承 Receiving, or Succeeding to.   Archaic Form

The derivation of this character is made sufficiently clear by the picture of two hands **Receiving** an object.

16. Sho 昌 Prosperous.   Archaic Form

If the upper figure of the archaic form is a picture of the sun, as is stated in the Setsu Mon, then its combination with a mouth and a volume of vapour, (breath or word) arising therefrom gives us a bright or cheerful word (a sunny smile), which indicates **Prosperity.** This curved line is "Ki" (paragraph 26) and the character may therefore signify a mystical connection between the sun, as giver of light, warmth, and therefore life, and the individual represented by "Mouth."

17. Cho 長 Long.   Archaic Form

Here the ideograph for man is surmounted by that for *above*, hence the meaning **Tall, Long.** See paragraph 27.

18. Tai 大 Great.   Archaic Form

This is simply a human figure with the arms and legs stretched out so as to occupy as much space as possible.

APPENDIX A. 257

19. Nyo 饒 Abundant.   Archaic Form

The upper part consisting of three lines (a triangle), signifies gathered (probably under one roof), or combined. The lower portion is a picture of a rice grain with a spoon, according to the Setsu Mon. The right hand radical conveys, according to the same authority, the notion of prominence or elevation, as it consists of three characters for earth, piled on the top of a bare mountain. It may therefore give the idea of having eaten too much food; it is suggested that the sound of the right hand radical corresponde l to the exclamation of a person who has eaten too much. Possibly the notion of earth heaped on a bare or rocky mountain was connected with the gathering of rice and hence the idea of **Abundance.** These explanations cannot be said to be entirely satisfactory.

20. Eki 益 Profit.   Archaic Form

The archaic form shews a vase or other food utensil, with water, or other fluid, above (overflowing?). It has thus the signification *abundant*, as in the previous character, and the idea of **Profit** in the modern sense may have been slowly evolved from the idea *increase*, which it still retains.

21. Jo, or Tei 貞 Chastity, Fidelity of a wife. Archaic Form

The primitive sketch represents the shell of the tortoise, which was used for divination by scorching with fire. The resulting cracks were of various shapes. The figure above the shell depicts such a crack. The answer was supposed to be infallible, and the process thus came to be regarded as the best illustration of truth and **Fidelity,** like Caesar's wife, "above suspicion".

22. Kwan 觀 Beholding.   Archaic Form

The upper portion probably signifies a stork, but it may also refer to an owl. If the two semi-circular figures mean mouths (see character Wa, paragraph 1.), then we may say that the upper portion of this character represented an owl, modified by two mouths to mean stork. The lowest portion is an eye, the two horizontal lines within the figure being the eyelids. Thus the whole character may mean *seeing* (the owl at night and the stork by day): or it might be that the two semi-circular figures are also intended for eyes, though this is less likely. In the other case, the character may be taken to be a picture of an owl with eyes in caricature and emphasised by the large eye underneath. The details are rather obscure, but even we moderns can gather from the *tout ensemble* the notion of **Beholding.**

23. Kwan 寬 Spacious, Liberal.   Archaic Form

It will be seen from the archaic form that there is something under a roof, but what that thing may be is an open question. There seems to be a quaint mixture of three things, which are used in an allegorical manner, namely legs, hands and an eye. The meaning might be thus expressed, room to move, to use the hands and to see. This seems to me more reasonable than the explanation that this interior figure is a combination of a goat and rabbit, with the inference that there is room for these very active creatures to roam about, hence wide, **Spacious,** with the later meaning, **Liberal.**

APPENDIX A.

24. En 延 Prolonged.   Archaic Form 延

According to the Setsu Mon, the left hand radical means a *Prolonged* walk. In the case of the character Tsu, paragraph 4, it was seen that the left hand radical depicted three legs as signifying that they were moving in the same time as two, therefore running. The same remark applies here. The lower leg is however prolonged under the right hand character and is assumed to imply a long walk.

Another interpretation is to the effect that one leg being lengthened means a slow or leisurely walk. The right hand radical is certainly a plant; the line above may refer to the stoppage of its growth, but it apparently means to lengthen. It would seem therefore that one radical emphasises the intention of the other to convey the idea of **Prolongation.**

25. Ki 喜 Gladness.   Archaic Form 喜

The archaic form shews a drum, or some musical instrument, surmounted by a plant, to indicate its erect position (may it not be music on the meadow?) Below is a laughing mouth, expressive of great joy and satisfaction (see the character Raku), a vivid picture of **Gladness.**

26. Ken 乾   Archaic Form

Heaven (when used in connection with Kon).

(The same character, when pronounced Kan, means dry. In divination, it sometimes refers to gold, the noblest metal.

This is a complicated character and the explanation is somewhat involved. The character Ken was used as

APPENDIX A.

an arbitrary symbol to indicate the mid-distance between due north and due west, the characters for which were already established, together with those for east and south. It is not at all unlikely that the character Ken was in existence before such distinctions as north-west, south-west, etc. were made. From its structure it appears that its use in divination preceded its application as a symbol for north-west. According to Kioshin, the author of the Setsu Mon, it consists of two radicals, but for purposes of description we may regard it as having four such components. (1) The upper left hand part of the archaic form portrays the sun, with a growing plant on the top, to signify its rising. In another archaic form, two round bodies of smaller dimensions probably represent stars. (2) The lower portion on the left is a mystical character composed of the numeral one and a curved line "Ki" which signifies vapour, breath or invisible force, (vital force, magnetism, vril or something of the kind). Together these two latter may be taken to signify energy in one, concentrated force. (3) The upper part of the right hand side, is said to mean innermost, or the very inside (viewed from without). It appears to have been originally the picture of a man (inside a house). As we are attempting an esoteric explanation, it may be safe to hint that this radical, which has the significance, when combined with the two former, of brightness, enlightement (perhaps revelation), may possibly refer to the innermost essence of things (noumenon). (4) The lower portion on the right hand side is given in the Setsu Mon as the second radical of this character. It represents an irresistable plant, whose growth may meet with obstruction, but which passes round the obstacle and grows on. Hence the meaning *irresistible.* In toto, this character, as I have remarked, has the signification

APPENDIX A.

Heaven, in combination with Kon (earth, in contrast to heaven). It is also said to mean Heaven when connected with the following character "Gen". The remarks in the foot note at page 75 may therefore be inapplicable.

27. Gen 元 Beginning.   Archaic Form

The character Gen has the same archaic meaning as Cho, though somewhat more archaic in form (paragraph 17). It represents *above* and *man*. It indicates the **Beginning** of Ki, energy, invisible force, something beyond man, whose beginning is outside his ken*.

28. Raku 樂 Pleasure, Music.   Archaic Form

I will here quote Professor Chamberlain. "On wood as a stand we see five drums,—one big drum in the centre and two small ones on either hand,—the Chinese idea of music and hence of enjoyment."—Introduction to the study of Japanese writing, page 105.

29. Mei 明 Enlightenment.   Archaic Form

This is a combination of the characters for the sun and moon, the *brightest* things known. The lines, or dots within these characters are stated by the Setsu Mon to also represent Ki (energy etc.) This is probably a later mystical interpretation.

30. Ji 治 Government, or Peace.   Archaic Form

The archaic form, meaning to regulate, presents two radicals. That on the left hand stands for water, but in

---
* There may be more than a coincidence in the fact that Ken to know and Ken to engender, to bring forth, to become, so closely resemble in sound the Chinese Ken and Gen.

China it may also mean a river. The right hand radical consists of two segments. The upper one signifies "My," or "Self", and the lower is a mouth. The two together mean *Satisfaction*.

In China where the irrigation of land is of paramount importance, the preservation of river banks and canals with dredging and other operations to regulate the flow of water has, from the most ancient times, been an important function of the government. It is said that nearly two thousand years B.C., the Hsia dynasty was founded by Yu, whose engineering works on the Yellow river were so much appreciated that he was made Emperor on the death of the former ruler Shun. No event produces more terror or distress in China than inundation or drought. Though the Setsu Mon is silent on the subject, I think that we may fairly conclude that the remedy to such disasters must have been closely associated in the minds of the teeming millions of agriculturists in China, with the notion of government. That the word to *regulate* should have acquired the signification to *govern*, is a fact of no little interest, shewing as it does that the civilisation of this ancient country was, nominally at least, based on the principle of the common weal. This character, with the preceding "Mei", form the name "Meiji", the present period of **Enlightened Government**.

31. Ho 保 Preservation.   Archaic Form

This character formerly signified rearing (fostering, nurturing). An infant on its entry to this vale of woe, guarded by an adult person, is graphically shewn in the archaic form. The propriety of youth being accompanied by a protector will be generally recognised. The excessively tender age of the infant in this case adds significance to the presence of the adult and clearly conveys

APPENDIX A. 263

the idea of **Preservation**. The above character "Ho", is used on the Tempo coin page 148. Compare with the "Ho", of paragraph 5.

32. It has been stated at page 22 that the word "sen" originally meant a fountain. The character was 泉, or 㐬 in the archaic form. The dot may represent the point of origin of the water, which divided into three streams. The horizontal line perhaps stands for the numeral 1, thus indicating a single origin. During the Shin Dynasty however, B.C. 246-210, a character (錢) having the same sound was employed, and is retained to this day as the character for sen. The archaic form is 錢 and consists of the radical, *metal*, on the left hand (see paragraph 2), with two weapons (primitive halberds), which in combination mean violence, cruelty, robbery. How they arrived at the signification, (in association with the radical for metal,) *farm implement*, except on the Biblical precedent of "spears" turned into "pruning hooks," one cannot imagine. Some of the archaic shapes of Chinese money might be taken for either one or the other and it is not unlikely that, as in still earlier times, a double function was assigned to these implements. The fact of the sound *sen* being the same in this character and that of the original word *fountain*, together with the coexistence of coin, in another part of the newly created Empire of China, shaped after swords, halberds, hoes and spades, doubtless brought about the general use of the character in its present form.

APPENDIX B.

見	宝	寳	寳	寶	寶
見	突	寳	寶	寶	寶
見	突	寳	寳	寶	寶
貝	寶	寶	寶	寶	寶
且	突	寳	寶	寶	寶
見	㠯	寶	寶	寶	寶
只	𣄼	寶	寳	寶	寶
貝	見	寶	寳	寶	寶

The above forms of the character Ho, are to be found on the coins of the Far East. The Archaic types will be recognized by reference to Appendix A.

APPENDIX C.

A list of the principal works by Japanese writers on the coins of Eastern Asia.

TITLE.	NUMBER OF VOLUMES.	AUTHER.	DATE.
Kwacho Ruien	2	Tennojiya Chozaemon	Tenwa (1681-3)
Seho Roku	5	Senoo Ryusai	Hoei (1704-9)
Hanji Roku	14	" "	Kyoho (1716-35)
Koho Dzukan	1	Nakatani Kozan	" "
Zoku Kwacho Ruien	2	Uno Somei	" "
Kisho Hyakuen	1	Kawamura Hadzumi	Temmei 6th (1786)
Wakan Sen I	1	Yoshikawa Iken	Kwansei 4th (1792)
Kwacho Sendzu	1	Hisano Kokkwan	Kwansei 11th (1799)
Shinsen Sempu	3	Kuchiki Masatsuna	Temmei 1st (1781)
Sempei Koi	1	Hisano Kokkwan	Bunkwa 4th (1807)
Kokon Senkwa Kan	20	Kuchiki Masatsuna	Kwansei 10th (1798)
Shin Kosei Kohodzukan	1	Kariya Kwaishi	Bunkwa 12th (1815)
Chin Sen Kihin Dzuroku	1	Omura Naritomi	Bunkwa 14th (1817)
Shinkwa Jorei	1	Finance Department	Meiji 4th (1871)
Meiji Shin Sen Sempu	3	Narushima Ryuhoku and Morita Jihei	Meiji 7th (1874)
Kwanei Shin Sen Sempu	2	Kameda Ichijo, Nakagawa Kinrei, Enomoto Bunshiro	Meiji 27th (1894)
Kwanei Sempu	1	Fujiwara Teikan	Written in the middle of the 18th century. Published in 1898.
Kosen Taisen	36	Imai Teikichi	Meiji 32nd (1899)
Gwa Sempu	2	Majima Kyou	" "
Kwanei Senshi	5	Enomoto Bunshiro	Meiji 31st (1898)
Kwocho Shenshi	1	Enomoto Bunshiro	Meiji 34th (1901)
Fugo Shenshi	3	Ipposha Kosho	Bunkwa (1804-16)
Kin Gin Dzuroku	7	Kondo Morishige	Meiwa 7th (1770)
Kin Gin Kwashi	3	Enomoto Bunshiro	Meiji 36th (1903)
Kimpu	1	Japanese Government	Meiji 1st (1868)
Dai Nihon Kwaheishi	13	Finance Department	Meiji 9th (1876)
Dai Nihon Kwahei Seidzu	1	" "	Meiji 11th (1878)
Kosen Kaushiki Kummo	1	Narushima Ryuhoku	Meiji 17th (1884)

MAGAZINES.

Tokyo Kosenkwai Zasshi
Kwaneisen Kenkyukwai Zasshi
Dai Nihon Kwahei Kenkyukwai Zasshi
Bisho Senkwai Tomoshu
Yokohama Kosen Taikwai Tomoshu
Tokyo Kosen Kyokwai Tomoshu

APPENDIX D.

NOTE ON ONO DOFU.

Yoshikawa Iken, in the Wakan Sen I, states that according to tradition, the later Wado sen were inscribed by the celebrated scholar Ono Dofu. It has been surmised that the Wado sen continued to be cast for upwards of two centuries and if so, Ono Dofu may have been concerned with their inscriptions, though it does not seem at all likely. If however the Wado coin ceased to be issued within fifty years after its first appearance, Ono Dofu could have had nothing to do with the writing of its inscription. It is a historical fact that Ono no Dofu lived in the early part of the tenth century and he may have been asked to write the characters for the Kengen Taiho, as stated at page 75. What is certain is that on the completion of the Seiryoden, a hall of the imperial palace, he wrote the poems on the *karakami* or sliding screens, which were ornamented with the figures of ancient sages. This was in A.D. 928, two hundred and twenty years after the Wado coin was first issued and one hundred and seventy after the issue of it is supposed to have been stopped.

APPENDIX E.

MEIJI CURRENCY.

The illustrations in chapter 6 shew the *copper* coins only as far as the eighth year, the *silver* coins of the third and seventh year and the *gold* coins up to the third year of Meiji. The gold coins have doubled in value, so that the twenty yen piece is now (though out of circulation) valued at forty yen. The silver yen and five sen, are also no longer current in Japan, the former being entirely replaced by gold, represented by notes, and the latter by nickel, though it is still to be seen in circulation.

APPENDIX F.

PRE-MEIJI GOLD AND SILVER CURRENCY.

Collections of the Oban, Koban and lesser coins have hitherto been made by the very wealthy and on a limited scale. The absence of Sabi, their secondary position as current coin and their comparatively recent origin, not to mention the high price of the Oban, have combined to inhibit interest in these really interesting forms of money. Although, in the course of collecting Japanese coin I have acquired a fair number, I confess that I have given them but little study and for the remarks on this subject have to acknowledge entire dependence on the following works, Dai Nihon Kwahei-shi, Dai Nihon Kwahei Seidzu, Kimpu, Kin Gin Dzuroku and Kin Gin Kwashi. The plates on these coins were not finished until my remarks were in print and hence a few more are exhibited than are treated of in the text. It some measure this defect is remedied by printing the name of each coin on the plate cover.

APPENDIX G.

GOVERNMENT ACTION REGARDING COUNTERFEITING, OVER A THOUSAND YEARS AGO.

Wado 2nd. A.D. 709. Imperial Edict. Those who counterfeit silver coin shall be enslaved and the *forged coin* given to the informant of the crime.

Wado 4th. A.D. 711. Imperial Edict. Forgers shall be beheaded and those who were accessory to the crime shall be made government slaves. Those belonging to the Goho (five homes) in which that of the forger is included, shall, provided they do not inform the government, be exiled. If proved to have no knowledge of the crime, their punishment shall be commuted five degrees.

Should the forger repent of his offence and surrender himself up to the government, even if the forged money has been used, he shall have the punishment commuted one degree. Should the money not have been used, he shall receive no punishment should he confess his crime and surrender himself up to the government. Probably the property and persons of the forgers were both held by government.

Wado 5th. A.D. 712. An amnesty having been declared, the punishment of forgers was remitted one degree.

Tempei Jingo, 2nd. A.D. 765. Edict. Forgers shall be enslaved and compelled to work in the government mints.

Jingo Keiun, 1st. A.D. 767. One Kimikiyo Maro (evidently a noble) and others, numbering 40, were exiled to the province of Dewa (northern part of the main island), the former being given the humiliating title of Izenibe (money forger).

APPENDIX G.

Hoki 3rd. A.D. 772. Edict. The regulations hitherto in force concerning the punishment of forgers, shall, be changed so as to enforce one degree less penalty, so that the punishment of exile shall take the place of beheading in the former regulations. Special care shall be taken that the degree of punishment shall be in fair and reasonable proportion to the gravity of the offence.

Ten-o 1st. A.D. 784. A general amnesty was extended to all but those who were guilty of forgery.

Enryaku 22nd and 23rd. A.D. 803-4. Amnesty. Forgers excepted.

Tencho 10th. A.D. 827. Amnesty. Forgers excepted.

Daido 4th. A.D. 909. Amnesty including forgers.

Jinjiu 3rd. 853. Amnesty to all criminals excepting forgers.

Jokwan 6th. 864. Amnesty; forgers excepted.

INDEX.

A

	Page.
Aho Muneyuki	76
Aidzu	174, 142
Ainu	8
Aki	139
Akita coins	139, 180, 207, 208, 209
An	185
Ancient Rock Alphabet	4

Anei
    Ni Shu Gin 196
Anglo-Saxons 13
Aniyama copper mine Akita 180
Annam 87
Ansei
    "Sho Ji" Koban...Chap. 6, Plate 18, No. 2.... 201
    Ni Bu Kin........Chap. 6, Plate 18, No. 3.... 200
    Ichi Bu Gin 200
    Ni Shu Gin 200
Arrow heads 2, 6
Asakusa mint 116, 117
Ashi Arai (Kwanei sen) 120
Ashikaga Mitsukane 92
Ahikaga Yoshimasa 86, 226
Ashio (Kwanei sen) 132
Aston, W. G. 9
Atai 19
Ateshi 19
Awata Mabito 29

B

Ban Sen 97, 111, 117
Barter 1
Beads 8

INDEX. 271

	Page.
Bean Money	202, 206
Benke	243
Benten	236, 241
Bishamon	236
Bita Sen	79, 97
Boeki Gin .... Chap. 6, Plate 22, No. 2	213
Buddhism	12, 53
Bunkyu Eiho	151
Bunkyu Tsuho	221
Bunroku Tsuho	104

Bunsei

Kin Koban	Plate 20, No. 2	197
Ni Bu Kin	Plate 20, No. 3	197
Isshu Kin	Plate 20, No. 4	197
Isshu Gin		197
Nishu Gin		198
Bun Sen	120 et seq.,	109
Bun Zaemon		122

C

Celtic Rings	5
Chamberlain, Professer	9, 49
Chikuzen Tsuho	169
Chin (precious)	24, 147, 251, 252
China (currency of)	15
China (Written language of)	Introduction viii
Cho Gin	202 et seq.
Cho Hei (Ryuhei Elho)	57
Cho Hei (Kwampei Taiho)	73
Cho Ho (Jingo Kaiho)	51
Chonen Taiho	65
Choroku Tsuho	86, 87
Cho To Ei (Ryuhei Eiho)	57
Coin collecting in Japan	Introduction xii
Coins absent from the Dolmens	14
Corea	8, 12
Counterfeiting	32, 268
Crystal beads	5
Cult of Shinto	83
Currency	22, 3

D

	Page.
Daibutsu	53, 109, 122
Daiji (Large character)........(Taiji)....57, 60, 66, 68	
Dazaifu	32
Daikoku Sama	223, 238
Dollar (trade)........Chap. 6, Plate 22, No. 2....	214
Dolmens of Europe and Japan	5
Do Sen	23
Dozan Shiho	184
Dream of Ieyasu	95

E

E Sen	225
Eidaka	95
Eiraku Tsuho	92
" Ban Sen.........Chap. 3, Plate 7	96
Eiri Te Sen............Chap. 4, Plate 11	157
Emperor	
Go Daigo	80
Go Hana Zono	86
Go Yo Zei	189
Heijo	57
Junnin	45
Kenso	15
Kwammu	52
Komei	212
Go Mizu no O	111
Nimmei	63
Reigen	121
Saga	58, 59
Sei Sho (of the Chinese Dynasty of Shu)	121
Shirakawa	90
Tai So, of the Kin Dynasty of China	159
Temmu	9
Empress Gemmyo	20
Koken (Shotoku)	38, 45
Meisei	111
En Kwan Kwampei:	72
Enki Tsuho	73
Enomoto Bunshiro, Dr	15, 163

F

	Page.
Fee	3
Five Provinces, The	54
Fujiwara Ason Nakamaro	38
" " Gyoyo	29
" no Ujime	70
" family of	82
Fukoku Kyohei (Mito sen)	222
Fukurokujin	236
Fundo Jirushi	191, 220
Furiki (Jingo Kaiho)	51
Futsu (common or ordinary)	34
Formosan Coins	156

G

Gamo, Family of	171
Gekitaku	58
Gembun	
Koban .... Chap. 6, Plate 20, No. 1 194,	195
Ichi Bu Kin	195
Genna Tsuho	108
Genroku	
Oban .... Chap. 6, Plate 7 and 8	192
Koban .... Chap. 6, Plate 17, No. 1	193
Ichi Bu Kin .... Chap. 6, Plate 17, No. 3	193
Ni Shu Ban Kin ... Chap. 6, Plate 17, No. 4	193
Genroku Kaichin	218
" Taichin	218
" Tokuho	219
Gindai Tsuho	219, 220
Ginei Tsuho	219
Gin Kwan (silver ring)	5
Go Shu	242
Go Yo Sen	144, 145
Gold and Silver Currency	186
Gold and Silver Ingots	191
Goto, Family of	189
Government mint at Shiba	118
Goza me (matting mark)	198
Gyosho (style of writing)	152

H

	Page.
Haha, or mother sen	146
Hai mon Sen	115
Hakke	182
Hakodate Tsuho	185
Haku Do Sen	174
Hamada Kenjiro	18
Hammer of Happiness	238
Hana	190
Hana Furi Gin	190
Hane (Hook)	34
Han Shu	165
Harima	32
Hashiba, Tokyo	148
Hatome, or Pigeon Eye Sen	165
Hen	34
Hidari Moji	88
Hideyoshi	96, 100, 190
Hideyoshi Cho Gin... Chap. 6, Plate 22, No. 1	202
Hiki (of cloth)	37
Hiragana	59, 234
Hitotsubashi	211
Hideya no Are	9
Ho, (Treasure)	24, 251-2
,, varieties of	264
Ho Cho Sei	107
Hoei Koban..........Chap. 6, Plate 17, No. 2	193
Hoei Tsuho	146
Hojo Family	84
Hojo Ujimasu	104
Hojo Ujiyasu	96
Hoernes Moritz	4
Honda	95
Hosokura Coin	179
Hotei	236
House of Shimadzu	101
Hyaku mon Tsuho	179

I

Ichi Bu Kin	192, 193, 195
" " Gin	198, 200, 209
Ichi Hyaku Ei Sen	220

INDEX. 275

	Page.
Iemitsu	216
Iemochi	211
Ietsuna	216
Ieyasu	100, 108
Images of Buddha, erection of	23, 53
Image of Buddha, destruction of	121
Imai Takechi, Introduction p. xx	
Ine (rice plant)	19
Inouye Geni	Introduction xx
Iron coins	128,134,135,136,137,138,141,142,143,158
Ishi me (stone mark)	188
Itakura Suwo no Kami	152
Izanagi	237
Izanami	237

J

Jingo	45
Jingo Kaiho (Introduction xi)	45
Jiu Hi Nan San (Mito coin)	228
Jiu Ni Zene (Twelve sen)	23
Jokwan Eiho	69

K

Kaei, Isshu Gin	199
Kagami Sen	245
Kagi (a key)	244
Kai (a shell)	4
Kaigen Tsuho	25, 26, 92
Kaika Jimpo	19
Kaiki Shoho	43, 44
Kajiki Sen	165 et seq.
Kaku (to write or scratch)	Introduction vii
Kameido mint	138, 140
Kami (god or goddess)	235
Kanragori	172
Kariya Kwaishi	Introduction xx
Kasa (head gear)	244
Katakana	39
Kawa (a river)	130
Kawamura Hadzumi	xix
Keian Tsuho	216

INDEX.

	Page.
Keicho Oban..........Chap. 6, Plates 5 and 6....	192
" Koban..........Chap. 6, Plates 16, No. 1..	192
Ichi Bu Kin	192
Keicho Tsuho....................................	106
Kengen Taiho	75
Kenkou Tsuho	80
Kibi Mabi....................................39,	49
Kin (weight)	53
Kin Kwan (Gold ring)...........................	5
Kin Tensho (coin)..............................	103
Kinder, Mr......................................	213
Kiri (Paulownia Imperialis)....................	97
Kinsei Empo....................................	158
Kirichin (exchange fee)........................	187
Kirikodama.....................................	5
Kirisen	187
Ko (ancient)...................................	27
Koban 188,192,193,194,197,199,201	
Kobo Daishi (Kukai)	59
Kobu Tsuho.....................................	166
Kofu Gold Coin	202
Kojiki 6,	9
Koma Sen...............................229 et seq.	
Koshin Sen	242
Kudatama	6
Kuchiki Masatsuna.................. Introduction xix	
Kurile Islands	7
Kusunoki Masashige............................	85
Kukai (Kobo Daishi)	59
Kwammon (one thousand mon)	212
Kwammon Gin Sen................................	17
Kwampei Taiho..................................	71
Kwandaka.......................................	95
Kwanto	92
Kwatsu En 41,	50
Kyoho Oban ....Chap. 6, Plates 9 and 10....	194
Kyoho Koban .... Chap. 6, Plate 19, No. 1....	
Kyoho Ichi Bu Kin....Chap. 6, Plate 19, No. 3....	
Kyoho Tsuho	216
Kyo sen (or Kyoto sen)......................94,	98

INDEX. 277

L

	Page.
Luchuan Coins	157 et seq.
Leaden Certificates	172
" Coin	178, 179, 183, 184

M

Magatama	5, 191
Majima	226
Mahâkâla	238
Mame Gin	202, 206
Manen	
Shin Koban	201
Ni Shu Kin	202
Mannen Tsuho	38, 244
Matsudaira Higo no Kami	174
Matsudaira Nobutsuna	121
Matsudaira Shungaku	152
Matskoka Judayu	168
Matsuri Sen	240
Mediaeval Coins	79
Meiji Tsuho	225
Minamoto	84
Mino (straw cape)	244
Mito Sen	171-2
Mito Shiken Sen	222, 223, 224
Mitsu Domoe	191, 246
Mitsutsugu (of family of Goto)	192
Morita Mr.	Introduction xx
Morioka Coin	179
Mogusa, (Artemesia Moxa)	Introduction xvii
Mumon Gin Sen	15, 16
Muneage	228
Muramatsu Mr	89, 157
Murdoch	106, 155, 168

N

Nagasaki	156
Nakagawa, Mr.	17
Nakatani Kozan	Introduction xix
Namba Go Yo Sen	145
Narushima Ryuhoku	24, 171

INDEX.

	Page
Nedan	19
Nembutsu (praying to Buddha)	233
Nengo	Introduction ix, page 63,64, 66
Nickel coin	213
Nihongi	9, 15
Nihon Shoki	15
Niji (two character) Hoei coin	148
Ni Jiu Ichi Nami (twenty one wave) sen	140 et seq.
Nikko Go Yo Sen	144
Nisui Ryuhei	56
Nobunaga (Ota)	86, 100, 188, 190
Noge Wado	33
Nyoki Jimpo	68

O

O Ashi	3
Oban, 188, 190, 192, 192-3, 194 and plates 1-14, chapter 6	
Ogasawara Dusho no Kami	152
Ogata (large size) coin	40, 61, 66, 74, 145
Omura Naritomi	Introduction xx
Ono Dofu	75 and Appendix D.
Ota Nobunaga	86, 100, 188, 190
Ota Tamesaburo	185

P

Pantheon (Japanese)	235
Pecuniary	3
Phoenix (or howo)	182
Polder (Mr. Van de)	213
Primitive Standards of Value	2
Protohistoric Period	7 et seq.
Puini (signor Carlo)	235

R

Raku (or fancy) Sen	247
Rice, current medium of exchange	19, 20
Rings of gold and silver	4, 5
Rock alphabet	4

INDEX. 279

	Page
Rokujo Sen	226
Ryogaeya (exchange office)	205
Ryo	189
Ryukyu Tsuho	162, 163, 164, 165
Ryuhei Eiho,	52

S

Sa (or left) Jin	69
Sabi	Introduction x, page 31, 159
Sadame (guaranteed)	197
Saidaiji Temple	43
Sanko Kaichin	228
Schoolcraft	4
Sei San Kyoku	175
Seiko Tsuho	161
Sen	22
Sendai Tsuho	176, 177
Senoo Ryusai	159
Shell money	3, 4
Shiba Shinsenza (mint)	118
Shibi Naisho	38
Shiken Sen	86, 108, 215 et seq.,
Shima Sen	52, 79, 87
Shimaya Sen	123
Shimesu	62, 68
Shi Mon sen	139 et seq.,
Shichifukujin (seven gods of luck)	235
Shinsho (style of writing)	107, 152
Shinto) religion)	236
Shojo	244
Shotai kyu	161
Shotoku	161
Shotoku	45
Shotoku Koban	194
Showa Shoho	63, et seq.
Siva	238
Shu	193
Shuku Riki Jingo	51
So Gyoku (two jewels)	228
Sosho	152
Standard of weight	5
Sugawara Kiyokimi	65

	Page.
Sugawara no Michizane	71, 234
Surface of Oban and Koban	188
Suwa Jinja	139
Sword guard of the Daimyo of Akita	181

T

Tai (sea bream)	237
Taihei Gempo	42
Taiji (large character)	60, 66, 68
Tajihi Mabito Myaki Maro	30
Taiko Hideyoshi	105, 191
Taiko Oban	190
Taiko Ichi Bu Kin	190
Taira (family of)	83, 84
Tajima Silver Coin	210
Takauji (Ashikaga)	85
Tane Sen	Introduction xiv, page 118
Tanuma Coin	195
Tasuki	167
Tatenuki (Fuju sen)	60
Teikyo Tsuho	217
Tenjin	71, 234
Tenkai	111
Tempo Oban	plates 11 and 12, chap 6
Koban (five ryo)	199
" (one ryo)	199
Ni Shu	199
Tsuho	148
Tennojiya Chozaemon	Introduction xviii
Tensho Oban	188 and plate 1, chap 6
Koban	190 and plate 2, chap 6
Tensho Tsuho	101
Tokugawa Ieyasu	100, 108, 109
Tokwan Tsuho	168
Torisumi Sen	124
Tosa Coins	169
To Sen Tsuho	221
Toyama (Daimyo of)	Introduction xviii
Toyotomi Hideyori	108
Trade Dollar	214
Tsuchi Me (hammer mark)	188
Tsume Jingo	247
Twelve Antique Sen	79

U

	Page.
Uchigata	Introduction xvlii
Unit of Value	2
Unno Somiu (or Somei)	159
Ushiwaka (Yoshitsune)	243
Usui Toge Kitte Sen	173

W

Wado Kaiho	24
Wado Kaichin	24
Wani	7
Wigmore, Mr. J. H.	92

Y

Yamagata Koban	208, 209
Yamato Minzoku	212
Yoko Ten (Horizontal dot) Mannen	40
Yokoyama, Mr.	16
Yonezawa Coin	174
Yoritomo	243
Yoshida Kenshuke	31
Yoshikawa Iken	46
Yoshimitsu	85, 93
Yoshimochi	93
Yoshitsune	243

CORRIGENDA.

Page 38. For Tempel Hojo *read* Tempel Hoji.
Page 61. For inposing *read* imposing.
Page 66. For bloster *read* bolster.
Page 93. For then *read* there.
Page 96. For his son Ujimasa *read* his brother &c.,
Page 104. For Ujimasu *read* Ujimasa.
Page 113. For Ryohei *read* Ryuhei.
Page 130. Figure 49 should shew the three strokes of the character "Kawa" only on the right side. The original coins are identical in writing, so that it was not necessary to do more than retouch the margin of the obverse in fig. 49.
Page 246. For Kinei Genpo *read* Shosei Gempo.
Page 228. (So) should be placed between "Jewels" and "Gyoku."
Page 231. For Nyu-I-Rin *read* Nyo-I-Rin.
Page 244. For everage *read* beverage.

For Product Safety Concerns and Information please contact our EU representative GPSR@taylorandfrancis.com
Taylor & Francis Verlag GmbH, Kaufingerstraße 24, 80331 München, Germany

www.ingramcontent.com/pod-product-compliance
Lightning Source LLC
Chambersburg PA
CBHW050833230426
43667CB00012B/1982